THE GOSPEL OF MATTHEW

An Exposition

THE GOSPEL
OF MATTHEW

An Exposition

by
CHARLES R. ERDMAN

PREFACE BY EARL F. ZEIGLER

THE WESTMINSTER PRESS

PHILADELPHIA

BS
2575
.E7
1966

Published by The Westminster Press®
Philadelphia, Pennsylvania
PRINTED IN THE UNITED STATES OF AMERICA

To
all who love
His appearing

PREFACE

The Gospel of Matthew was probably the most popular and useful of the four Gospels that circulated in the early church. It was natural that it should finally be selected to head the list. The Old Testament canon, as the books were finally arranged for use in the church, closed with Malachi. This prophet spoke of "the Lord whom you seek will suddenly come to his temple." The Gospel of Matthew opens to declare that this Lord has come in the person of "Jesus Christ, the son of David, the son of Abraham." As son of David, Jesus Christ was the royal heir—the Messiah. As son of Abraham, he was related to the father of the Jewish fellowship, but also to universal mankind—"by you [Abraham] all the families of the earth shall bless themselves" (Gen. 12:3). Thus the hopes of the Old Testament are fulfilled in the New; and the hopes of the world are revived in the reign of a universal King.

Matthew's Gospel is also a very contemporary writing for all who can still pray: "Thy kingdom come, thy will be done, on earth as it is in heaven." It breathes the spirit of hope and assurance as we read of the acclaim with which the infant Jesus was received by "Wise-men from the east" as well as common people. It continues to unfold the teachings, the marvelous works, the crucifixion, the resurrection, the ascension, the promise of coming again. It declares that this Jesus has been given all authority in heaven and in earth. Knowing this, believing this, we can face our world with courage and conviction. Jesus' commission is ours to obey—"Go . . . make disciples . . . , teaching them to observe all that I have commanded you; and lo, I am with you always." Jesus lived and died for the world into which he was born; he lives for the world in which we now live. If the early Christians were fortified and empowered, as they pored over the pages of Matthew's Gospel, shall we lose heart because we fail to read and understand what God is saying to us now through this Gospel?

Dr. Erdman's vivid and practical exposition of this Gospel will make it come alive to all who study to make themselves approved unto God, "rightly handling the word of truth."

During the period from 1916 to 1936 The Westminster Press published seventeen volumes comprising commentaries on all the New Testament books. The author and expositor of this notable series was Dr. Charles R. Erdman, then occupying the chair of practical theology in Princeton Seminary. Previously he had held two important pastorates in Philadelphia Presbyterian churches, and for a decade he was pastor of the First Presbyterian Church in Princeton while professor in Princeton Seminary. The General Assembly of the Presbyterian Church in the U.S.A. honored Dr. Erdman by electing him to the moderatorship in 1925. He also served the church at large as longtime president of the Board of Foreign Missions.

The volumes in the Erdman Commentary series have been in constant demand since these expositions were first published, and have been reprinted so often that the plates have become badly worn. The reprinting of Dr. Erdman's seventeen volumes in paperback editions has provided the opportunity for completely resetting type and creating new plates. Thus these aids to the study of the Scriptures will continue to be available to present and future generations of Bible students.

EARL F. ZEIGLER

FOREWORD

The hopes of the world are to be realized in the reign of a universal King. The seething unrest of nations, the savageries of war, the threatenings of anarchy increase the yearning for the rule of One whose wisdom is faultless, whose love is perfect, whose power is supreme. Such a Ruler is Christ, and under his scepter the earth is to attain its age of glory and of gold. It is inspiring, therefore, to read again that version of the Gospel story which emphasizes the royal features in the portrayal of our Lord. Such a review is certain to make his followers more loyal to his person, more devoted to his cause, and more eager to hasten the hour of his undisputed sway as King of righteousness and King of peace.

FOREWORD

INTRODUCTION

THE AUTHOR

Only by the power of Christ could a publican be transformed into an apostle. Such a change was experienced by Matthew, also called Levi, to whom tradition has assigned the authorship of the First Gospel. Even modern critics, who favor the theory that another writer compiled the book from various sources, believe that the great discourses which form a main feature of the Gospel came from the pen of the taxgatherer of Capernaum. These taxgatherers, or publicans, as collectors of revenue, were everywhere dreaded or despised. Throughout the whole Roman Empire they were accused of being extortionate, dishonest, and cruel. In the province of Judea they were looked upon with loathing, as traitors and renegades who were serving a hated and heathen oppressor. Even in Galilee, where one like Matthew may have been serving Herod Antipas and may have been collecting lawful customs from the caravans which moved along the great commercial highway, he would be regarded with suspicion and classed with social and religious outcasts. It is never quite fair, however, to condemn men by groups; at least we are certain that in this despised publican, Jesus Christ saw great possibilities of future usefulness. He found him at "the receipt of custom" and called him into the inner circle of his chosen companions. Matthew probably had seen Jesus before and had heard his impressive teachings, but in any case he rose up instantly and left all and followed him. He had much to leave, for he seems to have been a man of wealth and popular among men of his own class, as might be concluded from the fact that he gave a great feast, to celebrate his decision to serve Christ, and to introduce his old friends to his new Master. Wealth in a collector of customs and friendship with publicans do not indicate an irreproachable character; but Matthew seems to have had at least one virtue: he must have been, or have become, a modest man; for in reciting events of supreme importance in which he himself had played a part he makes no personal allusion. Whatever his character, his duties as a government official had disciplined him in system and accuracy and had developed a capacity for orderly thought and for methodical writing which fitted him for his immortal task as a biographer of Jesus Christ.

Strictly speaking, Matthew did not attempt to produce a life of his Master. No one of the Gospel writers had this in view. If so, they would not have passed with intentional silence the events of long years; they would not have omitted thrilling incidents which were known to all, but were recorded only by one or the other of the Four Evangelists; they would not so have centered the interest upon a few days at the close of the earthly ministry of our Lord.

THE PURPOSE

The purpose of this writer, like that of the other three, was to tell the "good news" of salvation wrought out by the life and death and resurrection of Christ. There is in reality only one gospel; it is found in four forms or versions, but the essential message is the same; the points in which all agree are of vastly more significance than those in which they differ. These differences, however, are of interest and importance and combine to form a more complete story. They are due to the varying experiences of each author and to some more or less definite but subordinate design in relating the "glad tidings" which are common to all.

Thus it has been said that Matthew wrote for Jews; Mark for Romans; Luke for Greeks; and John for the church. It might be more accurate to say that all four were intended primarily for Christian believers. Undoubtedly the Gospel of Matthew has a prevailing character which is properly termed Jewish. If, however, Matthew wrote to convince unbelieving Jews of the truth of Christianity, it is strange that he should have so emphasized the offense Jesus gave to the Jews by his disregard of their traditions, his denunciation of their rulers, his declaration of the rejection of Israel and of the salvation of Gentiles. Contrast, for example, the opening chapters of Matthew and those of Luke. In the former the Jews are disturbed by the coming of their king; their ruler seeks the life of the infant Jesus; Gentile Wise Men offer him princely gifts; and his parents are compelled to flee with him for safety into the land of Egypt. The latter story opens in the Temple at Jerusalem, where a godly priest is listening to the message of an angel. In the pious homes of Elisabeth and Mary, Hebrew saints are chanting their inspired canticles of praise to Jehovah and of gratitude for his goodness toward Israel, his chosen and beloved people. Such an approach to the Gospel story would be much more fitting for one who was seeking to conciliate and convince the Jews.

The Portrait of Jesus

Of course, Matthew was written by a Jew, and he must have had in mind his believing fellow countrymen; but the distinguishing marks of this Gospel may be explained from the fact that the aim of the writer was so to rehearse the story of salvation as to demonstrate the fact that Jesus of Nazareth was the Christ, the predicted Messiah, the King of the Jews, who had been rejected by his own nation, who was being accepted by Gentiles, and who someday was to return in power and great glory. As a result of this aim Matthew does possess traits which distinguish it from the other Gospels. In each the portrait of our Savior is identical, yet by each certain features are so emphasized that the picture is distinct.

1. The King

Thus Matthew is characteristically the Gospel of the King. The figure of Jesus is painted in colors of royalty. His ancestry is traced from a royal line; his birth is dreaded by a rival king, and Wise Men offer their royal gifts; his herald declares that his Kingdom is at hand. His temptation reaches its climax as he is offered the kingdom of the world; his great message to his followers, "the Sermon on the Mount," is like the manifesto of a king, setting forth the fundamental laws of his Kingdom. His miracles are his royal credentials; his parables are termed "mysteries of the Kingdom." Even outside his own land he is hailed as the "Son of David"; he claims freedom from paying tribute to "the kings of the earth," for he is the child of a King; he makes his royal entry into Jerusalem and claims sovereign power, and tells concerning himself the story of the marriage of the king's son; while facing the cross he predicts his return in glory and his universal reign. He claims power to command legions of angels. In the hour of his death the rocks are rent, the earth is shaken, the dead are raised; his resurrection is a scene of majestic power, emphasized by an earthquake, by the appearance of an angel, and by the terror of the guards; his last words are a kingly claim and a royal command, "All authority hath been given unto me. . . . Go ye therefore." The characteristic and significant phrase of the Gospel is in the legend "the kingdom of heaven." Here is a portrait in which even the minor touches are resplendent with purple and gold.

2. The Messiah

This King, however, is the "King of the Jews." Matthew is the Gospel of the Messiah. The appearance of this princely figure has been predicted by the Hebrew prophets. In fact, every important event in his career has been explicitly foretold: his birth of a virgin in the town of Bethlehem; his residence in Egypt, in Nazareth, and in Capernaum; his healing of the sick; his speaking in parables; his royal entry into Jerusalem; his desertion by his followers; his triumphant spirit in death. Allusions are made to sixty-five Old Testament passages, forty-three are verbally quoted, a number equal to that of all the other Gospels combined. Thus Matthew is the Gospel of fulfillment. It faces the Old Testament; it properly begins the New. The scenes are colored by Jewish customs; Jewish symbols and types abound. The Law, the Prophets, and the Psalms, all are shown to have pointed forward to Jesus of Nazareth. In him are found their significance, their meaning, and their goal; he is the expected Son of David, the son of Abraham; he is the predicted Messiah; he is the Christ of God. With all propriety Matthew is placed as the first Gospel, showing how the ancient Scriptures are linked with the good news of salvation in Jesus Christ.

3. Rejected

Matthew is further the Gospel of rejection. Of course the fact is essential to all the Gospels; but here it is presented continually. It colors all the teaching, it forms the background of every scene; its shadow is never lifted. Before Jesus is born, his mother is in danger of being repudiated by Joseph; at his birth Jerusalem is troubled and Herod seeks to take his life; on the plains of Bethlehem no angel choir sings, but mothers are weeping in anguish over their slaughtered babes; Jesus is hurried away to Egypt and hidden for thirty years in Nazareth; his forerunner is imprisoned, and beheaded in a dungeon. As Jesus points men to "the narrow way" he declares that few will find it. To the many he is to say as he sits in judgment, "I never knew you: depart from me"; men marvel at his miracles and offer to follow him, but he declares that the "Son of man hath not where to lay his head"; he warns his messengers that they, too, are to be rejected. His parables indicate that his Kingdom will not be realized on earth

until the present age ends; as soon as his disciples understand that he is the Messiah, he begins to express and
iterate the truth of his cruel sufferings and death; he relates
to the people his "parables of rejection"; he pronounces
his most solemn woes on the rulers of the people; he predicts the destruction of the city and the anguish of the
nation; in the hour of his death is heard that desolate cry,
"My God, my God, why hast thou forsaken me?" No
penitent thief is praying, no word of human sympathy is
spoken; those who pass by revile, the chief priests and
elders mock him; even after his death they set a seal and
a watch; even after his resurrection they hire soldiers to
hide his glory with their lie. In no Gospel is the attack of
his enemies so bitter; in no other is the King more definitely offered to the nation, and in none is his rejection so
cruel and so complete.

4. Returning

However, Matthew is likewise the Gospel of the returning King. No other Evangelist lays such stress on the
Second Coming of Christ. As he relates the great discourse concerning the return of our Lord which Mark and
Luke likewise record, Matthew alone adds the memorable
parable of the wise and foolish virgins, and of the talents,
and then draws the picture of the triumphant King seated
on his throne of judgment while all nations are gathered
before him and he determines who are to be received and
who are to be excluded from his Kingdom. He agrees
with Mark in recording for us the words spoken by our
Master to the high priest as he stands under the very
shadow of the cross. "Henceforth ye shall see the Son of
man sitting at the right hand of Power, and coming on the
clouds of heaven"; but he alone records the closing claim
of "all power in heaven and on earth." This is the Gospel
of triumph: the good news of the coming glory and the
universal sway of Christ the King.

THE METHOD

In ordering his literary material, Matthew uses a unique method. As he tells the story of redemption he does not consistently follow the order of time, but he groups similar events or teachings which may be logically related, and so heightens the effects. Thus we find collected in a single chapter seven of the fourteen parables which Matthew records, and in the same way in one group ten of the twenty miracles. So too the unique feature of the Gospel consists in five great summaries of the teachings of Christ; the Sermon on the Mount, the Instruction to the Disciples, the Parables of the Kingdom, the Woes Against the Pharisees, and the Discourses Relative to the Return of the King. Luke, by way of contrast, follows the order of time. He has been compared to a botanist who likes to follow a stream and to examine each flower in its native home; but Matthew prefers to gather the blossoms and to arrange them according to kind or color in great clusters of beauty.

THE OUTLINE

It is this method of Matthew which suggests one helpful way of analyzing his Gospel. Of course many will prefer to use the outline commonly applied to the writings of each of the first three Evangelists, namely, the division of the Gospel according to the time or place of the ministry of Christ. For example: Introduction to the Gospel, chs. 1:1 to 4:11; The Ministry in Galilee, chs. 4:12 to 18:35; The Journey Through Perea, chs. 19; 20; The Last Week in Jerusalem, chs. 21 to 28. Such a division is clear and satisfactory; but the outline here suggested is designed to fix the thought upon the great central Figure of the Gospel as he is presented in the character of a King, and to designate consecutively each group of teachings and incidents which Matthew combines under a single topic. Thus after the section dealing with the Birth, the Infancy, and the

Preparation of the King, chs. 1:1 to 4:11, there follow the Proclamation of the King, or the "Sermon on the Mount," chs. 4:12 to 7:29; the Credentials of the King, or the First Ten Miracles of our Lord, chs. 8:1 to 9:34; the Messengers of the King, or the Instructions to his Disciples, chs. 9:35 to 10:42; the Claims of the King, chs. 11; 12; the Parables of the King, ch. 13; the Withdrawal of the King, chs. 14:1 to 16:12; the Person and Work of the King, chs. 16:13 to 17:27; the Servants of the King, or Directions for his Followers, chs. 18 to 20; the Rejection of the King, chs. 21 to 23; the Prophecies of the King's Return, chs. 24; 25; and the Death and Resurrection of the King, chs. 26 to 28.

Such an outline may have the merit of emphasizing the apparent method of Matthew and of enabling the reader to see with increasing clearness the kingly majesty of Christ.

THE OUTLINE

IX

X

XI

XII

THE TRIAL, DEATH, AND RESURRECTION OF THE KING
Chs. 26 to 28

I
THE ANTECEDENTS
OF THE KING

Matt. 1:1 to 4:11

A. THE GENEALOGY Ch. 1:1-17

1 The book of the generation of Jesus Christ, the son of David, the son of Abraham.

2 Abraham begat Isaac; and Isaac begat Jacob; and Jacob begat Judah and his brethren; 3 and Judah begat Perez and Zerah of Tamar; and Perez begat Hezron; and Hezron begat Ram; 4 and Ram begat Amminadab; and Amminadab begat Nahshon; and Nahshon begat Salmon; 5 and Salmon begat Boaz of Rahab; and Boaz begat Obed of Ruth; and Obed begat Jesse; 6 and Jesse begat David the king.

And David begat Solomon of her that had been the wife of Uriah; *7 and Solomon begat Rehoboam; and Rehoboam begat Abijah; and Abijah begat Asa; 8 and Asa begat Jehoshaphat; and Jehoshaphat begat Joram; and Joram begat Uzziah; 9 and Uzziah begat Jotham; and Jotham begat Ahaz; and Ahaz begat Hezekiah; 10 and Hezekiah begat Manasseh; and Manasseh begat Amon; and Amon begat Josiah; 11 and Josiah begat Jechoniah and his brethren, at the time of the carrying away to Babylon.*

12 And after the carrying away to Babylon, Jechoniah begat Shealtiel; and Shealtiel begat Zerubbabel; 13 and Zerubbabel begat Abiud; and Abiud begat Eliakim; and Eliakim begat Azor; 14 and Azor begat Sadoc; and Sadoc begat Achim; and Achim begat Eliud; 15 and Eliud begat Eleazar; and Eleazar begat Matthan; and Matthan begat Jacob; 16 and Jacob begat Joseph the husband of Mary, of whom was born Jesus, who is called Christ.

17 So all the generations from Abraham unto David are fourteen generations; and from David unto the carrying away to Babylon fourteen generations; and from the carrying away to Babylon unto the Christ fourteen generations.

The opening chapters of Matthew may be regarded as an introduction to the Gospel. They concern the ancestry, birth, and infancy of Jesus, and the preparation for his public ministry. Each of these facts and events is so related as to reveal the distinct purpose of the writer and the distinguishing features of his narrative.

1. Matthew is the "Gospel of the King," and this "Book of the Genealogy of Jesus Christ," this birth roll, which begins the story, is emphatically the genealogy of a King. It is designed to show that Jesus was the lawful heir to the throne of David. It differs essentially from the genealogy recorded by Luke. The two lists of names diverge after the mention of David. Some have conjectured that Luke gives the natural as distinct from the royal line. Others have supposed that he gives the lineage of Mary. As to the true explanation of this divergence no agreement has been reached, but the important point is obvious. Luke, who paints the portrait of the ideal Man, traces the genealogy of Jesus to Adam, the father of the race; but Matthew, who draws for us the picture of the King, records the royal ancestry of Jesus. He traces the line from Abraham, but first mentions David, in whom the family attained the royalty which was lost at the captivity and regained in Christ. The genealogy omits several names in the royal line, but this does not destroy its value. It indicates, however, that the word "begat" does not mean, literally, "was the father of" but "was the legal ancestor," so that Joseph is shown to be the heir of David and because of his marriage to Mary, her Son becomes in all reality the "Son of David" the King.

2. Matthew, however, is the "Gospel of the Messiah." The King he described is emphatically the King of the Jews. In him the inspired prophecies are fulfilled. What

more fitting opening could be suggested than this genealogy which points backward over the whole history of the Hebrew people? It is no barren and lifeless list of names; it awakens the most sacred memories; it embodies the most glorious hopes; it forms the best conceivable link between the Old Testament and the New; it is not wanting in spiritual significance.

This genealogy is divided into three sections representing fourteen generations each. The division is characteristically Jewish, as it combines the divine number "three" with twice the sacred number "seven." These sections cover the three great periods of Jewish history before the time of Christ. The first is the period of the Patriarchs and Judges. Beginning with Abraham there appears the succession of heroes who made the name of Israel famous; mention is made of Ruth, whose romance forms the most charming idyll of the East, and of Jesse, and of David his royal son. The second period is that of the monarchy which attained its splendor in the days of David and Solomon. It is, however, a period of decline and failure. Something of revival and glory is suggested by the names of Jehoshaphat, Hezekiah, and Josiah; but the mention of Rehoboam, Ahaz, and Manasseh intimate the degeneration and apostasy which resulted in the tragedy of the captivity.

With few exceptions the persons named as belonging to the third period, covering the six hundred years between the monarchy and Christ, are shrouded in dateless and unbroken darkness. Thus the story outlined by the genealogy of Jesus is one of mingled pathos and glory, of heroism and disgrace; but its three chapters with their fascinating and diverse characters remind us that through the troubled centuries, through the changing scenes, by patriarchs, kings, and priests, by men illustrious and obscure, God was preserving a line and accomplishing a purpose, until at last appeared One who, as the "son of David," was destined to be the source and center of universal rule, and as the "son of Abraham," the source and center of universal blessing.

3. Matthew is also the "Gospel of Rejection." It is in harmony with this picture that the genealogy of Jesus contains names which the Jews might gladly have repudiated for their suggestions of disgrace and other names which recall apostasy from God, the breaking of his covenants, and the refusal of his offers of mercy. Most of all is it noticeable that Matthew includes four names which occasion surprise. They are the names of women and therefore unusual in such a Jewish genealogy, and they are the names of women, three of whom were guilty of gross sin and two were members of hated and heathen races. It may be that they were intended to suggest that the King whom the Jews rejected was a Savior who identified himself with sinful humanity, who offered pardon and high privilege to all penitent offenders, and who promised to Jew and Gentile alike the blessings of his transforming power; it even may be an intimation that, as the royal line had been preserved in extraordinary and irregular ways, so the last step would be the most marvelous of all, even the miraculous birth of Jesus, the Son of the Virgin Mary, the reputed Son of Joseph.

4. It may be suggested further that, as this Gospel so emphasizes the final triumph of the King, it is not unnatural that the royal line from which he came had for a time lost its glory and had been hidden in obscurity. Thus the Monarch who was despised and rejected and was nailed to a cross by his enemies, will ultimately appear as the true Son of David, and will restore the vanished glory as the rightful Heir of Solomon, as the Prince of Peace, as the universal King.

B. THE BIRTH OF JESUS Ch. 1:18-25

18 Now the birth of Jesus Christ was on this wise: When his mother Mary had been betrothed to Joseph, before they

*came together she was found with child of the Holy Spirit.
19 And Joseph her husband, being a righteous man, and
not willing to make her a public example, was minded to
put her away privily.   20 But when he thought on these
things, behold, an angel of the Lord appeared unto him in
a dream, saying, Joseph, thou son of David, fear not to take
unto thee Mary thy wife: for that which is conceived in her
is of the Holy Spirit.   21 And she shall bring forth a son;
and thou shalt call his name* JESUS; *for it is he that shall
save his people from their sins.   22 Now all this is come to
pass, that it might be fulfilled which was spoken by the Lord
through the prophet, saying,*

> *23 Behold, the virgin shall be with child, and shall bring
> forth a son,
> And they shall call his name Immanuel;*

*which is, being interpreted, God with us.   24 And Joseph
arose from his sleep, and did as the angel of the Lord commanded him, and took unto him his wife;   25 and knew
her not till she had brought forth a son: and he called his
name* JESUS.

The genealogy of Jesus declared him to be the Son of
David.   The story of his birth reveals him as the Son of
God.   It includes an explanation of the name which was
given and of the prophecy which was fulfilled.   The story
is brief, but it bears the features characteristic of Matthew,
the "Gospel of the King," of the predicted and rejected
Messiah; for it shows that the mother of Jesus is about to
be repudiated and that Joseph who was to be his legal
father is addressed as the "son of David," that Jesus is to
save "his people" and that an Old Testament prediction is
divinely fulfilled in his birth.

This account of the supernatural birth of our Lord is
given with inspired delicacy and reserve, yet with such
definiteness and clearness as to leave no doubt as to the
fact recorded.   The statement of the perplexity of Joseph,
the reference to Jewish law and custom, the divine guidance granted in the dream, the simple declaration of the
miraculous event, are all so natural and circumstantial as

to indicate that the writer was composing not a poetic idyll but sober history.

It is not necessary to believe that the deity or sinlessness of Christ were conditioned upon the miracle of his birth; it is conceivable that they might have been secured by some other method of incarnation; but surely, in the light of this miracle, they are more easily understood, and it is further true that doubt as to this miracle is usually accompanied by a denial of the divine person of our Lord or of the authority of Scripture.

Nor should this miracle be regarded as difficult to believe. Christ is himself the embodiment of miracle. In him the human and divine are inseparably united. If he has existed eternally as God, if his earthly ministry was attended by superhuman works, if he left the world by a supernatural resurrection and ascension, it is not incredible that his coming to earth was attended by miracle and mystery. The real importance of the event lies, however, not in the method, but in the result of the supernatural birth. This is emphasized by the announcement of the name of Jesus and by the interpretation of an inspired prophecy. "Jesus" is the Greek form of the Hebrew word "Joshua" ("Jehovah is salvation") and in the dream it is announced by the angel in the form of this memorable promise, "Thou shalt call his name JESUS; for it is he that shall save his people from their sins." Other men had borne that same name; notably, the great deliverer Joshua, who had gained the victory over the peoples of Canaan, and also the high priest who had aided in the restoration of Jerusalem; but now One was to appear who was to realize in its fullness all that the name implied; he was to save his people from all the guilt and power of sin.

This birth and this inspiring name were interpreted by Matthew as the fulfillment of an ancient prophecy. In the days of Ahaz, Isaiah had predicted that God was to grant deliverance to Judah from the kings of Israel and Syria, and that as a symbol of this divine intervention a virgin should bring forth a son who should be called "Immanuel," which means "God with us."   The ancient prophet may not have had in mind either a miracle or an event of the distant future, but the writer of the Gospel saw that the true meaning of his prediction was realized in the birth of Jesus, for he was no mere pledge of divine deliverance but himself a divine Savior, not only was his name a token of the presence of God, but he himself was manifest deity. The real significance of the birth of Jesus, as here related, lies therefore in the fact that the Son of Mary is also the incarnate God who is able to save those who put their trust in him, for he is all that his blessed name implies, our divine Savior, "JESUS."

C. THE VISIT OF THE WISE MEN Ch. 2:1-12

1 Now when Jesus was born in Bethlehem of Judæa in the days of Herod the king, behold, Wise-men from the east came to Jerusalem, saying, 2 Where is he that is born King of the Jews? for we saw his star in the east, and are come to worship him. 3 And when Herod the king heard it, he was troubled, and all Jerusalem with him. 4 And gathering together all the chief priests and scribes of the people, he inquired of them where the Christ should be born. 5 And they said unto him, In Bethlehem of Judæa: for thus it is written through the prophet,

6 And thou Bethlehem, land of Judah,
   Art in no wise least among the princes of Judah:
   For out of thee shall come forth a governor,
   Who shall be shepherd of my people Israel.

7 Then Herod privily called the Wise-men, and learned of them exactly what time the star appeared. 8 And he sent them to Bethlehem, and said, Go and search out exactly concerning the young child; and when ye have found him, bring me word, that I also may come and worship him. 9 And they, having heard the king, went their way; and lo, the star, which they saw in the east, went before them, till it came and stood over where the young child was. 10 And when they saw the star, they rejoiced with exceeding great joy. 11 And they came into the house and saw the young child with Mary his mother; and they fell down and worshipped him; and opening their treasures they offered unto him gifts, gold and frankincense and myrrh. 12 And being warned of God in a dream that they should not return to Herod, they departed into their own country another way.

Fancy has been allowed to play so freely with the story of the "Wise-men from the east" that in most minds it is difficult to dissociate the elements of fable from those of fact. It is commonly imagined that these Wise Men were kings, that they were three in number, that they were named Caspar, Melchior, and Balthasar, that one came from Greece, one from India, and the third from Egypt. All these statements belong to the realm of fiction, as do the descriptions of their journey and of their retinue, and the stories of their later life, and of their baptism by Thomas. It is even said that their bones were discovered in the fourth century by Saint Helena, were brought to Constantinople and deposited in the Church of Saint Sophia, subsequently transferred to Milan, and finally brought by Frederick Barbarossa to Cologne, where the three skulls are guarded today in a golden shrine in the great cathedral.

In reality nothing is known of these Wise Men in addition to the few brief statements here recorded by Matthew. Out of the mystery of their past they step upon the stage for only one short scene and then they disappear forever. However, the part they play is not unimportant and the lessons they bring are full of meaning.

Their designation as "Wise-men" is a translation of the Greek word "Magi," a name by which they are familiarly known, and from which have come such terms as "magic" and "magician." They were probably members of an Oriental priestly caste, who were familiar with astronomy or astrology, and who had been taught by Jews of the Dispersion to expect the coming of a Savior, a universal King.

Some sign in the heaven convinced them that such a Prince had appeared and they journeyed to Jerusalem, the capital city of the Jews, to render to the King who had been born the homage which was his due. The important point is that these men were heathen and that they represent the firstfruits of the Gentile nations. They symbolize the truth that in the great world today there are countless hungry hearts yearning for a divine Savior and ready to follow even faint and imperfect signs which may lead to his feet.

The background of the story is peculiarly dark. "When Herod the king heard it, he was troubled, and all Jerusalem with him." The cruel and suspicious tyrant feared that his power might be endangered by one who was reputed to be born "King of the Jews"; and the people themselves, who should have rejoiced in the announcement that their Deliverer had come, were distressed rather than gladdened by the arrival and the strange story of the Wise Men. Herod seems to have been the only one who was stirred to action or sufficiently concerned to aid the travelers in their quest. He summoned the Jewish leaders to learn from them where their promised Messiah was to be born. They knew exactly; they were familiar with the prophecy which pointed to Bethlehem, but they showed not the slightest interest in the possibility that their Messiah had appeared. It was Herod who closely questioned the Wise Men and sent them to report concerning "the young child," promising, hoary hypocrite that he was, to "come and worship him."

Thus it is now; many who are most familiar with the facts concerning Christ are least interested to accept him as their Lord, while some, like Herod, are hostile to him, fearing that to admit his claims may result in some personal loss.

Here, too, is a lesson in divine guidance. God gave the Wise Men a sign in the east; he led them to Jerusalem; he spoke to them from the Scripture; he directed them to Bethlehem, and finally showed them how to return to their homes in safety. Where hearts are eager to find the King, there are always provided signs which lead at last into his presence chamber. The method of guidance may be mysterious, the fact is certain. In the case of the Wise Men it is impossible to affirm what is meant by "the star, which they saw in the east." Was it a planet or a conjunction of planets, or one of those variable stars which sometimes flash forth with unwonted brilliance? An actual star might have guided them westward and southward, but how could a star move before them on that last brief journey and stand over a definite house in the little town of Bethlehem? It seems probable that the guidance was supernatural. Something like a star in appearance, but near the earth, may have been granted to lead those travelers to their sacred goal. It has been conjectured that it was the "cloud of glory" which had led the people through the wilderness, the chariot of Jehovah, the pavilion of the King. Here speculation is futile, the reality is plain; where men really are eager to learn the truth concerning Christ, providences are granted which give them occasion to rejoice "with exceeding great joy."

The third familiar lesson concerns the service of Christ. It is embodied in the picture of the Wise Men as "they fell down and worshipped him; and opening their treasures they offered unto him gifts, gold and frankincense and myrrh." When one sees the King in his beauty, when one recognizes in Christ the divine Savior, there is always awakened the desire to render to him priceless offerings. It is not necessary to regard the gifts of the Magi as symbols; but they were surely princely and precious. They rightly indicate that the acceptance of Christ involves the devotion to him of praise, and of love, and of treasure, and of toil, and of life.

When this story is compared with the early chapters of Luke it appears that the visit of the Wise Men must have occurred at least forty days after the birth of Jesus. There is no difficulty in harmonizing the accounts; but the contrasts emphasize the features which ever characterize the Gospel of Matthew. Here no humble shepherds are sent to find a "babe lying in a manger," but distinguished sages from foreign lands offer their princely gifts, while Herod the Great trembles on his throne. This is the "Gospel of the Messiah"; and here Jesus is declared to be the King of the Jews who was definitely predicted as the shepherd of Israel to be born "in Bethlehem of Judæa." This is the Gospel of "rejection," and here the rulers of Israel appear from the first as indifferent to his coming, and "all Jerusalem" is "troubled" by his birth. It is also the Gospel of the coming and the triumph of Christ; and here appear the representatives of the Gentile nations offering homage to him before whom all knees will bow, whom someday all will acknowledge as universal King.

D. THE FLIGHT INTO EGYPT Ch. 2:13-23

13 Now when they were departed, behold, an angel of the Lord appeareth to Joseph in a dream, saying, Arise and take the young child and his mother, and flee into Egypt, and be thou there until I tell thee: for Herod will seek the young child to destroy him. 14 And he arose and took the young child and his mother by night, and departed into Egypt; 15 and was there until the death of Herod: that it might be fulfilled which was spoken by the Lord through the prophet, saying, Out of Egypt did I call my son.

16 Then Herod, when he saw that he was mocked of the Wise-men, was exceeding wroth, and sent forth, and slew all the male children that were in Bethlehem, and in all the borders thereof, from two years old and under, according to the time which he had exactly learned of the Wise-men. 17 Then was fulfilled that which was spoken through Jeremiah the prophet, saying,

18 A voice was heard in Ramah,
Weeping and great mourning,
Rachel weeping for her children;
And she would not be comforted, because they are not.
19 But when Herod was dead, behold, an angel of the

*Lord appeareth in a dream to Joseph in Egypt, saying, 20
Arise and take the young child and his mother, and go into
the land of Israel: for they are dead that sought the young
child's life. 21 And he arose and took the young child and
his mother, and came into the land of Israel. 22 But when
he heard that Archelaus was reigning over Judæa in the
room of his father Herod, he was afraid to go thither; and
being warned of God in a dream, he withdrew into the
parts of Galilee, 23 and came and dwelt in a city called
Nazareth; that it might be fulfilled which was spoken
through the prophets, that he should be called a Nazarene.*

In addition to the story of the Wise Men, Matthew records only two other incidents in the infancy of Jesus: the
flight into Egypt occasioned by the cruel jealousy of
Herod, and the return to Palestine made possible by the
death of the murderous king. The hatred of Herod was
stirred to a rage by the failure of the Wise Men to report
to him of the Child whom they regarded as King of the
Jews, whom Herod desired to kill. When, therefore, he
learned that they had disappeared without returning to
Jerusalem, he sent forth his heartless command to slaugh-
ter "all the male children that were in Bethlehem, and in
all the borders thereof, from two years old and under";
he wished to make sure that the rival King, a mere helpless
babe, had been destroyed. Such a deed was wholly in accord with the character of Herod, who had recently murdered his own sons, Alexander and Aristobulus, for fear
that they might usurp his throne. Thus jealousy often appears as the most cruel of passions.

However, before the heartless edict of the king had been
issued, Joseph, with Mary and Jesus, had fled to Egypt.
How old the child then was, or how many years were spent
in exile, is quite unknown. Two facts, however, are emphasized by the writer: the story, like that of the Magi, is
one of divine guidance, and second, all its incidents are
declared to be in fulfillment of inspired prophecy. On the
departure of the Wise Men, Joseph was warned by a dream

to "take the young child and his mother, and flee into Egypt." On the death of Herod he was directed by a dream to "arise and take the young child and his mother, and go into the land of Israel." While he might have returned to Judea, "being warned of God in a dream, he withdrew into the parts of Galilee." Thus by means of his own choosing, God is ever guiding those who are devoted to the interests of his Son.

The divine element of the history is further revealed by the connection of the events with Old Testament prophecy. In this one brief paragraph three distinct quotations are made. Matthew is the Gospel of the Messiah, the Gospel of "rejection," the Gospel of fulfillment, and here all these features can be distinctly traced, while the last is made peculiarly prominent. The flight into Egypt is declared to fulfill the words of Hosea, "Out of Egypt did I call my son." Matthew does not quote the exact words, nor does he mean that the prophet intended them as a prediction, but that the history of Israel in being brought out of Egypt was a type and anticipation of this experience of the Messiah, the true Son of God. The second quotation is from Jeremiah, a highly figurative passage in which Rachel, the mother of Joseph and Benjamin, is pictured rising from her grave and lamenting the destruction of her descendants as she sees the files of captives who, by order of the king of Babylon, are being driven northward from the desolated city. Her anguish is said to find its counterpart, the picture of her agony is said to be fulfilled, in the grief of the bereaved mothers of Bethlehem.

The third prophecy is less definite; it probably refers to no specific prediction but to an intimation of several writers that the Messiah was to be "despised and rejected of men." This was actually the experience of Jesus; and one reason for his being despised was the fact of his long residence in the obscure and humble town of Nazareth. Yet his dwelling there was due to divine guidance. On his return from Egypt, Joseph would have lived in Judea; but there Archelaus was ruling in the place of his father and had begun his reign as a true son of Herod by the murder of three thousand citizens. Thus it came to pass that Joseph, "being warned of God in a dream, . . . withdrew into . . . Galilee, and . . . dwelt in . . . Nazareth"; and as a result Jesus was "called a Nazarene." This was a term of reproach and scorn, and the prophets had foretold that the Messiah would thus bear the contempt of men; but from despised Nazareth came forth One who finally will fulfill the prophecies of glory as he once did the predictions of shame, Jesus the Christ, the universal King.

E. THE HERALD OF THE KING Ch. 3:1-12

1 And in those days cometh John the Baptist, preaching in the wilderness of Judæa, saying, 2 Repent ye; for the kingdom of heaven is at hand. 3 For this is he that was spoken of through Isaiah the prophet, saying,

The voice of one crying in the wilderness,
Make ye ready the way of the Lord,
Make his paths straight.

4 Now John himself had his raiment of camel's hair, and a leathern girdle about his loins; and his food was locusts and wild honey. 5 Then went out unto him Jerusalem, and all Judæa, and all the region round about the Jordan; 6 and they were baptized of him in the river Jordan, confessing their sins. 7 But when he saw many of the Pharisees and Sadducees coming to his baptism, he said unto them, Ye offspring of vipers, who warned you to flee from the wrath to come? 8 Bring forth therefore fruit worthy of repentance: 9 and think not to say within yourselves, We have Abraham to our father: for I say unto you, that God is able of these stones to raise up children unto Abraham. 10 And even now the axe lieth at the root of the trees: every tree therefore that bringeth not forth good fruit is hewn down, and cast into the fire. 11 I indeed baptize you in water unto repentance: but he that cometh after me is mightier than I, whose shoes I am not worthy to bear: he shall baptize you in the Holy Spirit and in fire: 12 whose fan is in his hand, and he will thoroughly cleanse his threshing-floor; and he will gather his wheat into the garner, but the chaff he will burn up with unquenchable fire.

John the Baptist was the forerunner of Jesus; he prepared the way for the public ministry of our Lord; he was, in reality, the herald of the "King." This is evident from the word used to describe his work; he came "preaching," literally "heralding," and even the term "came" or "cometh" implies the "arrival of an official." This is evident also from the message he delivered, "Repent ye; for the kingdom of heaven is at hand"; the other Evangelists record the call to "repent"; but only Matthew adds the proclamation of the Kingdom. This is further evident from the prophecy quoted as fulfilled in his mission, "The voice of one crying in the wilderness, make ye ready the way of the Lord"; thus to John is assigned the role of a royal herald ordering the repair of the roads in view of the progress and near approach of the King; for, as in the Orient, where roads were few and poor, it was necessary to send an officer before a monarch to command the repair of the highways; so John by his call to repentance was preparing the people for the public ministry of Christ.

The time when John appeared is stated most definitely, "in those days," when Jesus was residing in Nazareth; but nearly thirty years had passed, and when at last Jesus was ready to leave his obscure home and to undertake his royal task, John was sent to arouse the expectation of the people and to make them eager for the coming of the King.

His mode of life was in keeping with the stern character of his office; he was clad in a rough garment of camel's hair cloth; "his food was locusts and wild honey." He was not teaching men to be ascetics; but as he was calling them from self-indulgence and from sin, he set an example of self-denial and of self-forgetful devotion to his task.

His success was immediate and surprising; the nation was aroused, and multitudes were baptized, not as a mere

Jewish rite symbolizing a purification which might be repeated daily, but as a sign of a definite break with a sinful past, of a crisis never to be experienced again.

Among the crowds John saw "many of the Pharisees and Sadducees coming to his baptism." They had not repented; they did not believe in John; they had no desire to do the will of God; they were ready to reject and to destroy the Christ whose coming John proclaimed. He addressed them in bitter rebuke and in tones of ironical surprise, "Ye offspring of vipers, can it be that ye are actually aroused and seek to escape the coming judgment as serpents flee before advancing flames?" Repentance must be sincere; it involves a change of heart and a corresponding life; "bring forth therefore fruit worthy of repentance." Inherited privileges, and membership in a religious sect will not suffice; "think not to say within yourselves, We have Abraham to our father"; God can prepare a people for himself out of most unpromising material, he "is able of these stones to raise up children unto Abraham."

Such in part was the rebuke addressed by John to the insincere and impenitent; Matthew continues to record the message intended for the multitudes as well. It consists of warnings and of promises. Repentance is absolutely necessary, for judgment is near. "The axe lieth at the root of the trees"; it is not to prune but to destroy; "every tree therefore that bringeth not forth good fruit is hewn down, and cast into the fire." The King is about to appear; he will baptize the penitent "in the Holy Spirit," not merely with the physical symbol of water but into spiritual fellowship with a divine Person, not merely to symbolize a turning from sin but to secure an actual deliverance from the guilt and power of sin.

Yet he is also to baptize "in fire." The coming judgment is described by the picture of a threshing floor; the penitent are like the wheat which will be garnered into the Kingdom, but the impenitent are like the chaff which will be burned up "with unquenchable fire."

Such is the proclamation of the herald: The King is coming to establish his Kingdom; but judgment will precede; turn from sin, accept the King, and share the glory of his reign.

How perfectly this story of the ministry of John corresponds with the uniform features of the First Gospel. Here appears the herald of the Messiah, his denunciation of the rulers intimates their future rejection of his Lord, his prediction of judgment points to the ultimate triumph and perfected Kingdom of Christ.

F. THE ANOINTING OF THE KING Ch. 3:13-17

13 Then cometh Jesus from Galilee to the Jordan unto John, to be baptized of him. 14 But John would have hindered him, saying, I have need to be baptized of thee, and comest thou to me? 15 But Jesus answering said unto him, Suffer it now: for thus it becometh us to fulfil all righteousness. Then he suffereth him. 16 And Jesus, when he was baptized, went up straightway from the water: and lo, the heavens were opened unto him, and he saw the Spirit of God descending as a dove, and coming upon him; 17 and lo, a voice out of the heavens, saying, This is my beloved Son, in whom I am well pleased.

There is something strikingly majestic in the appearance of Jesus as for the first time, in this Gospel of Matthew, he steps upon the scene; yet something equally humble. He unexpectedly presents himself before the great herald who has been proclaiming his coming and offers to submit to the baptism John is administering. His kingly superiority is shown by the surprise and hesitation of John and by his own word of command, "Suffer it now: for thus it becometh us to fulfil all righteousness." These are the first words from the lips of Jesus which Matthew records. They denote at once royal dignity and divine humility. The "suffer it now" is significant. John had hesitated to baptize Jesus, not that he then knew him to be the Messiah, but because he saw in him One of infinite moral superiority to himself. Jesus does not disclaim this superiority, he admits it; but he bids John, just for the time, to yield to him the inferior position, which he voluntarily assumes.

Yet, why should Jesus be baptized? He has answered, "to fulfil all righteousness," that is, that the righteous will of God, which Jesus alone understands, may be done in all its fullness. By his submission to baptism he set his seal of approval upon the work of John as being "not of men but of God," and attested the word of John that repentance and confession of sin are absolutely necessary for those who are to enter the Kingdom of Heaven.

Further, he thus identified himself with his people, not as himself sinful, but as sympathizing with sinners in their hatred of sin, in their sorrow for its burden, and in their hope and expectation of relief. Only those who sympathize can save.

Then, again, as baptism was for each penitent the beginning of a new life acceptable to God, so the baptism of Jesus was his entrance upon his public ministry; he had no life of sin to leave behind in the waters of Jordan, but there he did bring to an end the home life of Nazareth, the quiet peaceful years of preparation, and did accept as "the righteous will of God," the storm and strain and sacrifice of the work which he had come to do.

The essential features of the incident, however, were those which immediately followed, the vision of the descending Spirit, and the voice from heaven. The former was a symbolic indication of the divine power by which his ministry was to be accomplished, the latter was an assurance that he was the Messiah, the very Christ of God. Both were vitally related to his baptism. He had then yielded himself to his task, he is now prepared for his service; he had then dedicated himself to his work, he is now consecrated to his career. We are not to suppose that he before had lacked the presence of the Spirit, nor that he now assumed any new relationship to the Father; but at this hour of his baptism there came the new assurance of divine power and sonship. The vision was of "the Spirit of God descending as a dove," the symbol of gentleness and meekness, for the King was to be humble and lowly in spirit and ministry; the voice of the Father was heard to say, "This is my beloved Son, in whom I am well pleased," declaring Jesus to be the Messiah, the very Christ of God.

This was the true anointing of the King. As of old the chosen rulers of Israel were anointed with oil to suggest that the divine Spirit, thus symbolized, would grant them needed grace for the fulfillment of their tasks, so our Lord went forth from the scene of his baptism, anointed with the Holy Spirit, and fully equipped for his kingly ministry.

Thus for the followers of Christ, it is true that, while they all are granted the abiding presence of the Spirit, nevertheless, when they yield themselves anew to the service of their Lord, they are filled anew with his Spirit, empowered for their tasks and strengthened by a deeper assurance that they are indeed the sons of God.

G. THE TEMPTATION OF THE KING Ch. 4:1-11

1 Then was Jesus led up of the Spirit into the wilderness to be tempted of the devil. 2 And when he had fasted forty days and forty nights, he afterward hungered. 3 And the tempter came and said unto him, If thou art the Son of God, command that these stones become bread. 4 But he answered and said, It is written, Man shall not live by bread alone, but by every word that proceedeth out of the mouth of God. 5 Then the devil taketh him into the holy city; and he set him on the pinnacle of the temple, 6 and saith unto him, If thou art the Son of God, cast thyself down: for it is written,

He shall give his angels charge concerning thee:
and,

On their hands they shall bear thee up,
Lest haply thou dash thy foot against a stone.
7 Jesus said unto him, Again it is written, Thou shalt not

*make trial of the Lord thy God. 8 Again, the devil taketh
him unto an exceeding high mountain, and showeth him all
the kingdoms of the world, and the glory of them; 9 and
he said unto him, All these things will I give thee, if thou
wilt fall down and worship me. 10 Then saith Jesus unto
him, Get thee hence, Satan: for it is written, Thou shalt
worship the Lord thy God, and him only shalt thou serve.
11 Then the devil leaveth him; and behold, angels came
and ministered unto him.*

The most important, the most memorable, the most
mysterious battle in history, was the conflict between Jesus
and the devil. It is not to be supposed that this was the
first or last assault of the false against the rightful Ruler
of this world; but the experience which closed the forty
days spent by Jesus in the wilderness was a type and summary of all the attacks of Satan and a pledge and prophecy
of his final defeat.

The time is significant. "Then," when at his baptism
Jesus had been assured of his divine sonship and had become conscious of his supernatural powers, "Then was
Jesus . . . tempted," and to this new consciousness and
experience each attack of the enemy was related. The
seasons of highest spiritual exaltation are often followed by
those of greatest moral peril; after the opening skies the
descending Spirit and the heavenly voice come the whisper
of the demon and the serpent's hiss. So, too, every en-
larged power, every advancement in life, every increased
privilege, is accompanied by some new danger to the soul.

"Jesus was led . . . into the wilderness to be tempted,"
and the place is likewise suggested, for in the hour of
bitter struggle and testing the human heart is conscious of
peculiar loneliness and isolation; happy is he who is then
conscious of the presence of a divine Deliverer and of
angel ministers.

Jesus was "led up of the Spirit . . . to be tempted,"
for it was in accord with a divine purpose and its issue was
an unbounded benefit; Jesus was thus prepared to meet tri-

umphantly every temptation of his earthly ministry, and his followers are assured of his sympathy in their hours of deepest darkness and of his strength in places of most desperate need.

1. The first temptation was in the sphere of bodily appetite. After forty days of fasting there had come the reaction of ravenous hunger. "The tempter came and said unto him, If thou art the Son of God, command that these stones become bread." Why not? The desire for food was innocent, the need was imperative, and he had the power to secure instant relief; but had Jesus resorted to miracle to gratify his human desire and to relieve his personal needs, he would have separated himself from the experiences of men, he would have surrendered the very purpose of his mission; for him there would have been no suffering and in the end no cross, for us there now would be none to sympathize and none to save. A divine impulse had driven him into the wilderness as a divine purpose had brought him into the world, he must endure as a man, whatever the divine purpose may involve; there will be times and places for miracles, but never to gratify any selfish desire. Divine sonship secured superhuman powers, but it obligated perfect submission to the will of God. It is the custom of the tempter to entice men to gratify innocent desires in wrong ways; and many careers are ruined by devoting to selfish indulgence the powers which have been designed for higher service.

The real character of this temptation is revealed by the quotation which Jesus makes from the Old Testament. By one flash the battery of the enemy is unmasked and is silenced, "Man shall not live by bread alone, but by every word that proceedeth out of the mouth of God." Jesus recognized his need, but he was resolved to depend upon God for its supply. The devil had been tempting him to doubt the goodness or the power of God. Jesus declared that as his Father had sustained Israel in the wilderness, so now he would sustain his Son; then it had been by bread from heaven, how it now might be he did not know: he left that in the hands of God; he knew that he was in way of his Father's will and he knew that his Father would supply his need. To say that the phrase "Man shall not live by bread alone" implies that man has higher powers and capacities which physical food cannot satisfy is quite aside from the point. It was exactly physical food which Jesus had in mind; this was his need; and he resisted the temptation to an improper gratification of bodily appetite by his belief that God would supply every real need, and that however strong the demand of appetite might be, the way and the will of God were certain to secure satisfaction and the truest enjoyment of life.

2. The second temptation was in the sphere of intellectual curiosity. The devil had failed to make Jesus doubt; he takes him at his word and now tries to drive him to the other extreme of presumptuous trust. He leads him to "the pinnacle of the temple" and urges him to cast himself down. Why should he? Just to see what the experience would be. As he is the Son of God, he is tempted to test the providential care of his Father. He is asked to put himself in a situation of mortal peril and to trust in God to deliver him by supernatural power. To strengthen his suggestion the devil cites Scripture, as he always can for his purpose, "He shall give his angels charge concerning thee: and, on their hands they shall bear thee up." By this device Satan still seeks to destroy human souls. He urges men to "see for themselves," to increase their knowledge by experiences which needlessly endanger their purity, their credit, their health, their honor, to place themselves in moral peril, to live beyond their means, to undertake tasks beyond their strength. He does this even in the holiest places, even in full sight of the Temple where faith will be strongest, even in Christian service; he bids them to trust in God, and assures them that as children of God, as men of strong principles, as followers of Christ, no harm can possibly befall them, that God will work miracles and will preserve them.

Jesus met the temptation and the text by another quotation which showed that Satan had misapplied the Scripture, "Again it is written, Thou shalt not make trial of the Lord thy God." To compel God to rescue us, to put him to the test, to see whether or not he will act, is not faith but presumption, not belief but distrust. In the path of actual duty the child of God need not fear the most threatening perils, but one who puts himself in unnecessary danger cannot expect divine deliverance.

3. The third temptation is in the sphere of personal ambition. Jesus is offered "all the kingdoms of the world." It is noticeable that Matthew, the "Gospel of the King," unlike Luke, the "Gospel of the Ideal Man," places this temptation last, and brings the story thus to its climax. It was not unnatural that Jesus should desire universal rule; this he claimed; this he expected; this he will yet attain; but not on the devil's terms, "If thou wilt fall down and worship me." Of course not; what could be more abhorrent to the Son of God? He has ready his inspired reply, "Thou shalt worship the Lord thy God, and him only shalt thou serve." However, for even the followers of Christ, there is subtle power in this appeal of the tempter. He does not ask them to give up their high purposes of ultimate helpfulness and service to others and to the world; he only asks them to compromise with evil as a means of attaining the goal. He insists that the end will justify the means. He intimates that in the world of commerce, or society, or politics, evil methods are so much in vogue that success can be attained only by complicity with evil. He tells us that this is his world and we can rule only in so far as we make terms with him.

For Christ the issue was now clearly drawn, it was submission to Satan and an easy way to worldly popularity and temporary power, or it was loyalty to God with conflict and toil and tears and a cross, but then a universal and an eternal throne. That same choice is for his followers; for them unswerving loyalty is the way of the cross but that is the way of the crown.

"Then the devil leaveth him; and behold, angels came and ministered unto him."   Victory is possible, and after the conflict comes glad refreshment for all who fight with the sword of the Spirit and trust in the Son of God.

II
THE PROCLAMATION
OF THE KING
Chs. 4:12 to 7:29

A. THE CIRCUMSTANCES Ch. 4:12-25

12 Now when he heard that John was delivered up, he withdrew into Galilee; 13 and leaving Nazareth, he came and dwelt in Capernaum, which is by the sea, in the borders of Zebulun and Naphtali: 14 that it might be fulfilled which was spoken through Isaiah the prophet, saying,
15 The land of Zebulun and the land of Naphtali,
   Toward the sea, beyond the Jordan,
   Galilee of the Gentiles,
16 The people that sat in darkness
   Saw a great light,
   And to them that sat in the region and shadow of death,
   To them did light spring up.
17 From that time began Jesus to preach, and to say, Repent ye; for the kingdom of heaven is at hand.

18 And walking by the sea of Galilee, he saw two brethren, Simon who is called Peter, and Andrew his brother, casting a net into the sea; for they were fishers. 19 And he saith unto them, Come ye after me, and I will make you fishers of men. 20 And they straightway left the nets, and followed him. 21 And going on from thence he saw other two brethren, James the son of Zebedee, and John his brother, in the boat with Zebedee their father, mending their nets; and he called them. 22 And they straightway left the boat and their father, and followed him.

23 And Jesus went about in all Galilee, teaching in their synagogues, and preaching the gospel of the kingdom, and healing all manner of disease and all manner of sickness among the people. 24 And the report of him went forth into all Syria: and they brought unto him all that were sick,

holden with divers diseases and torments, possessed with
demons, and epileptic, and palsied; and he healed them.
25 And there followed him great multitudes from Galilee
and Decapolis and Jerusalem and Judæa and from beyond
the Jordan.

A distinguishing feature of the Gospel of Matthew is the
prominence of great discourses or collected sayings of
Jesus. The first and most familiar of these is popularly
known as "The Sermon on the Mount." It may be regarded as a proclamation or manifesto of the King, or as
the Magna Charta of his Kingdom. The closing verses of
chapter four indicate the circumstances under which these
sayings were delivered; the sermon itself is recorded in
chapters five, six, and seven.

1. Jesus had selected for himself a new home. Vs.
12-17. After his early experiences in Judea, after baptism
and temptation, he had returned to Galilee and settled for
a time in Nazareth, the home of his youth and early man-
hood; but as he was about to begin his public ministry,
"leaving Nazareth, he came and dwelt in Capernaum."
The occasion of his withdrawal to Galilee is declared to be
the arrest and imprisonment of John the Baptist. If his
herald is treated thus, what can the King expect? John
had severely rebuked the religious rulers in Jerusalem and
Judea; now that his career is ended their opposition is the
more likely to interrupt the work of Jesus. He retires to a
part of the country where their influence is less powerful.
Galilee was despised, as lacking in religious privileges; it
was, however, an attractive field for the proclamation of
the Kingdom. The thronging multitudes were keen, alert,
and intelligent; among them were many Gentiles who
would carry the good news into all the world; here Jesus
could collect a large company of followers before again offering himself to the nation, in Jerusalem, as the promised
Messiah.

The location of Capernaum "by the sea," and on the
border line of the two ancient tribes of Israel, "Zebulun
and Naphtali," is stated thus definitely to show how exactly

an inspired prophecy was fulfilled. Isaiah had predicted that these northern tribes which had suffered most severely should be granted deliverance from their enemies; in their "darkness" of despair should spring up the "light" of relief. Matthew declares that the prophecy is most truly fulfilled by the appearance in this region of Jesus, the "Light of the world" who would bring deliverance from the tyranny of sin. His coming was, as Matthew always indicates, the coming of a King, and the passage from Isaiah thus further describes him: "The government shall be upon his shoulder: and his name shall be called Wonderful, Counsellor, Mighty God, Everlasting Father, Prince of Peace."

Thus as Jesus now begins his ministry in Galilee it is described as a proclamation of his Kingdom, "From that time began Jesus to preach, and to say, Repent ye; for the kingdom of heaven is at hand." In the person of the King and in the proclamation of his Kingdom the light was shining which yet will banish all darkness from the world.

2. The first followers of Christ had also been summoned. Vs. 18-22. These were the brothers Peter and Andrew, and James and John. They previously had known Jesus, and believed him to be the Messiah; but now they were called from their homes and their usual course of life to devote all their time and energies to his service. The King needed men whom he could train as his heralds, and who could aid in proclaiming his Kingdom. He had summoned them with an imperial command, "Come ye after me," but he had added an inspiring promise, "I will make you fishers of men." Their work was to be somewhat similar in kind, requiring the same qualifications and abilities, but its results were to be infinitely more glorious. Promptly, they left their nets, the boat, and "their father, and followed him." Jesus is still summoning men to his service. His command involves sacrifice, but it should be promptly obeyed, for it promises fellowship with a King and the incomparable rewards and privileges of his Kingdom.

3. The Opening Ministry, vs. 23-25, probably a circuit

in Galilee, had also been accomplished, and it is recorded briefly, before the Sermon on the Mount, to suggest and summarize the conditions under which the Kingdom was being proclaimed.

The ministry was that of "teaching" and "preaching" and "healing." The last was unquestionably miraculous and it resulted in spreading the fame of Jesus through all the province of Syria, while from every part of Palestine actual multitudes thronged about him. It was at such a time and under such conditions that Jesus uttered those matchless precepts which are preserved for us in the Sermon on the Mount. The followers of Christ who go forth to preach and to teach and to heal in his name can expect to reach the multitudes only in case they observe the laws of his Kingdom and manifest in their lives the power of the King.

B. THE SERMON ON THE MOUNT Chs. 5 to 7

1. INTRODUCTION: THE CHARACTER AND BLESSEDNESS OF THE KING'S SERVANTS
Ch. 5:1-16

1 And seeing the multitudes, he went up into the mountain: and when he had sat down, his disciples came unto him: 2 and he opened his mouth and taught them, saying,

3 Blessed are the poor in spirit: for theirs is the kingdom of heaven.

4 Blessed are they that mourn: for they shall be comforted.

5 Blessed are the meek: for they shall inherit the earth.

6 Blessed are they that hunger and thirst after righteousness: for they shall be filled.

7 Blessed are the merciful: for they shall obtain mercy.

8 Blessed are the pure in heart: for they shall see God.

9 Blessed are the peacemakers: for they shall be called sons of God.

10 Blessed are they that have been persecuted for righteousness' sake: for theirs is the kingdom of heaven. 11

Blessed are ye when men *shall reproach you, and persecute you, and say all manner of evil against you falsely, for my sake.   12 Rejoice, and be exceeding glad: for great is your reward in heaven: for so persecuted they the prophets that were before you.*

13 Ye are the salt of the earth: but if the salt have lost its savor, wherewith shall it be salted? it is thenceforth good for nothing, but to be cast out and trodden under foot of men.   14 Ye are the light of the world.   A city set on a hill cannot be hid.   15 Neither do men light a lamp, and put it under the bushel, but on the stand; and it shineth unto all that are in the house.   16 Even so let your light shine before men; that they may see your good works, and glorify your Father who is in heaven.

The Sermon on the Mount is the supreme discourse in the literature of the world.   It is not, however, the sum and substance of Christianity.   It does set forth the fundamental laws of the Kingdom, but aside from the truth of the divine person and redeeming work of Christ, it would fill the heart of the hearer with bewilderment and despair.   It reveals a divine ideal and a perfect standard of conduct by which all men are condemned as sinful and to which men can attain only by divine help.   It is commonly called "The Sermon on the Mount" from the circumstance of the place where it was delivered.   This fact, however, is by no means essential, and the familiar title gives no conception of the sermon.   It might better be called "The Proclamation of the King," or possibly "The Sermon of True Righteousness," for surely its theme is the righteousness which the King requires.   It sets forth the fundamental law of his Kingdom.

The discourse opens with a description of the character and the blessedness of the followers of the King.   This introductory section contains those familiar promises commonly known as the Beatitudes, and also contains the parables of the salt of the earth and the light of the world.   The Beatitudes suggest ideal relations both to God and to man. The first of these sayings may be regarded as comprehensive, "Blessed are the poor in spirit." It indicates the humility and conscious dependence which characterize a right attitude toward God. The promise is that "theirs is the kingdom of heaven." They already enjoy something of its blessedness; but the riches of their inheritance belong to the future when the Kingdom shall be manifested in its perfection. These heirs of the Kingdom "mourn" for their sins and they are certain of a divine comfort. They are meek in their relation toward their fellowmen, but they are yet to "inherit the earth." They are hungering and thirsting after righteousness, but they are certain to be satisfied. They are "merciful" toward others, and they "shall obtain mercy" from God. They are "pure in heart," and consequently they now enjoy a divine fellowship and shall yet be blest with the vision beatific when they see the King in his beauty. They are eager to make peace among men and for such royal service they shall yet be acclaimed as the "sons of God."

It might be expected that persons of such character would enjoy peace and popularity in the world. For them no such experience is promised, in the present. On the contrary, they are to expect persecution. In a world which rejects the King his followers must expect to share his sufferings; but "theirs is the kingdom of heaven," and in the blessedness of that Kingdom their earthly distresses will be forgotten. This last Beatitude is directly applied to the disciples who were listening to the Master's word. They are bidden to rejoice when reproached and persecuted and slandered. They should count themselves happy not only because of the reward which awaits them in heaven, but also because they have the honor of belonging to the great army of prophets and saints and martyrs who before them have suffered for righteousness' sake and have won the crown of glory.

The blessedness of these followers of the King is not confined, however, to the future. It is their high privilege,

in the present, to exert upon the world in which they live
a saving and helpful influence. Yet this can be exerted
only when they are true to the requirements of the King,
and when they seek to make known his person and power.
"Ye are the salt of the earth." Their influence would keep
the world from corruption; but if so they must be true to
their own convictions; otherwise they would be like salt
which has lost its savor. "Ye are the light of the world";
but if their mission was to be performed, their light must
not be hid. Those who built a city upon a hill never intended it to be concealed, as those who lighted a lamp did
not hide it in under a measure. So those who had been
called to follow the King must manifest the righteousness
which he requires if they are to fill their rightful places and
to reflect glory upon their Father in heaven.

2. THE KING'S SERVANTS AND THE MORAL LAW
Ch. 5:17-48

a. The General Principle   Ch. 5:17-20

*17 Think not that I came to destroy the law or the
prophets: I came not to destroy, but to fulfil. 18 For verily
I say unto you, Till heaven and earth pass away, one jot or
one tittle shall in no wise pass away from the law, till all
things be accomplished. 19 Whosoever therefore shall
break one of these least commandments, and shall teach
men so, shall be called least in the kingdom of heaven: but
whosoever shall do and teach them, he shall be called
great in the kingdom of heaven. 20 For I say unto you,
that except your righteousness shall exceed the righteousness of the scribes and Pharisees, ye shall in no wise enter
into the kingdom of heaven.*

In setting forth the righteousness required by his followers, Jesus naturally explained, first of all, the relation
in which this righteousness stands to the demands of the
law as delivered by Moses and the prophets. The general
principle is that Jesus came not to amend or to abrogate

this law, but to interpret it and himself to realize its demands both in his own experience and increasingly in the experience of his followers. "Think not that I came to destroy the law or the prophets: I came not to destroy, but to fulfil."

Jesus regards this moral law as changeless and eternal. "Till heaven and earth pass away, one jot or one tittle shall in no wise pass away from the law, till all things be accomplished." In his Kingdom, eminence and power will depend upon the attitude one has shown toward this law, both in proclaiming it to others and in observing it himself; the highest place will be assigned to him who shall do and keep its commandments.

More specifically still, Jesus contrasts the righteousness he requires with that which was manifested by the scribes and Pharisees. For them it was a matter of external observance, of form or of pretense. Jesus insists that it must be a matter of the heart, of motive, and of desire, as well as of external performance. Above all it must be a righteousness which regards the will of God and seeks to please him, in contrast with actions which are designed to secure merely the approval of men. One who manifests a mere formal righteousness will be excluded from the Kingdom, "Except your righteousness shall exceed the righteousness of the scribes and Pharisees, ye shall in no wise enter into the kingdom of heaven."

b. The Five Illustrations   Ch. 5:21-48

(1) The Sixth Commandment   Ch. 5:21-26

21 Ye have heard that it was said to them of old time, Thou shalt not kill; and whosoever shall kill shall be in danger of the judgment: 22 but I say unto you, that every one who is angry with his brother shall be in danger of the judgment; and whosoever shall say to his brother, Raca, shall be in danger of the council; and whosoever shall say, Thou fool, shall be in danger of the hell of fire. 23 If

therefore thou art offering thy gift at the altar, and there
rememberest that thy brother hath aught against thee, 24
leave there thy gift before the altar, and go thy way, first
be reconciled to thy brother, and then come and offer thy
gift. 25 Agree with thine adversary quickly, while thou
art with him in the way; lest haply the adversary deliver
thee to the judge, and the judge deliver thee to the officer,
and thou be cast into prison. 26 Verily I say unto thee,
Thou shalt by no means come out thence, till thou have
paid the last farthing.

Jesus suggests five illustrations of his interpretation of
the moral law as contrasted with the false interpretations
of the scribes and Pharisees. The latter were concerned
merely with external acts; Jesus traces every deed to the
underlying motive and thought. The first illustration is
taken from the law against murder. The Pharisee might
suppose that he had not broken the Sixth Commandment
if his hands were not red with the blood of his brother.
Jesus declares that anger itself is a breach of this commandment, for if allowed to express itself in action it
would finally result in murder. He suggests three expressions of this evil and intimates for each an increasing severity of punishment. He who is "angry with his brother"
is declared to be in danger of condemnation by the local
court. He whose ill will is expressed in slander and contempt will be made to answer before the supreme council,
but he whose anger expresses itself in open abuse and in
charges of impiety shall be in danger of the sufferings of
hell. So serious is this offense that if one remembers, even
in the hour of worship, that he has given occasion to his
brother for such a feeling against himself, even at the risk
of apparent irreverence, he should leave the place of worship and seek for a reconciliation; then he can come and
worship with acceptance before God. Nor is there any
time to be lost; opportunities are fleeting; if one delays, it
may be too late and he will be compelled to bear the ut-
most penalty. Thus seriously, then, Jesus warns his fol-

lowers against the perils of anger. Thus perfect is the fulfillment of the "law against murder" which he required.

(2) The Seventh Commandment   Ch. 5:27-32

27 Ye have heard that it was said, Thou shalt not commit adultery: 28 but I say unto you, that every one that looketh on a woman to lust after her hath committed adultery with her already in his heart. 29 And if thy right eye causeth thee to stumble, pluck it out, and cast it from thee: for it is profitable for thee that one of thy members should perish, and not thy whole body be cast into hell. 30 And if thy right hand causeth thee to stumble, cut it off, and cast it from thee: for it is profitable for thee that one of thy members should perish, and not thy whole body go into hell. 31 It was said also, Whosoever shall put away his wife, let him give her a writing of divorcement: 32 but I say unto you, that every one that putteth away his wife, saving for the cause of fornication, maketh her an adulteress: and whosoever shall marry her when she is put away committeth adultery.

Jesus applies the same reasoning in reference to the Seventh Commandment. He declares that it is broken not merely by a sinful act but by every impure desire. He warns against allowing any occasion for evil thought. No matter how great the sacrifice involved, one must put out of his life all that might cause him to be tempted needlessly, anything which might endanger the purity of his soul; if necessary, even that which is as precious as the right eye, or as the right hand, must be sacrificed. It is far better, as our Savior says, "that one of thy members should perish, and not that thy whole body go into hell."

Nor can the securing of a divorce justify an act which is contrary to the moral law. No mere decree of a court can make right that which is in itself impure. To divorce an innocent wife or a husband and then to marry another, no matter what the civil law may declare, is a breach of the moral law which cannot be allowed in a follower of Christ.

(3) Oaths Ch. 5:33-37

33 Again, ye have heard that it was said to them of old time, Thou shalt not forswear thyself, but shalt perform unto the Lord thine oaths: 34 but I say unto you, Swear not at all; neither by the heaven, for it is the throne of God; 35 nor by the earth, for it is the footstool of his feet; nor by Jerusalem, for it is the city of the great King. 36 Neither shalt thou swear by thy head, for thou canst not make one hair white or black. 37 But let your speech be, Yea, yea; Nay, nay: and whatsoever is more than these is of the evil one.

The next example of the true interpretation of the moral law refers to the requirements both of the Third and the Ninth Commandments. It warns against both profanity and unfaithfulness to promises. It does not refer to oaths taken in courts of law. These safeguard and secure the truth which is regarded as sacred and is fully protected by the very interpretation of the law upon which Jesus here insists. The Pharisee, at least the formalist, regarded himself as bound by an oath provided it was stated in certain words. To his mind the slightest verbal change relieved him from all moral obligation. Then again he excused himself for his profanity in case he did not mention some special form of the divine name. He believed he could swear by the throne of God, or by the earth, or by Jerusalem; but Jesus suggests that all these are contrary to the Commandment which forbids us to take the name of the Lord in vain. He insists that our speech should be simple; that our language should be purged of extravagance; that our purposes, our thoughts, and our lives should be so sincere and so pure and so honest, that a simple "yes" or "no" in our social intercourse, and in our usual dealings with others should quite suffice to satisfy them of the truthfulness of our statements.

(4) The Law of Retaliation   Ch. 5:38-42

38 Ye have heard that it was said, An eye for an eye, and a tooth for a tooth: 39 but I say unto you, Resist not him that is evil: but whosoever smiteth thee on thy right cheek, turn to him the other also. 40 And if any man would go to law with thee, and take away thy coat, let him have thy cloak also. 41 And whosoever shall compel thee to go one mile, go with him two. 42 Give to him that asketh thee, and from him that would borrow of thee turn not thou away.

The next illustration of the perfect righteousness which Jesus requires of his followers is suggested by a contrast which he draws between his law of perfect love and the traditional interpretation of an Old Testament precept which was used by the Pharisees as an excuse for retaliation and revenge. According to the law of Moses the civil courts were to administer justice in accordance with the command, "An eye for an eye, and a tooth for a tooth." This simply meant that the penalty was to fit the crime. It is a fundamental principle of law in all lands and ages; but the Pharisee and the formalist whom he represented used this prescription for civil courts as a pretext for taking private revenge. It is necessary to have this distinction in mind when we read the Master's words, if we would be kept from fanaticism and folly. When he gives the command, "Resist not him that is evil," he has in mind no thought that men are to allow the innocent to be abused and the helpless to be killed, when it is possible to protect and to deliver them. In such defense it may even be necessary to lay down life. Our Master is insisting, however, that we are never to inflict suffering in a spirit of revenge. Evildoers must be punished, but the followers of Christ cannot be moved by malice. So, in the matter of injustice inflicted by legal process, rather than seek revenge one should be willing to make even greater sacrifice; or when suffering oppression from some civil power, instead of

seeking to retaliate, one should show a willingness to endure greater hardship; or, when one is asked to grant a
loan, while it would be folly to grant it in every instance,
the refusal must never be inspired by a desire for revenge.

(5) The Law of Love   Ch. 5:43-48

*43 Ye have heard that it was said, Thou shalt love thy
neighbor, and hate thine enemy: 44 but I say unto you,
Love your enemies, and pray for them that persecute you;
45 that ye may be sons of your Father who is in heaven:
for he maketh his sun to rise on the evil and the good, and
sendeth rain on the just and the unjust. 46 For if ye love
them that love you, what reward have ye? do not even the
publicans the same? 47 And if ye salute your brethren
only, what do ye more than others? do not even the Gentiles the same? 48 Ye therefore shall be perfect, as your
heavenly Father is perfect.*

The Old Testament plainly required one to observe the
law of love. No precept could be more familiar than this,
"Thou shalt love thy neighbor as thyself." However, in
order to excuse himself for his narrow exclusiveness and
national selfishness, the Jew had interpreted his "neighbor" as meaning only his fellow countrymen and, with
other nations in mind, he had stated the following rule to
guide his conduct, "Thou shalt love thy neighbor, and hate
thine enemy." Then further, he came to apply in private
life a precept which, at its best, was only a poor rule for
national guidance. Our Lord gives to the familiar precept
a very different interpretation and statement, "Love your
enemies, and pray for them that persecute you." He suggests that such conduct is princely and royal and is becoming to those who are sons of the heavenly Father, "For he
maketh his sun to rise on the evil and the good, and
sendeth rain on the just and the unjust." Jesus further insists that love for those who are kind and love for kindred
require no special grace and are deserving of no particular

reward. Even taxgatherers and pagans show such selfish or natural affection. It is for the follower of Christ to show the perfect love which can seek the highest welfare of enemies and can pray for the unkind; for this is like the perfect love of the Father.

3. THE KING'S SERVANTS AND RELIGIOUS OBSERVANCES
Ch. 6:1-18

a. Almsgiving   Ch. 6:1-4

1 Take heed that ye do not your righteousness before men, to be seen of them: else ye have no reward with your Father who is in heaven.
2 When therefore thou doest alms, sound not a trumpet before thee, as the hypocrites do in the synagogues and in the streets, that they may have glory of men. Verily I say unto you, They have received their reward. 3 But when thou doest alms, let not thy left hand know what thy right hand doeth: 4 that thine alms may be in secret: and thy Father who seeth in secret shall recompense thee.

The ideal life which Jesus demands of those who are to enter his Kingdom is tested by motive rather than by outward act. This is true in the matter of religious observances quite as much as in the acts which are demanded by the moral law. The real attitude toward God is certain to be expressed in some visible forms. Among these the three most common are almsgiving, prayer, and fasting. Here the general principle for the followers of Christ must be that the motive is a desire to please God and not to secure praise of men. This is what is intended by the first verse of the chapter, "Take heed that ye do not your righteousness before men, to be seen of them: else ye have no reward with your Father who is in heaven." Jesus does not mean that there is any virtue in secrecy, but he does warn us against the publicity which seeks to secure admiration and praise. He does intimate that any real expression of righteousness which is designed to be an act of worship must have as its motive trust in God and love toward him.

This general principle is illustrated first, in the case of charitable gifts. Jesus insists that these should not be attended with unnecessary publicity. He imagines the absurd case of a hypocrite, a mere actor, sounding a trumpet in the synagogue and in the streets to advertise his generosity and to secure glory of men. Such an expenditure of money and effort is not almsgiving; it is bargaining with the hope of selfish gain. It is an investment of certain funds with a hope of securing full value in human praise and adulation. It is perfectly possible to make such investments, "They have received their reward." On the contrary, Jesus insists, "When thou doest alms, let not thy left hand know what thy right hand doeth." He does not mean here to forbid care and system in giving charity, or in supporting religious causes. He means, however, to insist that in almsgiving our eyes are to be fixed not upon men but upon God; that we are not to seek for human praise and approval, but to remember that the "Father who seeth in secret shall recompense."

b. Prayer   Ch. 6:5-15

5 And when ye pray, ye shall not be as the hypocrites: for they love to stand and pray in the synagogues and in the corners of the streets, that they may be seen of men. Verily I say unto you, They have received their reward. 6 But thou, when thou prayest, enter into thine inner chamber, and having shut thy door, pray to thy Father who is in secret, and thy Father who seeth in secret shall recompense thee. 7 And in praying use not vain repetitions, as the Gentiles do: for they think that they shall be heard for their much speaking. 8 Be not therefore like unto them: for your Father knoweth what things ye have need of, before ye ask him. 9 After this manner therefore pray ye: Our Father who art in heaven, Hallowed be thy name. 10 Thy kingdom come. Thy will be done, as in heaven, so on earth. 11 Give us this day our daily bread. 12 And forgive us our debts, as we also have forgiven our debtors. 13 And bring us not into temptation, but deliver us from the evil one. 14 For if ye forgive men their trespasses, your heavenly Father will also forgive you. 15 But if ye forgive not men their trespasses, neither will your Father forgive your trespasses.

The same principle applies to prayer. Only a hypocrite will be moved to worship by a desire to win the approval of men. Jesus has no criticism to pass upon public prayer. What he, of course, condemns is ostentation and the desire to secure praise by the attitudes and forms of prayer. He counsels secrecy, believing that it aids one in fixing the thought upon the Father, to whom all prayer is rightly directed. The Father sees in secret and he will recompense.

So too, "vain repetitions" are to be avoided. This does not mean that one never is to ask a second time for that which he needs; but it is a warning against the belief that prayer is magical and that by continued iteration of a request God can be compelled to grant what he otherwise might deny. Jesus elsewhere encourages importunity in prayer; but he here insists that "vain repetitions" are worthy only of heathen and are unnecessary for his followers, for their Father knows what things they need even before they ask.

To guide his followers in the true spirit and form of prayer, Jesus then suggested that matchless prayer which is in itself a model, a formula, and a summary of all our rightful requests. We call it "The Lord's Prayer." It contains six petitions; three specially concern the cause and Kingdom of our Father; three express our personal needs. We pray that his name may be hallowed, that his Kingdom may come, that his will may be done as in heaven so on earth. We then request provision for our daily needs, pardon for our continual sins, and protection from moral peril. Jesus suggests that the spirit must be that of humble forgiveness, willing to overlook the offenses of others even as we expect our Father to forgive us.

c. Fasting   Ch. 6:16-18

16 Moreover when ye fast, be not, as the hypocrites, of a sad countenance: for they disfigure their faces, that they may be seen of men to fast. Verily I say unto you, They have received their reward. 17 But thou, when thou fastest, anoint thy head, and wash thy face; 18 that thou be not seen of men to fast, but of thy Father who is in secret: and thy Father, who seeth in secret, shall recompense thee.

A third religious form, very popular with the Jews among whom Christ lived, was that of fasting. If this is practiced in order to show to God our sorrow for sin; or if it is involved in our devotion to his service, it is right and commendable; but if it is employed as a means of winning the approval and praise of men, it is hypocrisy and pretense. Jesus insists that fasting, and all forms of self-denial, should be in secret; we are not to parade our sacrifices; we are not to make capital out of our devotion. We are to have regard only to the Father who is in secret, who sees in secret and who surely will reward.

4. THE KING'S SERVANTS AND THE WORLD'S GOODS
Ch. 6:19-34

19 Lay not up for yourselves treasures upon the earth, where moth and rust consume, and where thieves break through and steal: 20 but lay up for yourselves treasures in heaven, where neither moth nor rust doth consume, and where thieves do not break through nor steal: 21 for where thy treasure is, there will thy heart be also. 22 The lamp of the body is the eye: if therefore thine eye be single, thy whole body shall be full of light. 23 But if thine eye be evil, thy whole body shall be full of darkness. If therefore the light that is in thee be darkness, how great is the darkness! 24 No man can serve two masters: for either he will hate the one, and love the other; or else he will hold to one, and despise the other. Ye cannot serve God and mammon. 25 Therefore I say unto you, Be not anxious for your life, what ye shall eat, or what ye shall drink; nor yet for your body, what ye shall put on. Is not the life more than the food, and the body than the raiment? 26 Behold the birds of the heaven, that they sow not, neither do they reap, nor gather into barns; and your heavenly Father feedeth them. Are not ye of much more value than they? 27 And which of you by being anxious can add one cubit unto the measure of his life? 28 And why are ye anxious concerning raiment? Consider the lilies of the field, how they grow; they toil not, neither do they spin: 29 yet I say unto you, that even Solomon in all his glory was not arrayed like one of these. 30 But if God doth so clothe the grass of the field, which to-day is, and to-morrow is cast into the oven, shall he not much more clothe you, O ye of little faith? 31 Be not therefore anxious, saying, What shall we eat? or, What shall we drink? or, Wherewithal shall we be clothed? 32 For after all these things do the Gentiles seek; for your heavenly Father knoweth that ye have need of all these things. 33 But seek ye first his kingdom, and his righteousness; and all these things shall be added unto you. 34 Be not therefore anxious for the morrow: for the morrow will be anxious for itself. Sufficient unto the day is the evil thereof.

In describing the ideal life which he requires, Jesus gives two warnings in reference to the attitude of mind which should characterize his followers in their relation to worldly possessions. The first warning is against avarice, and the second against anxiety. The former is the special temptation of the rich; the latter of the poor. The former is forbidden on two or three different grounds. First, it is foolish to lay up treasures upon the earth, because earthly possessions are so uncertain and so soon pass away; and secondly, they tend to turn the mind away from God and his Kingdom. Then, again, the desire for wealth may become such a passion as to dull the moral sense; it may blind "the eye," whereas, a generous spirit clarifies the spiritual sight so that the whole being is full of light. Then, too, there is great peril lest a man may be possessed by his possessions. Avarice may transform one into a slave and may turn him from the service of God: "No man can serve two masters"; "ye cannot serve God and mammon."

On the other hand, Jesus warns us against anxiety. Of course he does not forbid foresight and prudence; but he would keep us from that carefulness and worry which destroy our peace and hamper our usefulness. He points us to the birds, to show that the heavenly Father will provide necessary food. He suggests the folly of anxiety which can shorten but can never lengthen the life of man. He bids us "consider the lilies of the field" in their beauty, in order to assure us that the heavenly Father will clothe those who trust in him. It is indeed a confident dependence upon the care of the heavenly Father which banishes anxiety. Jesus bids his followers to seek first the Kingdom of God and the righteousness which he requires, believing that all needful things will be granted them. He insists that they should not borrow trouble. He tells them that the morrow will have its own anxieties; that for each day there will be evil enough, but never too much, for those who put their trust in God.

5. The King's Servants and the World's Evil
Ch. 7:1-6

1 Judge not, that ye be not judged. 2 For with what judgment ye judge, ye shall be judged: and with what measure ye mete, it shall be measured unto you. 3 And why beholdest thou the mote that is in thy brother's eye, but considerest not the beam that is in thine own eye? 4 Or how wilt thou say to thy brother, Let me cast out the mote out of thine eye; and lo, the beam is in thine own eye? 5 Thou hypocrite, cast out first the beam out of thine own eye; and then shalt thou see clearly to cast out the mote out of thy brother's eye.

6 Give not that which is holy unto the dogs, neither cast your pearls before the swine, lest haply they trample them under their feet, and turn and rend you.

In relation to the evil that is in the world, Jesus gives
two warnings to his followers as he continues to describe
to them the ideal life which he desires them to lead. He
warns them, first, against censoriousness, and, second,
against carelessness. When Jesus said, "Judge not, that ye
be not judged," he did not mean that we can avoid form-
ing opinions of others, or that we should not condemn
what we know to be wrong. He is forbidding his followers
to be unkind in their judgments or to delight in unfavor-
able criticism. He condemns the spirit of faultfinding,
first, on the ground of its danger, "For with what judgment
ye judge, ye shall be judged," not only by our fellowmen,
who are sure to condemn us with as little charity as we
show toward them, but also by God himself, who will
judge us with that same severity which we have shown in
judging others. Further, Jesus suggests that this censoriousness is absurd. He draws the most ludicrous picture:
he suggests that it is ridiculous for one in whose eye there
is a "beam" to attempt to relieve one in whose eye there is
merely a splinter or a "mote." Still worse, it is mere hypocrisy, for in criticizing others we usually suggest that we
are greatly distressed by their weakness and faults, whereas
in our hearts there is a secret joy. If our sympathy were
real, we would first seek to remove our own imperfections,
particularly our uncharitableness and pride, and then we
would be fitted for the high service of enabling others to
overcome their defects.

The followers of Christ are not to be censorious or to
delight in unkind criticisms. However, they are not to go
to the other extreme and to become indifferent to the evil
that is in the world. They must discriminate carefully
between men of differing moral character, and must regu-
late accordingly their attitude toward them. This is particularly necessary for those who desire to communicate
spiritual truth. They must have regard to time and place
and to the nature and condition of those whom they approach and whom they seek to influence. If, for instance,

one seeks to cast a mote out of his brother's eye, he must act with tact and discretion. There are truths also which by some men could be neither understood nor appreciated. They would be rejected, scorned, despised, and their hearers would be insulted and abused. There is such a thing as "casting pearls before swine."

However, this caution must not be pressed too far. Christians must bear testimony even at the peril of their lives, and they are often surprised to find that those whom they, with hasty judgment, would have pronounced hopeless and hostile, are found to be quite ready and even eager to learn the good news concerning Christ.

6. THE KING'S SERVANTS AND THEIR RELATION TO GOD AND TO MEN   Ch. 7:7-12

7 Ask, and it shall be given you; seek, and ye shall find; knock, and it shall be opened unto you: 8 for every one that asketh receiveth; and he that seeketh findeth; and to him that knocketh it shall be opened. 9 Or what man is there of you, who, if his son shall ask him for a loaf, will give him a stone; 10 or if he shall ask for a fish, will give him a serpent? 11 If ye then, being evil, know how to give good gifts unto your children, how much more shall your Father who is in heaven give good things to them that ask him? 12 All things therefore whatsoever ye would that men should do unto you, even so do ye also unto them: for this is the law and the prophets.

The Sermon on the Mount here reaches its majestic climax as it discloses and emphasizes the relations which Christians should maintain toward God and toward their fellowmen. These are summed up in the exhortation concerning "prayer," and in the Golden Rule.

The former is not a message concerning the nature or place or philosophy of prayer, but it is, rather, an encouragement to the followers of Christ to maintain toward God a continual attitude of filial trust. The exhortations which

have preceded, warning against the perils of censoriousness and of carelessness, suggest the need of divine help.
Here Christ urges his followers to look to God at all times
for needed wisdom and strength and grace. "Ask, and it
shall be given you; seek, and ye shall find; knock, and it
shall be opened unto you." Nothing could be more simple
than the intercourse between earth and heaven which is
thus assured; and further confidence is inspired by the
comparison to an earthly parent who though only a man,
would not deceive or mock his son; how much more certainly will the "Father who is in heaven give good things
to them that ask him."

As this instruction concerning prayer inspires a right
attitude toward God, so the Golden Rule summarizes all
that Christ requires in relation to our fellowmen. It is an
expression of the law of love and it is, as Christ declares,
a fulfillment of all that is required by "the law and the
prophets." Some expressions of this Golden Rule, either
in a negative or in some other less perfect form, are found
reflected by Jewish teachers and even by heathen sages;
but it remained for the great King to proclaim in his manifesto the fundamental law, the observance of which would
end all the differences and discords between individuals,
between classes and parties, and between the nations of
the world, "All things therefore whatsoever ye would that
men should do unto you, even so do ye also unto them."

7. CONCLUSION: THE STRUGGLE, THE TEST, AND THE SECURITY OF THE KING'S SERVANTS   Ch. 7:13-29

13 Enter ye in by the narrow gate: for wide is the gate,
and broad is the way, that leadeth to destruction, and many
are they that enter in thereby. 14 For narrow is the gate,
and straitened the way, that leadeth unto life, and few are
they that find it.

15 Beware of false prophets, who come to you in sheep's
clothing, but inwardly are ravening wolves. 16 By their
fruits ye shall know them. Do men gather grapes of

thorns, or figs of thistles?   17 Even so every good tree bringeth forth good fruit; but the corrupt tree bringeth forth evil fruit.   18 A good tree cannot bring forth evil fruit, neither can a corrupt tree bring forth good fruit.   19 Every tree that bringeth not forth good fruit is hewn down, and cast into the fire.   20 Therefore by their fruits ye shall know them.   21 Not every one that saith unto me, Lord, Lord, shall enter into the kingdom of heaven; but he that doeth the will of my Father who is in heaven.   22 Many will say to me in that day, Lord, Lord, did we not prophesy by thy name, and by thy name cast out demons, and by thy name do many mighty works?   23 And then will I profess unto them, I never knew you: depart from me, ye that work iniquity.

24 Every one therefore that heareth these words of mine, and doeth them, shall be likened unto a wise man, who built his house upon the rock: 25 and the rain descended, and the floods came, and the winds blew, and beat upon that house; and it fell not: for it was founded upon the rock.   26 And every one that heareth these words of mine, and doeth them not, shall be likened unto a foolish man, who built his house upon the sand: 27 and the rain descended, and the floods came, and the winds blew, and smote upon that house; and it fell: and great was the fall thereof.

28 And it came to pass, when Jesus had finished these words, the multitudes were astonished at his teaching: 29 for he taught them as one having authority, and not as their scribes.

The sermon closes with three exhortations: one to seek for entrance into the Kingdom, one to beware of false teachers and false professions, and one to obey the commands of the King. Jesus employs three striking metaphors, the "two ways," the "two kinds of fruit," and the "two builders."

(a) In urging men to become his followers and to seek for an entrance into the Kingdom of Heaven, vs. 13-14, the figure of speech embodies three great contrasts, the wide and narrow gate, the death and life to which they lead, and the many and the few that enter in. Here the King plainly teaches that to follow him involves struggle, self-discipline, and effort. The right path is difficult to find and hard to keep; the broad path is popular and is easy to discover. It is not difficult for one to be lost; one only needs to follow the crowd. It is hard to be saved, it requires resolution, sacrifice, heroism; but the issue is life eternal.

(b) There are many false guides, vs. 15-20, who offer themselves; many religious leaders who masquerade under the name of Christian. They seem innocent enough but they are like wolves dressed in the fleeces of sheep. Their real purpose is selfish and destructive; they must be tested, not only by their lives and their deeds, but still more by the results of their corrupt and Christless teachings, "by their fruits ye shall know them."

Then, too, many others who profess to follow Christ need to be on their guard against self-deception. On that great day when the King will pronounce judgment and will determine who may enter and who must be excluded from his Kingdom, many will plead that they were regular in Christian worship and prominent in Christian work, to whom the King will say, "I never knew you: depart from me, ye that work iniquity." It is necessary not only to profess the name of Christ but truly to obey him and by his help to do the will of his Father who is in heaven.

(c) Therefore, in his final words of warning and exhortation, vs. 24-27, the King sets forth the absolute necessity of hearing and of doing his words, of accepting and of obeying his royal commands. He draws the picture of the two builders, one founding his house upon the rock, the other building upon the sand, and in the time of storm and flood one house stands firm and the other falls in complete ruin. So shall it be in the time of testing and of judgment, they who truly obey Christ will be safe. Their eternal destinies are built upon a rock, the servants of the King are secure.

(*d*) It is not strange that the multitudes marveled at the words of Christ. The world has been wondering at these words ever since. The crowds were astonished that he spoke with authority and not as their scribes; and he might well so speak, for these wonderful words are the proclamation of a King.

III

THE CREDENTIALS
OF THE KING

Chs. 8:1 to 9:34

A. THE FIRST GROUP OF MIRACLES
Ch. 8:1-17

1. CLEANSING THE LEPER   Ch. 8:1-4

1 And when he was come down from the mountain, great multitudes followed him. 2 And behold, there came to him a leper and worshipped him, saying, Lord, if thou wilt, thou canst make me clean. 3 And he stretched forth his hand, and touched him, saying, I will; be thou made clean. And straightway his leprosy was cleansed. 4 And Jesus saith unto him, See thou tell no man; but go, show thyself to the priest, and offer the gift that Moses commanded, for a testimony unto them.

Following the Sermon on the Mount, Matthew introduces ten miracles, which he arranges in three impressive groups. They form an integral part of the narrative. To deny the miracles or to remove them from the Gospel would leave an unmeaning and mutilated story. In the Sermon, Jesus claimed to be a divine and universal King; here he is shown to be worthy of submission and trust; the miracles are his credentials. We need not only the teaching of Christ, we need his healing touch; and each miracle is a parable of his saving power.

The first of these supernatural works related by Matthew is the healing of a leper. It is possible that here was an intimation that the first need of the nation was spiritual cleansing, and that this need must be supplied before the blessings of the promised Kingdom could be enjoyed. Surely, leprosy is the familiar and accepted type of sin. Its victim was a mass of festering sores; he was shut off from his fellowmen, regarded with loathing, and enduring a living death. Such was the case of the poor sufferer who came to Jesus, worshiping him and saying, "Lord, if thou wilt, thou canst make me clean." He believed in the power of Jesus, but he feared himself unworthy to be cured. Jesus "stretched forth his hand, and touched him," to show his sympathy, to strengthen the faith of the leper, and to assure us that he welcomes the foulest of sinners. Then Jesus spoke those majestic words, "I will; be thou made clean." How natural these words sound on the lips of Jesus! Can we imagine him saying, "I am sorry for you, but I can give you no help; I advise you to adopt some remedy or to resort to some human physician"? Belief in a divine Savior makes it easy to accept the truth of his divine works. "Straightway his leprosy was cleansed." The completeness and instantaneousness of the cure form a striking feature of the miracle, and suggest to us the power of Christ to give immediate relief from the stain and guilt and power of sin.

Jesus forbade the man he had healed to tell others of his cure. What he meant was to avoid a noisy publicity which might have aroused fanaticism and created such excitement as to interfere with his teaching. Today he desires all who are cured to testify of his grace. He commanded the man to show himself to the priest and to observe the customs commanded by Moses. Jesus did not hesitate to break a ceremonial law in touching the man when this was necessary for his cure; he told the man to keep the ceremonial law, when no higher law interfered and when a failure might have resulted in misunderstanding and offense.

2. HEALING THE PARALYTIC   Ch. 8:5-13

5 And when he was entered into Capernaum, there came unto him a centurion, beseeching him, 6 and saying, Lord, my servant lieth in the house sick of the palsy, grievously tormented. 7 And he saith unto him, I will come and heal him. 8 And the centurion answered and said, Lord, I am not worthy that thou shouldest come under my roof: but only say the word, and my servant shall be healed. 9 For I also am a man under authority, having under myself soldiers: and I say to this one, Go, and he goeth; and to another, Come, and he cometh; and to my servant, Do this, and he doeth it. 10 And when Jesus heard it, he marvelled, and said to them that followed, Verily I say unto you, I have not found so great faith, no, not in Israel. 11 And I say unto you, that many shall come from the east and the west, and shall sit down with Abraham, and Isaac, and Jacob, in the kingdom of heaven: 12 but the sons of the kingdom shall be cast forth into the outer darkness: there shall be the weeping and the gnashing of teeth. 13 And Jesus said unto the centurion, Go thy way; as thou hast believed, so be it done unto thee. And the servant was healed in that hour.

Leprosy was a type of the loathsomeness of sin; paralysis may be regarded as a symbol of its helplessness. As the cure of the former reveals the power of Christ, this story emphasizes the necessity of faith in him. The centurion, or Roman military commander, of Capernaum, was evidently a man of the same high character attributed to all similar soldiers in the New Testament. Moved by sympathy for this suffering servant he appealed to Jesus for relief, and on receiving the promise of the Master to "come and heal," he gave his surprising reply, revealing his remarkable faith. He declared that as he himself knew what it was to obey, and be obeyed, so he was certain that Jesus had need only to speak a word, not to come to his house, and his command would be fulfilled and the servant would be healed. His humility and his trust were so extraordinary that Jesus declared, "I have not found so great faith, no, not in Israel." Then Jesus added a word which must have startled the Jews. Using as a figure of speech the picture of a banquet to describe the joys of the Kingdom of Heaven, he declared that many Gentiles would be admitted to the Kingdom, while from it many Jews would be excluded. The faith of such a Roman centurion was a prophecy of such Gentile converts, and in response to his faith Jesus spoke the word of blessed assurance, "Go thy way; as thou hast believed, so be it done unto thee." Thus, this Gospel, which is said to have been "written for the Jews," contains unsurpassed promises of future blessings for all the nations of the world.

3. CURING PETER'S WIFE'S MOTHER Ch. 8:14-17

14 And when Jesus was come into Peter's house, he saw his wife's mother lying sick of a fever. 15 And he touched her hand, and the fever left her; and she arose, and ministered unto him. 16 And when even was come, they brought unto him many possessed with demons: and he cast out the spirits with a word, and healed all that were sick: 17 that it might be fulfilled which was spoken through Isaiah the prophet, saying, Himself took our infirmities, and bare our diseases.

The third example of the power of Jesus over disease was given in the home of his disciple, Simon Peter. Here the sufferer was distressed by a fever, a form of disease which may suggest the anxiety, the fear, the worry, the temper, the haste, which may be found in the homes of even the closest followers of Christ. The touch of Jesus' hand bespoke his sympathy and love; and it was a touch of power, for, "the fever left her." Yet it did not leave her weak and helpless, as fever is wont to do. The cure was immediate and complete, for "she arose, and ministered unto him." In countless homes today, hearts soothed by the healing touch of Christ are rendering to him the service of grateful love.

The report of this cure, or of similar miracles, brought to Peter's door a great multitude of those who suffered from demons and disease, and Jesus healed them all. In this gracious ministry, Matthew, whose Gospel is linked to the Old Testament by continual quotations, finds fulfillment of the prediction of Isaiah, "Himself took our infirmities, and bare our diseases." The prophecy was fulfilled partly in the burden of sympathy felt for those he was healing; more perfectly was it fulfilled when finally he "bare our sins in his body upon the tree."

B. THE IMPULSIVE SCRIBE AND THE RELUCTANT DISCIPLE   Ch. 8:18-22

18 Now when Jesus saw great multitudes about him, he gave commandment to depart unto the other side. 19 And there came a scribe, and said unto him, Teacher, I will follow thee withersoever thou goest. 20 And Jesus saith unto him, The foxes have holes, and the birds of the heaven have nests; but the Son of man hath not where to lay his head. 21 And another of the disciples said unto him, Lord, suffer me first to go and bury my father. 22 But Jesus saith unto him, Follow me; and leave the dead to bury their own dead.

Between the first and the second group of miracles, Matthew mentions two incidents which likewise reveal the divine nature of Christ and also indicate the effect his miracles were having on the multitudes. Each instance shows the power of Christ to read the hidden thoughts of the human mind and to penetrate to the motives which lie back of words and deeds. More definitely do these incidents indicate the growing popularity of Jesus; they show that men were feeling eager to become his followers or were trying to excuse themselves for refusing to submit to his will.

In the first case a scribe comes to him with fervor declaring, "I will follow thee withersoever thou goest." He had supposed such companionship would be delightful, popular, easy. Jesus declares that it will mean hardship, self-denial, a cross, "Foxes have holes, and the birds of the heaven have nests; but the Son of man hath not where to lay his head." Nothing further is heard of this eager young man. Jesus wishes followers, but he wants them to count the cost; he warns against rashness and inconsiderateness among those who are contemplating his service.

Another seems ready to follow, but declares that he first must go and bury his father. It was probably a mere pretense or a poor excuse for refusal or delay. There is something of severity in the stern reply of the Master, "Follow me; and leave the dead to bury their own dead." Nothing should be allowed to keep men from following Christ. No matter how tender the tie or how sacred the duty, that which keeps one from him keeps him among the spiritually dead, and will result ultimately in his being buried by "the dead."

C. THE SECOND GROUP OF MIRACLES
Chs. 8:23 to 9:8

1. STILLING THE STORM   Ch. 8:23-27

23 And when he was entered into a boat, his disciples followed him. 24 And behold, there arose a great tempest in the sea, insomuch that the boat was covered with the waves: but he was asleep. 25 And they came to him, and awoke him, saying, Save, Lord; we perish. 26 And he saith unto them, Why are ye fearful, O ye of little faith? Then he arose, and rebuked the winds and the sea; and there was a great calm. 27 And the men marvelled, saying, What manner of man is this, that even the winds and the sea obey him?

In the first group of miracles Jesus is seen to have power to cure bodily disease; in the second he is shown to have power over the forces of nature, over unclean spirits, and even power to forgive sins.

Storms were common on the surface of the little lake which Jesus often crossed with his disciples; and storms are frequent in the lives of all his followers. To accompany the Master does not exempt men from struggles, and tempests, from black skies, and hungry waves. Yet this was no usual storm. Even the sturdy fishermen of Galilee were fearful. With the King on board the boat, they should have felt secure. He was calm and untroubled. "The boat was covered with the waves: but he was asleep."

It was foolish to be afraid; but it was wise to come to the Master with their fears. They awoke him, saying, "Save, Lord; we perish." We can be certain that he will bring us relief if we cry to him in any hour of need: but it may be necessary for him to rebuke us. Stronger faith might lessen our fear. He said unto them, "Why are ye fearful, O ye of little faith?" Then, when he had rebuked his followers, "he arose, and rebuked the winds and the sea; and there was a great calm." Surely this King who is the "Ruler of all nature" can deliver from all possible perils those who put their trust in him. Such experiences must have strengthened the faith of his followers; but the first effect upon the witnesses was deep wonder. They "marvelled, saying, What manner of man is this, that even the winds and the sea obey him?"

2. CASTING OUT DEMONS   Ch. 8:28-34

28 And when he was come to the other side into the country of the Gadarenes, there met him two possessed with demons, coming forth out of the tombs, exceeding fierce, so that no man could pass by that way. 29 And behold, they cried out, saying, What have we to do with thee, thou Son of God? art thou come hither to torment us before the time? 30 Now there was afar off from them a herd of many swine feeding. 31 And the demons besought him, saying, If thou cast us out, send us away into the herd of

swine. 32 And he said unto them, Go. And they came out, and went into the swine: and behold, the whole herd rushed down the steep into the sea, and perished in the waters. 33 And they that fed them fled, and went away into the city, and told everything, and what was befallen to them that were possessed with demons. 34 And behold, all the city came out to meet Jesus: and when they saw him, they besought him *that he would depart from their borders.*

Jesus had just shown his power over the forces of nature; he now exhibits his authority over the unseen world of spirits. He crossed to the east side of the lake; and "there met him two possessed with demons, coming forth out of the tombs, exceeding fierce, so that no man could pass by that way." These men were not merely insane, they were demoniacs. However, both insanity and demon-possession are symbols of the more terrible tyranny of sin. Men who are slaves of passion, of lust, of appetite, of envy, and of greed, like the Gadarenes among the tombs, dwell in places of uncleanness and death, and endanger all who come near them.

The demons recognized Jesus as the Son of God; they dreaded his power; they realized that he would deliver the men they were tormenting; and therefore they requested that they might enter a herd of swine which was seen feeding at some distance. When permission was granted, "the whole herd rushed down the steep into the sea, and perished in the waters."

It often has been asked why Jesus caused or allowed such a destruction of property. It might be difficult to answer were it not that all the miracles of our Lord were acted parables, intended to teach spiritual truths. On the very surface of this narrative it is evident that the destruction of the swine was related to the deliverance of the men; they were helped to realize that their condition had been desperate and their deliverance was real; it revealed to them the power of Christ and led them to trust in him. Most of all it is evident that the destruction of the swine was an arresting message to the men of the neighboring city, both of their possible danger from evil spirits and of the deliverance which Jesus could give from all the tyrannies of suffering and of sin; but "they besought him that he would depart from their borders." Some there are today who fear that the presence of Jesus may cause them some loss of property or at least may rebuke them for their sin. Some regard the King not with loving reverence but only with fear and dread.

3. FORGIVING SINS   Ch. 9:1-8

1 And he entered into a boat, and crossed over, and came into his own city. 2 And behold, they brought to him a man sick of the palsy, lying on a bed: and Jesus seeing their faith said unto the sick of the palsy, Son, be of good cheer; thy sins are forgiven. 3 And behold, certain of the scribes said within themselves, This man blasphemeth. 4 And Jesus knowing their thoughts said, Wherefore think ye evil in your hearts? 5 For which is easier, to say, Thy sins are forgiven; or to say, Arise, and walk? 6 But that ye may know that the Son of man hath authority on earth to forgive sins (then saith he to the sick of the palsy), Arise, and take up thy bed, and go unto thy house. 7 And he arose, and departed to his house. 8 But when the multitudes saw it, they were afraid, and glorified God, who had given such authority unto men.

Jesus had shown that he was able to deliver from the dominion of unclean spirits; he now shows that he has power to forgive sin. The occasion was the healing of a man who was "sick of the palsy." This disease was more pitiful than mere paralysis. The control of the muscles was lost, but there were sudden paroxysms of pain, which became more frequent and more agonizing until the poor sufferer found relief in death. The paralytic whom Jesus healed was suffering from the far more terrible malady of sin, of which his disease was the dreadful symbol and probably the result.

Therefore Jesus considered the deeper need and said to the sick of the palsy, "Son, be of good cheer; thy sins are forgiven." "And behold, certain of the scribes said within themselves, This man blasphemeth." They were quite right; Jesus was guilty of blasphemy and worthy of death, unless, and there is no other alternative, he was himself divine. That he was divine he proved, first, by reading the thoughts of his enemies, and secondly, by curing the sufferer of his disease. Neither pronouncing pardon for sin nor securing instant relief from palsy lies within the power of man. He who could perform the latter had the right to do the former. Therefore Jesus said to the sick of the palsy, "Arise, and take up thy bed, and go unto thy house." The cure was immediate; the demonstration was complete, "He arose, and departed to his house."

The effect upon the multitudes was mingled fear and joy. They feared as they found themselves in the presence of a divine King, but they rejoiced that he possessed the right and the authority to grant forgiveness of sins. For all who submit to his will, fear passes into gratitude and praise.

D. THE CALL OF MATTHEW AND THE QUESTION ABOUT FASTING Ch. 9:9-17

9 And as Jesus passed by from thence, he saw a man, called Matthew, sitting at the place of toll: and he saith unto him, Follow me. And he arose, and followed him.

10 And it came to pass, as he sat at meat in the house, behold, many publicans and sinners came and sat down with Jesus and his disciples. 11 And when the Pharisees saw it, they said unto his disciples, Why eateth your Teacher with the publicans and sinners? 12 But when he heard it, he said, They that are whole have no need of a physician, but they that are sick. 13 But go ye and learn what this meaneth, I desire mercy, and not sacrifice: for I came not to call the righteous, but sinners.

14 Then come to him the disciples of John, saying, Why do we and the Pharisees fast oft, but thy disciples fast not?

15 And Jesus said unto them, Can the sons of the bride-chamber mourn, as long as the bridegroom is with them? but the days will come, when the bridegroom shall be taken away from them, and then will they fast. 16 And no man putteth a piece of undressed cloth upon an old garment; for that which should fill it up taketh from the garment, and a worse rent is made. 17 Neither do men put new wine into old wine-skins: else the skins burst, and the wine is spilled, and the skins perish: but they put new wine into fresh wine-skins, and both are preserved.

Between the second and third groups of miracles there are introduced two incidents which in themselves intimate the divine power of Christ. The first was the call to discipleship of a publican, or collector of customs, by the name of Matthew, the man to whom the authorship of this Gospel is assigned.

His occupation was such as to place him among the class of social outcasts, but One who could cleanse the leper and heal the paralytic evidently was able to transform a despised publican into an apostle, an evangelist, and a saint.

The faith of Matthew was shown by his immediate response, by the evident sacrifice he made in leaving all to follow the Master, and further by his inviting his old friends to a great feast at which Jesus was the guest of honor. It is not difficult to draw parallels which may suggest how sincerity in accepting Christ today may be manifested.

The enemies of Jesus were ready with their criticism. They complained that he ate with publicans and sinners. This was the occasion for uttering one of his most suggestive sayings, "They that are whole have no need of a physician, but they that are sick." Here Jesus asserts his absolute power to give moral healing. He implies that if the Pharisees were morally sound as they professed, they should not begrudge his going to the morally sick, as they regarded publicans to be.

Jesus did not declare the Pharisees to be sound; that
was their estimate of themselves. They really deserved
a rebuke, and so he quotes from the Old Testament,
"I desire mercy, and not sacrifice." A sacrifice might be
a mere external form; the important thing in the sight of
God is a right heart. The Pharisees were formally right in
their avoidance of sinners; but they showed their evil
hearts by their lack of sympathy, and by their enmity
against Christ. Then Jesus adds, "I came not to call the
righteous, but sinners." He does not mean to affirm that
any class of men are truly righteous; he wishes to emphasize that his ministry is for sinners. As Matthew invited
outcasts to his feast so Jesus, as the divine Host, is ever
calling even the worst of sinners to share the blessings of
his Kingdom.

The liberty which Jesus felt in the matter of mere ceremonial observance was further emphasized by his reply
to the question as to why he did not require his followers
to observe frequent fasts. He declares that fasting as a
religious rite is perfectly proper if a genuine expression of
religious feeling, but as a matter of rule, or requirement, or
a ground of merit, it is futile and absurd. So, for his
disciples, it would be most unfitting to fast while he, the
heavenly Bridegroom, was with them; when they should
be separated from him, then they might fast. Yet, even
then, these matters of ceremony would have little importance. He had not come to make a few additions to the
Jewish ritual, as a man might put a patch on an old garment. Nor yet could the old forms of Judaism contain the
spirit of the Gospel he proclaimed. As new wine, fer-
menting and expanding, would burst leathern bottles already stretched or worn by age, so the religion of Christ
could not be confined to any set of ceremonies and should
not be confused with any ritual. It was a new life im-
parted by faith in him. It controlled men, not by rules,
but by motives. Its symbol was not a fast but a feast.

E. THE THIRD GROUP OF MIRACLES
Ch. 9:18-34

1. RAISING THE DEAD AND STOPPING THE ISSUE OF BLOOD   Ch. 9:18-26

18 While he spake these things unto them, behold, there came a ruler, and worshipped him, saying, My daughter is even now dead: but come and lay thy hand upon her, and she shall live. 19 And Jesus arose, and followed him, and so did his disciples. 20 And behold, a woman, who had an issue of blood twelve years, came behind him, and touched the border of his garment: 21 for she said within herself, if I do but touch his garment, I shall be made whole. 22 But Jesus turning and seeing her said, Daughter, be of good cheer; thy faith hath made thee whole. And the woman was made whole from that hour. 23 And when Jesus came into the ruler's house, and saw the flute-players, and the crowd making a tumult, 24 he said, Give place: for the damsel is not dead, but sleepeth. And they laughed him to scorn. 25 But when the crowd was put forth, he entered in, and took her by the hand; and the damsel arose. 26 And the fame hereof went forth into all that land.

The first group of miracles demonstrated the power of Jesus over bodily disease; the second, over disorder in the physical, spiritual, and moral world; the third reveals his power over death. The same story is related by Mark and Luke, who tell us that Jairus was the name of the ruler whose little daughter Jesus raised from the dead. In all three Gospels the story is interwoven with the account of another miracle which relates the healing of a woman upon whom death had set its seal. The story as told by Matthew is much more brief and omits many of the features mentioned by the other writers. Matthew wishes to fix the thought upon the long series of marvels which are here reaching their climax. He does not wish to distract the thought by needless details, but only to increase the impression already produced as to the kingly power and

authority of Christ. Even in this brief scene the movement of the Lord is majestic. The ruler approaches him
with a request which is beyond the power of man, but
Jesus indicates that the petition will be granted. The helpless woman touches his garment and Jesus turns to her
with the princely assurance that even her imperfect faith
has resulted in a perfect cure. At the house of the ruler in
the midst of the tumult of mourning, he speaks the mysterious words of hope, "The damsel is not dead, but sleepeth." He knew that life had left the body, but in view of
his purpose and with confidence in his power he spoke a
message, the full import of which gives absolute assurance
of life beyond the grave, and has comforted countless
mourners with its consolation and cheer, "Not dead, but
sleepeth."

The ridicule of the crowd, so rude and heartless, contrasts with the kingly sympathy of Christ and attests the
reality of the miracle. No doubt the little girl was dead;
to deny the fact, if that had been the meaning of Jesus,
was absurd. What he really meant becomes evident at
once. Dismissing the noisy throng he takes the maiden by
the hand and instantly she rises, fully restored to life and
strength. No wonder "the fame hereof went forth unto
all that land." Surely such a King is worthy of trust and
homage.

2. GIVING SIGHT TO THE BLIND AND SPEECH TO THE DUMB   Ch. 9:27-34

27 And as Jesus passed by from thence, two blind men
followed him, crying out, and saying, Have mercy on us,
thou son of David. 28 And when he was come into the
house, the blind men came to him: and Jesus saith unto
them, Believe ye that I am able to do this? They say unto
him, Yea, Lord. 29 Then touched he their eyes, saying,
According to your faith be it done unto you. 30 And their
eyes were opened. And Jesus strictly charged them, saying, See that no man know it. 31 But they went forth, and

spread abroad his fame in all that land.

32 And as they went forth, behold, there was brought to him a dumb man possessed with a demon. 33 And when the demon was cast out, the dumb man spake: and the multitudes marvelled, saying, It was never so seen in Israel. 34 But the Pharisees said, By the prince of the demons casteth he out demons.

After Jesus has shown his power over death, the miracle of giving sight to the blind and speech to the dumb may seem less marvelous. It is probable, however, that Matthew places these in this third group of miracles as they show how Jesus restored faculties which in reality were dead. Surely the blind and dumb are accepted pictures of men who need the power of Christ to enable them to see spiritual realities and rightly to praise the goodness and love of God. The faith of the blind men whom Jesus healed seems to have been real but it was imperfect. They refused to obey him when he had requested that they should not disclose his healing power. The motive of his command may not be clear; probably he wished to avoid arousing any sudden outbreak of fanatical enthusiasm which might have arrested the progress of his mission. It is always wise to obey the commands of the King.

We are told again that at these surprising miracles "the multitudes marvelled," but we read that the Pharisees were aroused to such envious and bitter hatred that they brought against Jesus their most bitter charge, "By the prince of the demons casteth he out demons." It cannot be denied even by his enemies that the power of Christ was supernatural. There is, then, no other alternative, it was either demonic or divine.

IV
THE MESSENGERS
OF THE KING
Chs. 9:35 to 10:42

A. THE OCCASION OF THEIR COMMISSION
Ch. 9:35-38

35 And Jesus went about all the cities and the villages, teaching in their synagogues, and preaching the gospel of the kingdom, and healing all manner of disease and all manner of sickness. 36 But when he saw the multitudes, he was moved with compassion for them, because they were distressed and scattered, as sheep not having a shepherd. 37 Then saith he unto his disciples, The harvest indeed is plenteous, but the laborers are few. 38 Pray ye therefore the Lord of the harvest, that he send forth laborers into his harvest.

This portion of the Gospel opens with a summary of the Galilean ministry of Jesus, similar to that which precedes the Sermon on the Mount and the account of the ten great miracles which were recorded as "credentials of the King." This summary properly introduces the record of the commission which Jesus gave to his twelve disciples. It shows the occasion and motive of their mission. It pictures the great crowds which were thronging about Jesus as well as the unreached multitudes which had become so great as to demand helpers who might preach in the name of the Master. It looked forward likewise to the time when the rejected King would be taken from his followers and when the whole burden of testimony would rest upon them. It is the fact that the present and the more distant needs were in mind at the same time, which explains many of the difficulties which the commission to the apostles contains. Some of the exhortations and warnings belong to the days of the earthly ministry of our Lord; and others have their application to all the intervening ages and to the experiences of his followers even in years yet to come. The immediate motive, however, which compelled Jesus to act, was his deep compassion for the multitudes. He saw that they were "distressed"; that is, they were harassed by cares and doubts and fears; they were "scattered" or "prostrate," downcast and hopeless; they were "as sheep not having a shepherd"; that is, they were in need of a guide, protector, and leader. They were perplexed and knew not which way to turn; they were hungry and knew not how the longing of their souls could be satisfied. It is a striking picture of the world today. Its multitudes are likewise helpless. They are in need of that which the Good Shepherd alone can provide. When we sympathize with the Master and look upon the crowds as he saw them, we feel something of his passion and eagerness to offer relief and to send forth those who can testify in his name. It was his yearning over the multitudes which led Jesus to urge his disciples to pray. He changes the metaphor, but the need implied is obvious: "The harvest indeed is plenteous, but the laborers are few. Pray ye therefore the Lord of the harvest, that he send forth laborers into his harvest." He is telling us that the grain is ripe and unless workers can be secured, the harvest will be lost. For this loss none feels so deep a sorrow as the Lord himself. It is his harvest and he longs for reapers. They were few in the days of Jesus; they ever have been too few; but the need can be supplied more nearly if the followers of the King will heed his command and unite in prayer for more laborers. Of course such a petition implies and secures a deepening interest on the part of the petitioners. When Jesus urged his disciples to pray, he was about to send them forth to work.

B. THE NAMES OF THE TWELVE
Ch. 10:1-4

1 And he called unto him his twelve disciples, and gave them authority over unclean spirits, to cast them out, and to heal all manner of disease and all manner of sickness.

2 Now the names of the twelve apostles are these: The first, Simon, who is called Peter, and Andrew his brother; James the son of Zebedee, and John his brother; 3 Philip, and Bartholomew; Thomas, and Matthew the publican; James the son of Alphæus, and Thaddæus; 4 Simon the Cananæan, and Judas Iscariot, who also betrayed him.

Before Matthew records the list of the memorable names of the immediate and chosen apostles of Christ, he states the character of the work which they were called to do. They were given "authority over unclean spirits, to cast them out, and to heal all manner of disease and all manner of sickness." These miracles would serve as credentials of their commission. It was a unique privilege. Other great leaders had wrought miracles, but none had given this power to their followers. The works of mercy and of grace performed by the Twelve would win for them willing hearers and would secure ready acceptance for the good news they proclaimed.

The names of the twelve apostles are arranged in three groups of four names each. These same groups and in the same order appear in all the lists recorded by the different Evangelists. It is possible that the groups are arranged in accordance with the comparative intimacy with Christ which different apostles enjoyed. At least it is certain that the four first named were the most intimate companions and most trusted messengers of Jesus. Peter is mentioned first, not merely because his name begins the list but to suggest that he was first in prominence. Closely associated with him were Andrew, his brother, and James and John, the sons of Zebedee. It had been the privilege of Andrew to bring Peter to Jesus; James had the honor of being the first martyr among the band of apostles; John was the "disciple whom Jesus loved" and who seemed most fully to return this affection and to understand the divine nature of his Lord.

Philip is named with Bartholomew; the latter we are probably to identify with Nathanael, the Israelite without guile, whom Philip had introduced to his Lord. Thomas is known as the "doubting disciple"; he really had as much loyalty and faith as his companions, but he wished proof of his own choosing and was a man characterized by melancholy and by a certain stubbornness of temperament. Matthew, in only this list of the disciples is called "the publican." It is an intimation that he himself wrote the record. The name "publican" implied something of opprobrium and was therefore given him by none of the other Evangelists. He seemed to glory in the fact that Jesus had done so much for him and had called him from the task of a publican to the work of an apostle.

James, the son of Alphaeus, is not to be confused either with the brother of John, nor yet with the brother of Jesus. The last mistake is very commonly made, but this apostle who was elsewhere called "James the Less" followed and trusted Jesus during those long years which "the brother of Jesus" passed in unbelief. It was after the resurrection that "the brother of our Lord" became a disciple and rose to prominence in the early church, and finally wrote the epistle which bears his name. The Thaddaeus here mentioned is the same as the "Judas the son of James" mentioned by Luke and the "Judas (not Iscariot)" mentioned by John. "Simon the Cananæan" or "Zealot," was so named either because he belonged to the party of extreme nationalists among the Jews, or else, which is less likely, because of his own burning enthusiasm for his Lord.

Judas was possibly called "Iscariot" to suggest that he came from the town of Kerioth. If so, he was the only disciple who belonged to Judea, and therefore from the first may have had less sympathy with Christ than his eleven comrades. Of this there is no certainty. It is noticeable, however, that whenever he is named, it is always with some reminder of the dark crime inseparable from his memory, as Matthew here adds, "who also betrayed him." That Jesus should have selected such a man to be his follower has often occasioned wonder and surprise. We are probably to conclude, however, that his character was at first full of promise and that his career is simply a warning of what may be possible for anyone who attempts to follow Christ and who still allows the mastery of some besetting sin.

Such in brief are the twelve men whom Jesus sent out as his messengers. They were probably men of moderate ability, of modest means, and had no place in the great world of history. They were of diverse characters; some of them are so unknown that they are to us mere names; yet through them was laid the foundation of the greatest movement and the most important institution of all time. It is for the followers of Christ to be loyal to him and then, whatever their talents or limitations, however prominent or obscure their positions, they can be certain that he will accomplish through them a work which only eternity can measure.

C. THE MISSION   Ch. 10:5-15

5 *These twelve Jesus sent forth, and charged them, saying, Go not into any way of the Gentiles, and enter not into any city of the Samaritans: 6 but go rather to the lost sheep of the house of Israel. 7 And as ye go, preach, saying, The kingdom of heaven is at hand. 8 Heal the sick, raise the dead, cleanse the lepers, cast out demons: freely ye received, freely give. 9 Get you no gold, nor silver, nor brass in your purses; 10 no wallet for your journey, neither two coats, nor shoes, nor staff: for the laborer is worthy of his food. 11 And into whatsoever city or village ye shall enter, search out who in it is worthy; and there abide till*

*ye go forth. 12 And as ye enter into the house, salute it.
13 And if the house be worthy, let your peace come upon
it: but if it be not worthy, let your peace return to you.
14 And whosoever shall not receive you, nor hear your
words, as ye go forth out of that house or that city, shake
off the dust of your feet. 15 Verily I say unto you, It shall
be more tolerable for the land of Sodom and Gomorrah in
the day of judgment, than for that city.*

Here Matthew records the charge definitely intended
for the twelve apostles and applicable to the task which
immediately awaited them. It includes first of all a statement of the scope of their mission. It was not to be to
the Gentiles or the Samaritans, but only to the shepherd-
less sheep of the "house of Israel." Later on these same
apostles would be sent to Samaria and the "uttermost part
of the earth," but for the present they were to prepare
the way for the King who likewise limited his ministry to
his own people. It is true that he also brought his
message to Samaritans and once crossed the border into
a heathen land. He also indicated on more than one
occasion that his work was for the Gentiles who would
ultimately receive him as King. However, during the days
of his earthly ministry, he restricted himself and usually
labored within the same bounds which he designates as
the field of temporary service for his followers.

The message they were to deliver was identical with his
own, "The kingdom of heaven is at hand." Later on they
were to state more explicitly that he himself was the King,
and finally they were to be witnesses of his atoning work
and his glorious resurrection; but on this first mission
they were to call men to repentance and to promise them
the blessings of the coming Kingdom.

Their message was to be attended by works of mercy.
They were not only to heal the sick, to cleanse the lepers,
to cast out demons, but even to raise the dead. There is
something very startling in this commission and it is not
strange that a ministry so attested awakened wonder and

belief in countless multitudes. As to their recompense and reward, Jesus declares, "Freely ye received, freely give." This does not mean that they were not to receive support in their labor. The contrary is at once stated; but it does imply that they were not to use their mission as a means of acquiring wealth. The good news that had been gratuitously bestowed should not be employed as a means of gain.

They were to take with them for their journey nothing which might needlessly encumber them. The specific directions of the Master were not intended to produce discomfort or involve distress, but only to free them from needless care. They were to be discreet as to the place where they abode. They were to be courteous in their attitude toward those by whom they might be entertained; but they were to waste no time on fruitless soil. If they were not received as messengers of the King, they were at once to seek some new field of labor. However, they were to give a solemn warning to such unbelievers and were to shake off the dust of their feet as though they had been treading on polluted ground. It is evident that these injunctions were intended only for the days when the apostles were preparing the way for the earthly labors of their Lord. Many of these directions were purely temporary. Jesus wished to impress upon them the fact that the time of his ministry would be brief, that the message which they bore was important, and that refusal to accept the good news was a serious offense, so that he could close the special injunctions by the statement that it would be more tolerable for the land of Sodom and Gomorrah in the day of judgment than for one of these unbelieving cities to which Jesus sent his first messengers.

D. THE SUFFERING Ch. 10:16-23

16 Behold, I send you forth as sheep in the midst of wolves: be ye therefore wise as serpents, and harmless as doves. 17 But beware of men: for they will deliver you up to councils, and in their synagogues they will scourge you; 18 yea and before governors and kings shall ye be brought for my sake, for a testimony to them and to the Gentiles. 19 But when they deliver you up, be not anxious how or what ye shall speak: for it shall be given you in that hour what ye shall speak. 20 For it is not ye that speak, but the Spirit of your Father that speaketh in you. 21 And brother shall deliver up brother to death, and the father his child: and children shall rise up against parents, and cause them to be put to death. 22 And ye shall be hated of all men for my name's sake: but he that endureth to the end, the same shall be saved. 23 But when they persecute you in this city, flee into the next: for verily I say unto you, Ye shall not have gone through the cities of Israel, till the Son of man be come.

In the warning which Matthew records as intended for the messengers of the King, there is much which evidently applies to the experiences of a later day, and to those who, through the passing centuries, have endured hardship for the sake of Christ. The testimony of the Master prepared his followers not only for the unbelief and the indifference of those to whom they testified, but also for the active persecution and cruel hostility of bitter enemies. His messengers were to go forth "as sheep in the midst of wolves." They needed, therefore, to be wise as serpents and harmless as doves. They were to be delivered to councils for trial; they were to be cruelly scourged in public; they were even to testify before the governors and kings of heathen lands. When brought to trial, however, they were not to be anxious as to the message which they should deliver. The Master himself would furnish for them words of wisdom. The very Spirit of God would speak through them.

Their suffering would involve the treachery of even the nearest kindred; brother would betray brother, the father his child, and children would cause the death of their own parents. For the sake of his name, the messengers of Christ would be hated of all men, but their distress would issue in eternal salvation. When persecuted they were not needlessly to imperil their lives; they were not to seek the glory of martyrdom. However, the time of their distress was not unlimited. Deliverance was always imminent. The period allotted for their labors should be regarded as brief. Their task would not be complete until the Son of Man appeared. For the followers of Christ experiences are various; they change with the revolving years; but in no age need they be surprised at the hostility of the world; in every hour of darkness they may be cheered by the hope of the coming of the King.

E. THE ENCOURAGEMENT   Ch. 10:24-33

24 A disciple is not above his teacher, nor a servant above his lord. 25 It is enough for the disciple that he be as his teacher, and the servant as his lord. If they have called the master of the house Beelzebub, how much more them of his household! 26 Fear them not therefore: for there is nothing covered, that shall not be revealed; and hid, that shall not be known. 27 What I tell you in the darkness, speak ye in the light; and what ye hear in the ear, proclaim upon the house-tops. 28 And be not afraid of them that kill the body, but are not able to kill the soul: but rather fear him who is able to destroy both soul and body in hell. 29 Are not two sparrows sold for a penny? And not one of them shall fall on the ground without your Father: 30 but the very hairs of your head are all numbered. 31 Fear not therefore: ye are of more value than many sparrows. 32 Every one therefore who shall confess me before men, him will I also confess before my Father who is in heaven. 33 But whosoever shall deny me before men, him will I also deny before my Father who is in heaven.

Not only did the Master comfort his followers by the assurance of a coming deliverance, but he told them that it would be their distinction to suffer as he had suffered. It need not surprise them if the servants met with the same treatment which was given to their Lord. If men called him "Beelzebub," they would use no less reproachful titles in addressing his followers. Just what that particular epithet may have meant, it is impossible to determine; but the warning was clear that they should share in the hatred which had been shown toward him. They were encouraged, however, not to fear. Three times the exhortation was repeated. In spite of their sufferings they were not to be terrified, because their testimony would be made only the more powerful because of their distress. They were not to fear the most cruel enemies, for these might kill the body, but their trust was in One whose power was not limited to the present life. He could "destroy both soul and body in hell." A reverent fear of him would destroy all fear of men. They were further encouraged by the assurance that this heavenly Father would care for them. He knew of the fall of the sparrow and regarded the smallest portions of the bodies of his children; he would certainly protect and deliver them in the time of danger. Most of all, should they be encouraged by the glory which would await them as they stood at last before the throne of the Father in heaven. Those who had been loyal to Christ on earth would then receive a glorious recognition and would be acknowledged as the true children of God. Whatever may be involved in an open confession of Christ should be cheerfully and heroically endured. Needed strength will be given in the present and in the future the blessedness of heaven.

F. THE CROSS   Ch. 10:34-39

34 Think not that I came to send peace on the earth: I came not to send peace, but a sword. 35 For I came to set a man at variance against his father, and the daughter against her mother, and the daughter in law against her mother in law: 36 and a man's foes shall be they of his own household. 37 He that loveth father or mother more than me is not worthy of me; and he that loveth son or daughter more than me is not worthy of me. 38 And he that doth not take his cross and follow after me, is not worthy of me. 39 He that findeth his life shall lose it; and he that loseth his life for my sake shall find it.

In warning his messengers of the suffering which might attend their ministry, Jesus speaks with definiteness and assures them of its certain bitterness. If they are to testify to an unbelieving and impenitent world, they must expect opposition, persecution, and pain. The final issue of the mission of Christ will be universal peace, but that will not result from the first proclamation of his demands. There will arise, rather, a sharp division between those who accept and those who reject him. The presence of Christ always occasions separations. Some are for him and some are against him. "Think not," the Master warns his followers, "that I came to send peace on the earth: I came not to send peace, but a sword." These separations will appear even in the most sacred circles. A man will be "at variance against his father, and the daughter against her mother"; "a man's foes shall be they of his own household." No tie, however tender, should be allowed to keep one from fidelity to Christ. "He that loveth father or mother more than me is not worthy of me." The sacrifice may involve life itself, "He that doth not take his cross and follow after me, is not worthy of me." The cross here indicates an instrument of death. It is used, here, for the first time in the story. Matthew may be regarded as the "Gospel of rejection." At the end of his earthly pathway Jesus saw a dark cross on the horizon. Under the shadow of that cross most of his work was done. It was not unnatural, therefore, that his followers should likewise endure something of his suffering and even for his sake should lay down their lives. The Master seems to picture a long procession of men and women each bearing a cross to the place of death. He indicates, however, that such sacrifice will result in the largest life both here and hereafter. "He that findeth his life shall lose it; and he that loseth his life for my sake shall find it."

G. THE SYMPATHY   Ch. 10:40-42

40 He that receiveth you receiveth me, and he that receiveth me receiveth him that sent me. 41 He that receiveth a prophet in the name of a prophet shall receive a prophet's reward: and he that receiveth a righteous man in the name of a righteous man shall receive a righteous man's reward. 42 And whosoever shall give to drink unto one of these little ones a cup of cold water only, in the name of a disciple, verily I say unto you he shall in no wise lose his reward.

The final words of this commission, addressed by the King to his messengers, embody another statement of encouragement. He has already assured them of the protection of the Father and of the glory which he will bestow. He now declares that they will not be without sympathy from men; and he indicates the blessedness of those who in any age show kindness and give relief to such as are testifying for him. He declares that one who receives his messenger is in a real sense receiving the King himself, and that whoever receives a prophet who is speaking for the King, shall partake in the reward of the prophet; that he who receives a righteous man, that is, one who is proclaiming the law of the King and is presumably observing that law himself, will partake in the reward of the righteous. He even promises that one who gives a cup of cold water to a disciple, because he is a disciple, will receive a sure reward. It is not given to all men to be public messengers like the twelve apostles, but all can share in their work and can become partakers of their glory and their joy by showing for them sympathy and by offering to them help and relief in the name of their Lord.

V
THE CLAIMS
OF THE KING
Chs. 11; 12

A. THE MESSIAH PREDICTED BY JOHN
Ch. 11:1-19

1 And it came to pass when Jesus had finished commanding his twelve disciples, he departed thence to teach ʼ *and preach in their cities.*

2 Now when John heard in the prison the works of the Christ, he sent by his disciples 3 and said unto him, Art thou he that cometh, or look we for another? 4 And Jesus answered and said unto them, Go and tell John the things which ye hear and see: 5 the blind receive their sight, and the lame walk, the lepers are cleansed, and the deaf hear, and the dead are raised up, and the poor have good tidings preached to them. 6 And blessed is he, whosoever shall find no occasion of stumbling in me.

7 And as these went their way, Jesus began to say unto the multitudes concerning John, What went ye out into the wilderness to behold? a reed shaken with the wind? 8 But what went ye out to see? a man clothed in soft raiment? Behold, they that wear soft raiment are in kings' houses. 9 But wherefore went ye out? to see a prophet? Yea, I say unto you, and much more than a prophet. 10 This is he, of whom it is written,

Behold, I send my messenger before thy face,
Who shall prepare thy way before thee.

11 Verily I say unto you, Among them that are born of women there hath not arisen a greater than John the Baptist: yet he that is but little in the kingdom of heaven is greater than he. 12 And from the days of John the Baptist until now the kingdom of heaven suffereth violence, and men of violence take it by force. 13 For all the prophets and the law prophesied until John. 14 And if ye are willing to receive it, this is Elijah, that is to come. 15 He that hath ears to hear, let him hear. 16 But whereunto shall I liken this generation? It is like unto children sitting in the marketplaces, who call unto their fellows 17 and say, We piped unto you, and ye did not dance; we wailed, and ye did not mourn. 18 For John came neither eating nor drinking, and they say, He hath a demon. 19 The Son of man came eating and drinking, and they say, Behold, a gluttonous man and a winebibber, a friend of publicans and sinners! And wisdom is justified by her works.

In chapters eleven and twelve of his Gospel, Matthew reveals the increasing hostility to Christ shown by his enemies. It is more and more obvious that the King is to be rejected. This forms the continual background of the picture. On the other hand, Jesus is here making with ever-increasing clearness his claims to be the Messiah, the King of Israel, the predicted Savior of the world. In recording these claims Matthew is, therefore, furthering the specific purpose of his Gospel. In earlier chapters Jesus has borne similar testimony to himself and in later chapters this testimony will become ever more definite and complete. Yet as it is the custom of Matthew to group materials under certain definite topics, in order to heighten the effect, so here is a series of incidents, in each one of which the King makes a startling claim. First of all, when John the Baptist sends from prison to ask whether or not Jesus is the coming One, the predicted Messiah, Jesus sends as his reply a description of the gracious work which he is performing and particularly of the glad tidings which he is preaching even to the poor. These should be signs to reassure John, and in spite of the long delay on the part of Christ in publicly manifesting himself as the Messiah, John should not doubt the truth which he had himself publicly proclaimed. Then, as the messengers are leaving, Jesus turns to the multitudes to bear his matchless testimony to the character and work of John. The people, who had heard the bold preaching of the herald, were probably ready to point at him the finger of scorn as he has sent a message which implies something at least of doubt as to the truth of his own testimony; but Jesus declares that John is the greatest among men. His greatness consists partly in his character, but more definitely in his career. He was great as a man but still greater as the messenger of the Messiah. His moral greatness is set forth by an implied negative answer to two questions: First, he was a man of courage, for very obviously he was not like a "reed shaken with the wind." In spite of opposition and peril and in the face of the king he had stood firm as a rock. He also was a man of consecration; he was not a man who wore "soft raiment," that is, who sought only comfort and gratification. At any sacrifice he had pursued his great mission. It was indeed this mission which constituted his essential greatness. Unlike other prophets who had predicted the coming of Christ, John enjoyed the unique privilege of actually pointing to Jesus and declaring him to be the Messiah. He was indeed the messenger of whom the prophet Malachi had spoken, "Behold, I send my messenger before thy face, who shall prepare thy way before thee." It was because John was his herald that Jesus declared of him, "Verily I say unto you, Among them that are born of women there hath not arisen a greater than John the Baptist." How great then was Jesus; what does he claim to be? If to point to Jesus as the Christ is the greatest task ever assigned to man, is not Jesus "the Christ," and is he not greater than man? Is not this claim clearly involved in the praise which Jesus bestowed upon John the Baptist?

The Master adds a gracious and mysterious word, "He that is but little in the kingdom of heaven is greater than he." It must at least mean that present messengers of Christ know more of his person and work than even John the Baptist knew; and more definitely still, that however great may be the privilege of any messenger in this present time, it will not compare with the glory of the least of those who are admitted to the Kingdom of Heaven. In that perfected Kingdom the relative position of John is not implied. That will be determined by the comparative faithfulness of those who like John have been privileged to witness for the King.

As has been suggested, the background of this glorious claim is the dark picture of the rejection of Jesus. As the forerunner was imprisoned, so Jesus is to be disowned and crucified. Both in the person of the herald and in the person of the King himself "the kingdom of heaven suffereth violence." If John who came in the spirit and power of Elijah was allowed to languish in prison, the King saw clearly that for himself there was ready a cross. With the thought of his own rejection coupled with that of John, Jesus spoke the parable of the "children sitting in the marketplaces" who were complaining that their companions were unwilling in their childish games to imitate either funerals or weddings. John had come with his solemn call to repentance, and men turned from him as from a gloomy fanatic, declaring "He hath a demon." Jesus came eating and drinking, showing the glad life which befitted his good news; but they declared that he was "a gluttonous man and a winebibber." Neither one was able to please the unbelieving generation of Jews. They were both rejected, not because of their manner of life, but because John insisted upon repentance, and because Jesus claimed to be the Christ, the Messiah, the divine King.

B. THE JUDGE OF THE IMPENITENT
Ch. 11:20-24

20 Then began he to upbraid the cities wherein most of his mighty works were done, because they repented not. 21 Woe unto thee, Chorazin! woe unto thee, Bethsaida! for if the mighty works had been done in Tyre and Sidon which

were done in you, they would have repented long ago in
sackcloth and ashes.   22 But I say unto you, it shall be
more tolerable for Tyre and Sidon in the day of judgment,
than for you.   23 And thou, Capernaum, shalt thou be
exalted unto heaven? thou shalt go down unto Hades: for
if the mighty works had been done in Sodom which were
done in thee, it would have remained until this day.   24
But I say unto you that it shall be more tolerable for the
land of Sodom in the day of judgment, than for thee.

Jesus implies a further claim when he turns to pronounce
his solemn woes upon Chorazin and Bethsaida and Capernaum.   Who but a divine King could venture to pronounce such penalties upon these cities; who would venture to declare the relative punishments which would be
meted out in the Day of Judgment?   More definite still
was the implication that, if failure to believe in him was
declared to be a cause for eternal punishment, then surely
he must be the Christ, the Savior, who was in his person
all that he suggested and declared.   Can we imagine any
other man than he solemnly stating that if men did not
believe in him and accept him as a Lord and Savior, they
should suffer the doom of hell?   Who must it be who makes
such claims for himself?   It is well to note here that Jesus
pronounces his woes not merely upon the wicked, the im-
moral, the depraved, but upon those who are indifferent
to his claims.   Again it should be noted that Jesus insists
that the larger the opportunity for belief, the greater is the
condemnation upon those who reject him.   Capernaum is
to be brought down unto Hades because the city has been
exalted to heaven in the privilege it had enjoyed in witness-
ing the mighty works of Christ.   His miracles were his
credentials.   Whatever view may be taken by modern
men of these wonderful works, Jesus declares that they
bore definite testimony to his claims and that those who
beheld them were under greater condemnation for their
unbelief.   It is certainly true today that a larger knowledge of Christ and of his power places upon men a greater

responsibility to accept him as Lord and Master and to render him homage as to the universal King.

C. THE REVEALER OF THE FATHER
Ch. 11:25-30

25 At that season Jesus answered and said, I thank thee, O Father, Lord of heaven and earth, that thou didst hide these things from the wise and understanding, and didst reveal them unto babes: 26 yea, Father, for so it was well-pleasing in thy sight. 27 All things have been delivered unto me of my Father: and no one knoweth the Son, save the Father; neither doth any know the Father, save the Son, and he to whomsoever the Son willeth to reveal him. 28 Come unto me, all ye that labor and are heavy laden, and I will give you rest. 29 Take my yoke upon you, and learn of me; for I am meek and lowly in heart: and ye shall find rest unto your souls. 30 For my yoke is easy, and my burden is light.

It is at this time that Jesus gives expression to truths which embody such definite claims of a unique relationship to God that they are regarded by many as equal to the similar statements in the Gospel of John. They should be weighed carefully by those who insist that the first three Gospels do not testify to the divine nature of Christ. Jesus here returns thanks that the truth concerning himself, while hidden from "the wise and understanding" has been revealed to "babes." Jesus does not mean that intellectual attainment necessarily stands in the way of faith in him; but he does imply that it is not necessary. Even the most ignorant and untutored are able to apprehend the saving truth concerning Christ. Their ignorance is no advantage; yet it is no disqualification. Jesus is returning thanks that saving knowledge is not dependent upon worldly wisdom. He goes on to state that no one really understands him excepting the Father, and that no one really knows God excepting those to whom Jesus himself is willing to reveal him. As we remember this claim of a unique and incomparable knowledge of the Father and of an ability to reveal this knowledge to whomsoever he will, we can fully understand the difficult but precious and incomparably beautiful invitation, familiar to every believing heart, "Come unto me, all ye that labor and are heavy laden, and I will give you rest." To those who are burdened by the legal requirements of the professed teachers of religion, to those whose hearts were heavy with doubt and sorrow and fear, Jesus gives this gracious call, to come to him, as to one who can reveal to them the Father in all his grace and goodness and love. He urges all to become his disciples, "Take my yoke upon you, and learn of me." In contrast to the teachers of the day, he declares that he is "meek and lowly in heart." He offers to all men rest, not from physical burdens, not from struggles and distresses, but in spite of all these, rest for the soul. He strengthens his invitation by the blessed assurance that the yoke he asks us to bear is "easy"; the "burden" which he places upon us is "light." This is an incomparable invitation; and does it not embody a matchless claim? Who among all the characters that have stepped upon the stage of human history could venture to say for a single moment what Jesus here says? On the lips of any other speaker would it not sound hollow, futile, absurd? As the words fall from his lips they touch the soul with all the sweet cadences of a heavenly melody, with all the assurance of divine reality. He who spoke these words must have been the Son of God, he must have been the divine King.

D. THE LORD OF THE SABBATH Ch. 12:1-21

1 At that season Jesus went on the sabbath day through the grainfields; and his disciples were hungry and began to pluck ears and to eat. 2 But the Pharisees, when they saw it, said unto him, Behold, thy disciples do that which it is not lawful to do upon the sabbath. 3 But he said unto them, Have ye not read what David did, when he was hun-

gry, and they that were with him; 4 how he entered into
the house of God, and ate the showbread, which it was not
lawful for him to eat, neither for them that were with him,
but only for the priests? 5 Or have ye not read in the law,
that on the sabbath day the priests in the temple profane
the sabbath, and are guiltless? 6 But I say unto you, that
one greater than the temple is here. 7 But if ye had known
what this meaneth, I desire mercy, and not sacrifice, ye
would not have condemned the guiltless. 8 For the Son of
man is lord of the sabbath.

9 And he departed thence, and went into their synagogue: 10 and behold, a man having a withered hand.
And they asked him, saying, Is it lawful to heal on the sabbath day? that they might accuse him. 11 And he said
unto them, What man shall there be of you, that shall have
one sheep, and if this fall into a pit on the sabbath day,
will he not lay hold on it, and lift it out? 12 How much
then is a man of more value than a sheep! Wherefore it
is lawful to do good on the sabbath day. 13 Then saith
he to the man, Stretch forth thy hand. And he stretched
it forth; and it was restored whole, as the other. 14 But
the Pharisees went out, and took counsel against him, how
they might destroy him.

15 And Jesus perceiving it withdrew from thence: and
many followed him; and he healed them all, 16 and
charged them that they should not make him known:
17 that it might be fulfilled which was spoken through
Isaiah the prophet, saying,

18 Behold, my servant whom I have chosen;
My beloved in whom my soul is well pleased:
I will put my Spirit upon him,
And he shall declare judgment to the Gentiles.
19 He shall not strive, nor cry aloud;
Neither shall any one hear his voice in the streets.
20 A bruised reed shall he not break,
And smoking flax shall he not quench,
Till he send forth judgment unto victory.
21 And in his name shall the Gentiles hope.

The opposition to Jesus became most bitter and intense
when he defended his disciples for having broken a minute

traditional rule as to the observance of the day of rest. His followers had been guilty of appeasing their hunger by picking ears of ripened grain, an act which the Pharisees interpreted as breaking the law of the Sabbath. In his reply Jesus declared that this law, which is sacred and divine, can be broken to perform a work of necessity, as was done in the case of David, who in a time of necessity broke a law relative to Temple worship. Furthermore, as Jesus reminds his enemies, the priests in the Temple continually break the law of Sabbath rest and are guiltless. The defense seems to be complete but Jesus startles his hearers by adding, "But I say unto you, that one greater than the temple is here." What more blasphemous utterance could be imagined? The Temple embodied all that was most sacred in the life of the nation; yet Jesus declares of himself that he is greater than all the worship and symbols and laws of the house of God. He even goes farther still, and declares that he is "lord of the sabbath." No wonder that such claims goaded his enemies to madness. There seems to be no alternative. Either Jesus was a blasphemer or he was divine.

While Jesus has answered the Pharisees, he has not made himself liable to arrest, so they further observe him to see whether he will not himself break the Sabbath law. There is in the synagogue, where Jesus has gone to worship, a poor cripple whom Jesus heals. As he does so he explains the other ground on which Sabbath rest may be broken. It is on the ground of mercy. He does not suggest that the law of Sabbath rest has been abrogated. His own example would take us on the Sabbath day to the house of God. It would show us that this day is divinely appointed for worship and for rest, but that the two possible grounds for breaking this rest are works of necessity and mercy. His gracious healing of the cripple on the Sabbath was regarded as involving work and so as sinful. Such was the interpretation of his enemies. His followers regarded it as a demonstration of deity. A choice must be made. "The Pharisees went out, and took counsel against him, how they might destroy him."

Jesus, however, meekly withdrew from the hatred and opposition of the rulers, and Matthew declares that this was in fulfillment of the prediction which described the Messiah as one who would be meek and gentle, who would "not strive; nor cry aloud." He would not break the "bruised reed" nor quench the "smoking flax." A time would come, however, when he would appear in triumph and in victory. Even though his own nation might reject him, the day would come when in his name the Gentiles would hope and would find in him the King of life.

E. THE AGENT OF THE HOLY SPIRIT
Ch. 12:22-37

22 Then was brought unto him one possessed with a demon, blind and dumb: and he healed him, insomuch that the dumb man spake and saw. 23 And all the multitudes were amazed, and said, Can this be the son of David? 24 But when the Pharisees heard it, they said, This man doth not cast out demons, but by Beelzebub the prince of the demons. 25 And knowing their thoughts he said unto them, Every kingdom divided against itself is brought to desolation; and every city or house divided against itself shall not stand: 26 and if Satan casteth out Satan, he is divided against himself; how then shall his kingdom stand? 27 And if I by Beelzebub cast out demons, by whom do your sons cast them out? therefore shall they be your judges. 28 But if I by the Spirit of God cast out demons, then is the kingdom of God come upon you. 29 Or how can one enter into the house of the strong man, and spoil his goods, except he first bind the strong man? and then he will spoil his house. 30 He that is not with me is against me; and he that gathereth not with me scattereth. 31 Therefore I say unto you, Every sin and blasphemy shall be forgiven unto men; but the blasphemy against the Spirit shall not be forgiven. 32 And whosoever shall speak a word against the Son of man, it shall be forgiven him; but whosoever shall speak against the Holy Spirit, it shall not

*be forgiven him, neither in this world, nor in that which
is to come. 33 Either make the tree good, and its fruit
good; or make the tree corrupt, and its fruit corrupt: for
the tree is known by its fruit. 34 Ye offspring of vipers,
how can ye, being evil, speak good things? for out of the
abundance of the heart the mouth speaketh. 35 The good
man out of his good treasure bringeth forth good things:
and the evil man out of his evil treasure bringeth forth
evil things. 36 And I say unto you, that every idle word
that men shall speak, they shall give account thereof in
the day of judgment. 37 For by thy words thou shalt be
justified, and by thy words thou shalt be condemned.*

The casting out of demons caused the multitudes to
marvel and to question whether Jesus was not possibly
the promised Messiah; for the Pharisees it was the occasion of a desperate and vicious charge; the reply of Jesus
embodied one of his most definite claims. That miracles
were being performed, his enemies could not deny; the
superhuman power must have been divine or demonic; the
Pharisees were driven to accept the latter choice; they declared that Jesus cast out demons by the aid of the devil.

Jesus showed the charge to be absurd by reminding
them that if Satan was casting out his own agents it was
like casting out himself; he would be destroying his own
kingdom, which would be ridiculous to suppose.

Further, Jesus appealed to the fact that there were many
Jews who, as exorcists, claimed to be casting out demons
and were approved by the Pharisees; to single out Jesus for
attack was an evidence of injustice and malice.

Then Jesus declared plainly that his works were wrought
by the Spirit of God and were evidences that, in his person, the Kingdom of God was manifest among them, and
that the power of Satan was being overthrown. The two
kingdoms were opposed to each other and men must
choose on which side to stand. If not on the side of Jesus
then the Pharisees must be on the side of Satan. Thus
Jesus turned the charge upon his enemies.

He did more. He declared that their charge was a sin

which could not be forgiven; it was "blasphemy against the Spirit"; it was attributing to Satan the power of God. In the present day it is popular to say that "resisting the Holy Ghost," or "sinning away the day of grace" is "the unpardonable sin." This is both a confusion of ideas and a misinterpretation of the words of Jesus. He declared that a person might be forgiven for misunderstanding his mission and message, for even speaking against him as "the Son of man," but maliciously to ascribe his power to the devil, and thus to "speak against the Holy Spirit," could be forgiven "neither in this world, nor in that which is to come."

Such an atrocious charge could come only out of an evil heart. The miracles of Jesus were gracious and could come from only a pure source, like good fruit from a good tree; on the other hand, the venomous attack of his enemies revealed them to be a brood of vipers, incapable of bringing forth anything but evil. Blasphemy is not a mere utterance of the lips; it is serious because it is an expression of the heart; for even their light and careless words men are responsible; how great then is the guilt of such a cruel slander!

The Pharisees brought the charge against Jesus; he replied that in so doing they were guilty of an unpardonable sin against the Holy Spirit; therefore, in what unique relation to the Holy Spirit did Jesus claim to stand? Could any other man who ever lived make the same assertion about himself? If too, in his person, the Kingdom was present, was not this the Spirit-anointed King, the Messiah, whom Matthew distinctively depicts?

F. THE PROPHET AND THE KING
Ch. 12:38-45

38 Then certain of the scribes and Pharisees answered him, saying, Teacher, we would see a sign from thee. 39 But he answered and said unto them, An evil and adulterous generation seeketh after a sign; and there shall no sign be given to it but the sign of Jonah the prophet: 40

*for as Jonah was three days and three nights in the belly of
the whale; so shall the Son of man be three days and three
nights in the heart of the earth. 41 The men of Nineveh
shall stand up in the judgment with this generation, and
shall condemn it: for they repented at the preaching of
Jonah; and behold, a greater than Jonah is here. 42 The
queen of the south shall rise up in the judgment with this
generation, and shall condemn it: for she came from the
ends of the earth to hear the wisdom of Solomon; and behold, a greater than Solomon is here. 43 But the unclean
spirit, when he is gone out of the man, passeth through
waterless places, seeking rest, and findeth it not. 44 Then
he saith, I will return into my house whence I came out;
and when he is come, he findeth it empty, swept, and gar-
nished. 45 Then goeth he, and taketh with himself seven
other spirits more evil than himself, and they enter in and
dwell there: and the last state of that man becometh worse
than the first. Even so shall it be also unto this evil generation.*

The demand for a sign was a cruel and studied insult.
It reflected upon the miracles already wrought; it implied
that Jesus lacked credentials; it intimated that he was
making claims he could not vindicate. However, it is
echoed today by men who claim that they have not proof
enough for believing in Christ, or are asking for evidence
of some different kind to justify their unbelief.

Jesus replied that the trouble was with his enemies; their
hearts were not right toward God or they would have accepted the testimony already given. He called them an
"adulterous generation," one unfaithful to God, and declared that no greater sign would be given them but one,
the sign of his own resurrection; it would be a miracle even
greater than that of Jonah. They were more guilty than
the men of Nineveh, who repented at the preaching of
Jonah; for he was "greater than Jonah." The example
of the Queen of Sheba condemned them, for she eagerly
sought for the wisdom of Solomon, and he was "greater
than Solomon." Are not these claims astonishing? In
this chapter Matthew records the claims of the great Priest,

"One greater than the temple is here," and of the great Prophet, "a greater than Jonah is here"; but, true to his unfailing purpose, he reverses the order of Luke, and the order of time, and reaches his climax in the claim of the King to be the true Son of David, "a greater than Solomon is here."

To illustrate the unbelief of his people Jesus tells the story of the unclean spirit, who for a time left the man he had been tormenting, but returned with seven other demons "more evil than himself." So Israel, possessed by unbelief, had been cured for a time and turned from idolatry, but God had not been admitted to the empty heart of the nation, and now their attitude toward Christ showed that unbelief possessed them more cruelly and completely than ever before.

It is a parable, too, of many modern experiences. Men turn from sin and find temporary freedom; but unless Christ is admitted to the citadel of the soul as Lord and Master, defeat and failure and more bitter captivity are sure to follow; reformation is not regeneration; resolution is not conversion; repentance may not be united with faith; morality is not religion.

G. THE SON OF GOD   Ch. 12:46-50

46 While he was yet speaking to the multitudes, behold, his mother and his brethren stood without, seeking to speak to him. 47 And one said unto him, Behold, thy mother and thy brethren stand without, seeking to speak to thee. 48 But he answered and said unto him that told him, Who is my mother? and who are my brethren? 49 And he stretched forth his hand towards his disciples, and said, Behold, my mother and my brethren! 50 For whosoever shall do the will of my Father who is in heaven, he is my brother, and sister, and mother.

Matthew has emphasized the opposition to Jesus and also his unique claims. This seventh and last incident reveals the most trying form of opposition and implies the supreme claim. His mother and his brothers have come to take him from his work, fearing that his mind has become unbalanced by his incessant toil. It is the most difficult and delicate dilemma in which our Lord has ever been placed. He cannot offend the members of his household; on the other hand, he cannot allow his task to be interrupted and himself to be led away like a poor sick child. By a single stroke he extricates himself and at the same time gives a message of inspiring helpfulness to his followers in all coming time. He does not deny the sacredness of natural ties, nor the tenderness of human relationships. He does not disclaim his mother or his brothers; he enlarges the family circle and declares spiritual ties are the most real and that all who do the will of God are most intimately related to himself. However, it is to his disciples that he points most definitely as he declares: "Behold, my mother and my brethren! For whosoever shall do the will of my Father who is in heaven, he is my brother, and sister, and mother." Those who follow Christ are those who do the will of God; not those who reject him or doubt him or refuse to believe him. There was no discourtesy shown to the members of his home circle, but there was a gentle rebuke which they alone understood, for they did not then believe in him. His word may contain a tender note of warning to some of his followers to-day. If they are true followers, they must be doing the will of God. He does not say "The same is my Father." He is claiming for himself a unique relationship with God and is declaring that those are most nearly related to him who are doing the will of his own Father. Who, then, is this teacher who claims such divine perfection that those who are most truly godly are nearest to himself? Who is this who claims such a distinct relationship with the Father? It is the one of whom Matthew has here been writing, the predicted and rejected King, the Son of Man, who is also the Son of God.

VI
THE PARABLES
OF THE KING
Ch. 13

A. THE SOWER Ch. 13:1-23

1 On that day went Jesus out of the house, and sat by the sea side. 2 And there were gathered unto him great multitudes, so that he entered into a boat, and sat; and all the multitude stood on the beach. 3 And he spake to them many things in parables, saying, Behold, the sower went forth to sow; 4 and as he sowed, some seeds fell by the way side, and the birds came and devoured them: 5 and others fell upon the rocky places, where they had not much earth: and straightway they sprang up, because they had no deepness of earth: 6 and when the sun was risen, they were scorched; and because they had no root, they withered away. 7 And others fell upon the thorns; and the thorns grew up and choked them: 8 and others fell upon the good ground, and yielded fruit, some a hundredfold, some sixty, some thirty. 9 He that hath ears, let him hear.

10 And the disciples came, and said unto him, Why speakest thou unto them in parables? 11 And he answered and said unto them, Unto you it is given to know the mysteries of the kingdom of heaven, but to them it is not given. 12 For whosoever hath, to him shall be given, and he shall have abundance: but whosoever hath not, from him shall be taken away even that which he hath. 13 Therefore speak I to them in parables; because seeing they see not, and hearing they hear not, neither do they understand. 14 And unto them is fulfilled the prophecy of Isaiah, which saith,

> *By hearing ye shall hear, and shall in no wise understand;*

And seeing ye shall see, and shall in no wise perceive:
15 *For this people's heart is waxed gross,*
   And their ears are dull of hearing,
   And their eyes they have closed;
   Lest haply they should perceive with their eyes,
   And hear with their ears,
   And understand with their heart,
   And should turn again,
   And I should heal them.
16 *But blessed are your eyes, for they see; and your ears,*
for they hear. 17 For verily I say unto you, that many
prophets and righteous men desired to see the things which
ye see, and saw them not; and to hear the things which ye
hear, and heard them not. 18 Hear then ye the parable of
the sower. 19 When any one heareth the word of the king-
dom, and understandeth it not, then *cometh the evil* one,
and snatcheth away that which hath been sown in his heart.
This is he that was sown by the way side. 20 And he that
was sown upon the rocky places, this is he that heareth the
word, and straightway with joy receiveth it; 21 yet hath he
not root in himself, but endureth for a while; and when
tribulation or persecution ariseth because of the word,
straightway he stumbleth. 22 And he that was sown
among the thorns, this is he that heareth the word; and
the care of the world, and the deceitfulness of riches, choke
the word, and he becometh unfruitful. 23 And he that
was sown upon the good ground, this is he that heareth the
word, and understandeth it; who verily beareth fruit, and
bringeth forth, some a hundredfold, some sixty, some
thirty.

It is the usual method of Matthew to secure a heightened
effect by massing material which is of the same character.
Thus we find here a group of parables, as before we found
a group of miracles. These parables are seven in number,
arranged in divisions of four and three. They are all
closely related and seem to have been delivered on the
same day when Jesus had been so cruelly assailed by his
enemies and when his rejection by the nation had been so
clearly foretold. The parables relate to the period of time

between his rejection and his final return to inaugurate his perfected Kingdom.

Matthew is not only the Gospel of rejection, but it is the Gospel of fulfillment, and accordingly it is stated that the practice of Jesus in teaching by parables was in accordance with inspired prophecy, vs. 34-35; and in explaining to his disciples the reason for his use of parables, Jesus quotes at great length from the prophecy of Isaiah stating that ancient predictions were thus definitely fulfilled. The purpose was fourfold: First of all, parables were illustrations which made spiritual truth more plain and clear to the mind of the hearer. Second, they put the truth in portable form so that it easily could be carried away and remembered. Third, they were designed to avoid offense to those who were hostile and who were not prepared to receive the truth; and fourth, they were used, as Isaiah declared, as a judgment upon those who were willfully blind. They shrouded the truth from such as lacked spiritual qualifications for its reception.

Again Matthew is the "Gospel of the King" and these parables are designated as the "Mysteries of the Kingdom." A "mystery," according to New Testament usage, does not refer to something which cannot be understood, but it denotes a truth which once was hidden but now has been revealed. The truth of this chapter relates to the "kingdom." It would be unwise to insist upon an exact definition of this term which would fit all the phrases of the chapter. In some instances it seems to refer to the will or reign of God; in others to the society in which the sovereignty of God is recognized, as the Christian church or Christian civilization. It is probably best to understand the phrase as Matthew commonly employs it, to denote the perfected reign of Christ which is to be established at the end of the present age. In these parables are found statements concerning the nature, the reception, and the results of the proclamation of this Kingdom by the King and his followers.

Thus in the case of the parable of the sower, our Lord declares that its teaching concerns "the word of the kingdom." The main point of the parable is to show that the effect of the word is dependent on the state of the heart. The parable is sometimes called "the parable of the soils," for it illustrates the various spiritual conditions found among men to whom the word is preached. In some cases this "word of the kingdom," whether preached by Christ or his followers, falls on hearts which are pictured by the hard, trodden footpath which runs through a field of grain. No possible impression can be made. The word finds no entrance and Satan snatches it away as a bird would pick up the grain which has fallen by the wayside.

Other hearers are compared to the "rocky places" where a thin layer of earth covers a bed of rock. Seed which falls into such soil springs up the more quickly because of the warmth of the underlying rock, but as the roots cannot strike downward, the grain soon withers beneath the glare of the sun. So there are hearers who receive with enthusiasm the message concerning the Kingdom but when confronted with the persecution which the followers of Christ must bear, they quickly desert his cause.

Then there are hearers who are compared to the seed which falls where thorns are growing. It springs into life but has no room for development. Such hearers are so preoccupied by worldly interests, by wealth and pleasure, that they can bear no spiritual fruit. There are those, however, who are likened to the "good ground" on which the seed falls and a harvest results, thirty, sixty, or a hundredfold. So there are honest and good hearts ready to receive this "word of the kingdom," to meditate on it, to give their best efforts to its cultivation and development, until in their lives a golden harvest is produced.

Such a parable is a warning to all who hear the Gospel message. They need to take heed how they hear. Yet further, it is an encouragement to all who proclaim the good news. They need not expect that every hearer will be eager for the message, nor that all who accept it will prove true to Christ. They are, however, to believe that if they faithfully perform their tasks, the Lord of the harvest will produce results which will bring an infinite reward.

B. THE TARES; THE MUSTARD SEED; AND THE LEAVEN Ch. 13:24-43

24 Another parable set he before them, saying, The kingdom of heaven is likened unto a man that sowed good seed in his field: 25 but while men slept, his enemy came and sowed tares also among the wheat, and went away. 26 But when the blade sprang up and brought forth fruit, then appeared the tares also. 27 And the servants of the householder came and said unto him, Sir, didst thou not sow good seed in thy field? whence then hath it tares? 28 And he said unto them, An enemy hath done this. And the servants say unto him, Wilt thou then that we go and gather them up? 29 But he saith, Nay; lest haply while ye gather up the tares, ye root up the wheat with them. 30 Let both grow together until the harvest: and in the time of the harvest I will say to the reapers, Gather up first the tares, and bind them in bundles to burn them; but gather the wheat into my barn.

31 Another parable set he before them, saying, The kingdom of heaven is like unto a grain of mustard seed, which a man took, and sowed in his field: 32 which indeed is less than all seeds; but when it is grown, it is greater than the herbs, and becometh a tree, so that the birds of the heaven come and lodge in the branches thereof.

33 Another parable spake he unto them; The kingdom of heaven is like unto leaven, which a woman took, and hid in three measures of meal, till it was all leavened.

34 All these things spake Jesus in parables unto the multitudes; and without a parable spake he nothing unto them: 35 that it might be fulfilled which was spoken through the prophet, saying,

I will open my mouth in parables;
I will utter things hidden from the foundation of the world.

36 Then he left the multitudes, and went into the house: and his disciples came unto him, saying, Explain unto us the parable of the tares of the field. 37 And he answered and said, He that soweth the good seed is the Son of man; 38 and the field is the world; and the good seed, these are the sons of the kingdom; and the tares are the sons of the evil one; 39 and the enemy that sowed them is the devil: and the harvest is the end of the world; and the reapers are angels. 40 As therefore the tares are gathered up and burned with fire; so shall it be in the end of the world. 41 The Son of man shall send forth his angels, and they shall gather out of his kingdom all things that cause stumbling, and them that do iniquity, 42 and shall cast them into the furnace of fire: there shall be the weeping and the gnashing of teeth. 43 Then shall the righteous shine forth as the sun in the kingdom of their Father. He that hath ears, let him hear.

As in the previous parable, it is evident that when our Lord speaks of "the kingdom of heaven," he means the proclamation of that Kingdom and the results of this message. As he explained to his followers, "The field is the world," it is not the church, nor civilization, but the whole world of men to whom the gospel is being preached. As a result of this proclamation many will be transformed and prepared to take their places in the coming Kingdom. However, at the same time, the enemy of mankind is at work. He is sowing tares and as a result there are found in this world those whom our Lord declares to be the "sons of the evil one." Side by side with the "sons of the kingdom" they grow and develop. It is impossible to effect a separation between them. They continue together "until the harvest." In this present age good and evil, virtue and vice, sin and holiness, continue in spite of their antagonism and contrast. It is only at the "end of the world," when the harvest takes place, that the Lord of the harvest will command the reapers to gather the tares to be burned and to gather the wheat into his garner. Universal righteousness and peace cannot be expected until the King comes to bring the right to its ultimate triumph. "Then shall the righteous shine forth as the sun in the kingdom of their Father."

Between the statement and the interpretation of the parable of the sower, which illustrated the mingled good and evil of the present age, our Lord introduced two minor parables which he does not explain. The first is that of the mustard seed and the second that of the leaven. As the parable of the sower and the parable of the tares were interpreted by our Lord to refer to the effect of his preaching and that of his followers during the present age, so it is probable that these two parables have the same purport. There are some who understand the growth of the mustard seed to suggest the sudden but unsubstantial development which characterizes certain present forms of what they designate "the kingdom"; and, as leaven is usually in the Scripture a symbol of corruption, the latter parable is taken to denote the false doctrine which often permeates the teaching of professed Christians. These interpretations are quite in accord with the mingling of good and evil, set forth by the previous parables. It is much more common however, to find in the "mustard seed" a symbol of the small beginnings and wide extension of the message of the Kingdom and of its effects; and to regard the leaven as typifying its silent work and permeating power.

C. THE TREASURE; THE PEARL; THE NET
Ch. 13:44-50

44 *The kingdom of heaven is like unto a treasure hidden in the field; which a man found, and hid; and in his joy he goeth and selleth all that he hath, and buyeth that field.*

45 *Again, the kingdom of heaven is like unto a man that is a merchant seeking goodly pearls:* 46 *and having found one pearl of great price, he went and sold all that he had, and bought it.*

47 *Again, the kingdom of heaven is like unto a net, that*

*was cast into the sea, and gathered of every kind: 48
which, when it was filled, they drew up on the beach; and
they sat down, and gathered the good into vessels, but the
bad they cast away. 49 So shall it be in the end of the
world: the angels shall come forth, and sever the wicked
from among the righteous, 50 and shall cast them into the
furnace of fire: there shall be the weeping and the gnashing
of teeth.*

The familiar parables of the hid treasure and of the
pearl of great price are sometimes taken to illustrate how
precious to the mind of Christ are his people and his
church, for which he gave up the glories of heaven and
laid down his own life. This teaching is quite in accord
with other Scripture, but it may be wiser to find here illustrations of the fact that one who really understands the
gospel message will be ready to make any possible sacrifice
that he himself may become an heir of the Kingdom. He
may have heard this message when busied in his usual tasks
in the field or in the home; or he may be like the merchant
who was seeking goodly pearls, he has a yearning for that
which is highest and best; at last he finds in the gospel of
Christ the thing which satisfies his soul, and at the cost of
all that he may have held dear, he takes Christ as his Lord
and accepts his promise of eternal life.

The last parable of the seven, like the two great parables
which Jesus himself interprets, seems to show clearly that
good and evil will be found, at the very end of the age,
even among those who have been reached by the gospel
of Christ. The word of the Kingdom seems to be in its
effect like a great net, gathering fish of all kinds out of
the sea, but as the age comes to its close there is at last a
separation: the angels come forth and sever the wicked
from among the righteous. Thus there are those who appreciate the word of the Kingdom and who submit to the
King, but there are others, even nominal followers of his,
for whom there await only condemnation and punishment.

D. THE RESPONSIBILITY OF THE DISCIPLES AND THE REJECTION OF JESUS
Ch. 13:51-58

51 Have ye understood all these things? They say unto him, Yea. 52 And he said unto them, Therefore every scribe who hath been made a disciple to the kingdom of heaven is like unto a man that is a householder, who bringeth forth out of his treasure things new and old.

53 And it came to pass, when Jesus had finished these parables, he departed thence.

54 And coming into his own country he taught them in their synagogue, insomuch that they were astonished, and said, Whence hath this man this wisdom, and these mighty works? 55 Is not this the carpenter's son? is not his mother called Mary? and his brethren, James, and Joseph, and Simon, and Judas? 56 And his sisters, are they not all with us? Whence then hath this man all these things? 57 And they were offended in him. But Jesus said unto them, A prophet is not without honor, save in his own country, and in his own house. 58 And he did not many mighty works there because of their unbelief.

Having ended his seven striking parables, Jesus reminds his immediate disciples of the responsibility which rests upon them as upon men who have received truths which the greatest men, the prophets and the righteous of past ages, would gladly have heard. It is for them, as for all followers of Christ, to make known the great teachings concerning his Kingdom. Each is to be like a householder who brings forth "out of his treasure things new and old." That is, they are to proclaim new truths concerning the Kingdom which the world otherwise would never know, and they are to proclaim old truths in new forms even as Jesus taught in parables to make clear his message; and they are to teach old truths in new relations. The gospel is the same in every age, but each age demands special applications of this old gospel for its new needs.

It is in keeping with this story that this chapter of parables, which indicates a partial rejection and a partial acceptance of the message of the Kingdom during this present age, closes with this story of the rejection of Jesus in his own home. Here for a second time in Nazareth, where he had spent so many years of his life, he is met with cruel unbelief. Here he pronounces that word of rebuke, "A prophet is not without honor, save in his own country, and in his own house." This is not because a prophet is well known in his own country, but because he is not really known. They thought they knew him, because they were acquainted with his brothers and his sisters. They failed to appreciate what his works suggested as to his unique nature. They refused to admit his claims. Those who had the best opportunity of knowing him rejected the King. It is this incident which prepares the way for the next section of the Gospel which shows Jesus in retirement, withdrawing from unbelieving Israel and seeking in secret to instruct his disciples and those who like them believed and trusted him.

VII
THE WITHDRAWAL
OF THE KING
Chs. 14:1 to 16:12

A. JOHN THE BAPTIST BEHEADED
Ch. 14:1-12

1 At that season Herod the tetrarch heard the report concerning Jesus, 2 and said unto his servants, This is John the Baptist; he is risen from the dead; and therefore do these powers work in him. 3 For Herod had laid hold on John, and bound him, and put him in prison for the sake of Herodias, his brother Philip's wife. 4 For John said unto him, It is not lawful for thee to have her. 5 And when he would have put him to death, he feared the multitude, because they counted him as a prophet. 6 But when Herod's birthday came, the daughter of Herodias danced in the midst, and pleased Herod. 7 Whereupon he promised with an oath to give her whatsoever she should ask. 8 And she, being put forward by her mother, saith, Give me here on a platter the head of John the Baptist. 9 And the king was grieved; but for the sake of his oaths, and of them that sat at meat with him, he commanded it to be given; 10 and he sent and beheaded John in the prison. 11 And his head was brought on a platter, and given to the damsel: and she brought it to her mother. 12 And his disciples came, and took up the corpse, and buried him; and they went and told Jesus.

To record the death of John the Baptist just at this point in the story is a stroke of genius. The death of his herald was a certain portent of the rejection and crucifixion of the King. Its recital forms a fitting transition to this portion of the "Gospel of the Rejection" which deals with the temporary retirement of Jesus and the crisis of his struggle with the Pharisees in Galilee.

In itself the incident is one of tragic interest and deep moral significance. The picture of Herod shows the peril of trifling with conscience. Herodias reveals the deadly power of revenge. Both are contrasted with the moral grandeur of John; both are connected with the career of Jesus. This Herod Antipas is to be distinguished from Herod the Great and from Herod Agrippa; yet all are involved in a common infamy. Herod the Great slaughtered the babes of Bethlehem in hope of destroying the true King; Herod Antipas murdered John the Baptist, the herald of the King; Herod Agrippa killed James and imprisoned Peter, two of the chief messengers of the King.

The real instigator of the crime was Herodias whom Herod married although her husband, the brother of Herod, was still living. John the Baptist, with the courage of a great prophet who does not fear to rebuke sin in high places, had won the enmity of Herodias by condemning this guilty alliance. She hated him not only for his rebuke, but because his influence threatened to foil the ambition which had led her to desert her husband in order to secure a position of royalty. Herod imprisons John but hesitates to put him to death both for fear of the people and because he himself regards John with something of reverence and awe. Herodias plots to secure a cruel revenge. While Herod is celebrating his birthday in revelry with his companions, Salome, the daughter of Herodias, is sent in to dance immodestly before the king. In his drunken delight he promises with an oath to reward her with any gift she may name. Prompted by her mother she requests the head of John the Baptist. The king is entrapped but he is a moral coward. He fears to withdraw his rash oath lest he should be ridiculed by his companions. He violates his conscience. He issues the fatal command. He wins the contempt of his comrades and secures the scorn and condemnation of a world. It is not the last time that an indecent dance has wrought the downfall of a king. It is not the last time that a man has been more afraid of a sneer than a crime. It is not the last time that the vanity and malice of a woman have compassed the death of a prophet.

Herodias gloats over her bloody prize. Herod has silenced the voice of John; he cannot still the voice of conscience. Again and again the buried memory of his crime rises up to torment him. And now more terrible still he comes to believe that John himself has risen up from the grave to confront him and possibly to destroy him; for he hears of the miracles of Jesus and his awakened conscience fills him with horror; he believes that none but John could perform such works. He identifies John with Jesus. It is not strange that Jesus now sees clearly what "the princes of this world" have in store for him and that he now seeks places of seclusion where he can instruct his disciples and prepare them for his last struggle with the rulers and for the hour when he will follow his forerunner in the experience of a violent and cruel death.

B. THE FIVE THOUSAND FED Ch. 14:13-21

13 Now when Jesus heard it, he withdrew from thence in a boat, to a desert place apart: and when the multitudes heard thereof, they followed him on foot from the cities. 14 And he came forth, and saw a great multitude, and he had compassion on them, and healed their sick. 15 And when even was come, the disciples came to him, saying, The place is desert, and the time is already past; send the multitudes away, that they may go into the villages, and buy themselves food. 16 But Jesus said unto them, They have no need to go away; give ye them to eat. 17 And they say unto him, We have here but five loaves, and two fishes. 18 And he said, Bring them hither to me. 19 And he commanded the multitudes to sit down on the grass; and he took the five loaves, and the two fishes, and looking up to heaven, he blessed, and brake and gave the loaves to the disciples, and the disciples to the multitudes. 20 And they all ate, and were filled: and they took up that which re-

*mained over of the broken pieces, twelve baskets full. 21
And they that did eat were about five thousand men, besides women and children.*

When Jesus learned that John had been put to death,
and possibly had been told that Herod believed John was
risen, and identified Jesus with the man he had murdered,
our Lord withdrew from the scenes where multitudes had
been attending his ministry to seek in seclusion both an
opportunity to rest with his disciples, who had just returned
from their great mission, and also to instruct them in
reference to his own person and work and approaching
death. He entered into a boat and crossed to the northern
shore of the lake to a desert place where he might be un-
interrupted. However, when the crowds heard where he
was they followed him from all the neighboring cities; his
heart was touched with compassion; he healed their sick
and then he performed what is often regarded as his most
remarkable miracle. With five loaves and two fishes he
fed five thousand men, besides women and children. It is
the one miracle which is recorded in all the Four Gospels.
Here for the first time the story of Matthew unites with that
of John. The fact is not of great importance until we
remember that in the latter Gospel an interpretation is
given and the meaning of the miracle is set forth in the
sermon which our Lord delivers, subsequent to the miracle,
when he declares himself to be "the bread of life." The
account in Matthew reveals the deep sympathy of our Lord
and his divine power; but read in the light of the Fourth
Gospel the miracle becomes a parable concerning his person and work. It illustrates his saying, "I am the bread
of life: he that cometh to me shall not hunger, and he that
believeth on me shall never thirst." The multitudes did
not understand the truth thus depicted; nor was it then disclosed to his disciples, but to every follower of Christ today this record brings among others the following familiar
and important messages:

1. We must seek to relieve the physical wants of men, but we must be more concerned still with their deeper spiritual needs, of which the hunger and thirst of that fainting multitude were symbolic.

2. We must believe that Jesus Christ can supply these needs of the soul, this hunger of the heart, this fainting for spiritual food. It is the divine Christ who foresaw his rejection and death; it is the Christ who was crucified and who rose again who alone can supply this need. Jesus did feed a multitude by the sea, but his real mission was to give his life for the salvation of the world.

3. Faith is the condition of receiving the life which Christ provides. One must identify himself with this Savior if he is to find the satisfaction which is promised; as Jesus declared we must "eat the flesh of the Son of man and drink his blood." There must be an appropriation of the grace which Christ supplies for every need. There must be a dependence upon him for the satisfaction of every spiritual want.

4. Christ expects his followers to help him in the work and to bear the truth concerning himself to all the world, even as of old he bade the disciples bear to the multitudes the broken bread. Faith naturally results in a desire to share and not simply to keep. The gospel message is a trust. The messengers of the King must be eager to complete his work.

5. The blessing of Christ preceded and seems to have produced the miracle. It is certain that his blessing can secure great results from the simplest efforts in his service. When we hesitate because conscious that our gifts are small and our endeavors are weak, we must remember the five loaves and the two fishes which were offered to the Lord and which he used to feed the multitude.

6. We must be ready also to carry out his commands and to obey his suggestions. It required the obedience of faith on the part of the disciples to become real assistants in that great work of grace. If we expect our efforts to be

blessed, we also must both trust and obey.

7. We must be careful also as to the fragments and allow nothing to be wasted of all that our Lord provides for body, or mind, or soul. We must treat with contempt nothing which he gives, however small. The fragments in reference to which Jesus gave such careful commands were not the crumbs left by the eaters, but the portions which had been broken by Christ and his disciples. They were to be kept to supply future needs, but they also would be for days to come reminders of the miraculous power of their Lord. There are many suggestions both in the written word and in our daily experiences to remind us of the grace of our Lord; but none is more important than the memorial feast which he ordained, at which, as we partake of the broken bread, we are reminded anew of his body which was broken for us, and of the life he has given that we by faith in him may truly live.

C. JESUS WALKS ON THE WATER
Ch. 14:22-36

22 And straightway he constrained the disciples to enter into the boat, and to go before him unto the other side, till he should send the multitudes away. 23 And after he had sent the multitudes away, he went up into the mountain apart to pray: and when even was come, he was there alone. 24 But the boat was now in the midst of the sea, distressed by the waves; for the wind was contrary. 25 And in the fourth watch of the night he came unto them, walking upon the sea. 26 And when the disciples saw him walking on the sea, they were troubled, saying, It is a ghost; and they cried out for fear. 27 But straightway Jesus spake unto them, saying, Be of good cheer; it is I; be not afraid. 28 And Peter answered him and said, Lord, if it be thou, bid me come unto thee upon the waters. 29 And he said, Come. And Peter went down from the boat, and walked upon the waters to come to Jesus. 30 But when he saw the wind, he was afraid; and beginning to sink, he

cried out, saying, Lord, save me. 31 And immediately Jesus stretched forth his hand, and took hold of him, and saith unto him, O thou of little faith, wherefore didst thou doubt? 32 And when they were gone up into the boat, the wind ceased. 33 And they that were in the boat worshipped him, saying, Of a truth thou art the Son of God.

34 And when they had crossed over, they came to the land, unto Gennesaret. 35 And when the men of that place knew him, they sent into all that region round about, and brought unto him all that were sick; 36 and they besought him that they might only touch the border of his garment: and as many as touched were made whole.

It would be difficult to imagine a more beautiful sheet of water than that which is known as the Sea of Galilee. Of course, it is not a sea but a lovely inland lake. It is only about thirteen miles in length and seven miles in breadth. Its clear water is supplied and again drained by the river Jordan. It lies six hundred and fifty feet below the level of the sea, and to the north rises the summit of Mt. Hermon, which is clad in perpetual snows. Because of such a situation great currents of air frequently roll down from the surrounding hills and sweep the surface of the lake with sudden and fierce storms. It was in such a tempest that the disciples were found on that night when Jesus was seen walking toward them upon the surface of the water. This was a striking and marvelous miracle. Many have denied its reality. There is no reason, however, for doubt. It is attested by Mark and John. In neither of these accounts, however, does the form of Jesus appear more majestic and more kingly. He had commanded his followers to precede him across the lake while he remained to dismiss the multitudes which he had fed with the five loaves. At nightfall he had gone up on the hillside to pray. In the deepening darkness the disciples were faced by a raging wind. During the long hours they struggled wearily at the oars and with little progress. Suddenly they saw Jesus drawing near "walking upon the sea"; his appearance awakened more terror than the storm and "they cried out for fear"; but his word of cheer brought relief and confidence, so that Peter asked permission to come to his Master likewise walking upon the waters. Matthew alone records this incident of the faith and the failure of Peter. He tells us of his bold attempt, of his rising fear, his peril, his rescue, and his return to the boat with the Master, and then describes the stilling of the storm and the worship offered to Jesus as the Son of God. The whole picture reveals the One whom Matthew continually paints as the universal King, the "Ruler of all nature."

It is not strange that so striking a story has been interpreted by Christians as symbolizing their spiritual experiences. It certainly is true that obedience to Christ does not secure freedom from the storms and tempests and trials of life. He had commanded the disciples to cross the sea, for he knew that it would be better for them than to remain among the crowds who had, as John declares, such wrong conceptions of his person and work. The place of storm and trial is often the place of greatest moral security.

It is also true that the followers of Christ can always believe in his presence amidst the night and the storms. This is perhaps the supreme lesson in the story. At first the Lord may not be recognized; the form in which he comes may even increase our fear, but his word however voiced brings hope and even in the midnight and the tempest the assurance of his presence brings confidence and peace.

The experience of Peter may illustrate how faith can triumph over all obstacles, how doubt brings disaster, and how Christ is ever ready to save. It was not mere pride and presumption which led Peter to attempt to walk on the sea; it was simply the response of his faith to the word and example of his Lord. He was not rebuked by Christ for his request but for his unbelief. Today our Lord does not correct his followers for trying to imitate his moral purity or for endeavoring to walk as he walked, but he does grieve at our imperfect faith. It is when we take our eyes off from him and think of our own weakness, and worry about our temptations, that we are imperiled. He must regret our doubt and fear, but as we put our trust in him he stretches out his hand and by a touch he gives us strength to walk in safety by his side. The Christian life is a continual triumph over natural tendencies which would draw us down. To walk really with Christ in holiness and purity and love is a continual miracle. Christ does not rebuke us for attempting too much, but for trusting him too little; and even when our faith has brought us to a position of peril or of shame, he is ready to rescue and relieve.

In reviewing this surprising miracle which Matthew has given in such fullness, it has not been unusual to find a symbol of the truth concerning the rejected and returning King whom Matthew is ever throwing into such bold relief. As Jesus fed the five thousand and then went up into the mountain to intercede for his disciples and then came walking on the waves to rescue them and bring them peace, so Christ having offered himself to the world as "the bread of life" has ascended to intercede for us; and someday he will come again; even now he may be drawing near; over all the turmoil and distress of nations he may be making his majestic approach, and when he appears the night will end and all the storms will cease.

The obvious purpose of the miracle was to relieve the disciples from fear and danger, and to give them ground for a larger trust in their Master. If, however, we are seeking for symbols, surely the closing paragraph of the story is a picture of the present ministry of Christ; amid the thronging multitudes of suffering men he is standing today, a presence unseen but real, full of compassion and ready to relieve the moral and spiritual ills of those who put forth the hand of faith; even though their trust is weak and they touch but the border of his garment, as many as touch are healed.

D. CEREMONIAL AND REAL DEFILEMENT
Ch. 15:1-20

1 Then there come to Jesus from Jerusalem Pharisees and scribes, saying, 2 Why do thy disciples transgress the tradition of the elders? for they wash not their hands when they eat bread. 3 And he answered and said unto them, Why do ye also transgress the commandment of God because of your tradition? 4 For God said, Honor thy father and thy mother: and, He that speaketh evil of father or mother, let him die the death. 5 But ye say, Whosoever shall say to his father or his mother, That wherewith thou mightest have been profited by me is given to God; 6 he shall not honor his father. And ye have made void the word of God because of your tradition. 7 Ye hypocrites, well did Isaiah prophesy of you, saying,

8 This people honoreth me with their lips;
But their heart is far from me.
9 But in vain do they worship me,
Teaching as their doctrines the precepts of men.
10 And he called to him the multitude, and said unto them, Hear, and understand: 11 Not that which entereth into the mouth defileth the man; but that which proceedeth out of the mouth, this defileth the man. 12 Then came the disciples, and said unto him, Knowest thou that the Pharisees were offended, when they heard this saying? 13 But he answered and said, Every plant which my heavenly Father planted not, shall be rooted up. 14 Let them alone: they are blind guides. And if the blind guide the blind, both shall fall into a pit. 15 And Peter answered and said unto him, Declare unto us the parable. 16 And he said, Are ye also even yet without understanding? 17 Perceive ye not, that whatsoever goeth into the mouth passeth into the belly, and is cast out into the draught? 18 But the things which proceed out of the mouth come forth out of the heart; and they defile the man. 19 For out of the heart come forth evil thoughts, murders, adul-

*teries, fornications, thefts, false witness, railings: 20 these
are the things which defile the man; but to eat with un-
washen hands defileth not the man.*

No sooner has Jesus crossed to the scenes of his earlier
labors on the west side of the lake than the Pharisees and
other religious leaders from Jerusalem make a bitter attack
upon him.   They declare that his disciples did not wash
their hands when they ate bread.   They did not mean that
their hands were actually unclean, but that the companions of Jesus had neglected the ceremonial washing which
Jewish tradition required.   The charge may seem trivial.
In fact there is something ludicrous in the picture of distinguished teachers making the long trip from Jerusalem
solemnly to prefer such a charge against a great Prophet
whose words and works were filling the land with wonder.
However, to the mind of the Pharisees, the traditions of the
elders were matters of great importance.   These traditions
consisted in the collected interpretations of the Old Testament law which had been given by the rabbis.   They had
come to be regarded as of more importance and authority
than the law itself.   To neglect these traditions was to
these old formalists the most serious of sins.   This particular requirement as to the washing of the hands before par-
taking of food was for some reason regarded as peculiarly
sacred.   The story is told of an imprisoned rabbi who was
allowed the most meager amount of bread and water for
his daily ration, that he used the water for bathing his
hands instead of drinking it, saying that he had rather die
than transgress the institutions of his ancestors.

The charge gave to Jesus an opportunity for rebuking
the Pharisees, and also for showing the difference between
ceremonial and real defilement; between that which is spiritual and that which is material; between purity of the soul
and the observance of a form; between true religion and
false.

The Pharisees had accused the disciples of acting contrary to a human tradition.   Jesus shows that it may be

possible in obeying human tradition to transgress divine law. He cites an instance of what seems to have been a common practice among the Pharisees. According to an accepted tradition, if one pronounced over any property the word "Corban," which means a "gift," this property was regarded as dedicated to God. No matter how thoughtlessly or deceitfully the word might have been spoken, the vow must be kept. Even though a father or mother was in need of food, they might be allowed to starve but the oath could not be broken. It is even suggested that a son might use such devoted possessions for his own comfort and enjoyment; but the law of God which required one to honor his father and his mother might freely be set aside in order that the tradition of men might be sacredly observed. Jesus declares that this is the very essence of hypocrisy. He reminds the Pharisees that scrupulous observance of religious forms may be accompanied by utter disregard of moral law. This has been the peril of formalists and ritualists and hypocrites of all ages. In condemning the Pharisees, Jesus quotes an appropriate passage from the prophet Isaiah: "This people honoreth me with their lips; but their heart is far from me. But in vain do they worship me, teaching as their doctrines the precepts of men."

During this discussion with the Pharisees a crowd gathered. Jesus turned to them with the significant words involving the whole principle at stake, "Not that which entereth into the mouth defileth the man; but that which proceedeth out of the mouth, this defileth the man." The Pharisees had believed that the touch of a hand which was ceremonially unclean would defile the food which would in turn render the eater unclean. Jesus suggested that the serious matter is not such ceremonial defilement but the uncleanness which results from evil thoughts and from the impure heart.

It is easy to understand why the Pharisees were scandalized at such teaching. It seemed to run counter to the precepts of Moses in reference to clean and unclean food and so to contradict all the elaborate interpretations imposed by Jewish traditions. The anger of the Pharisees was reported to our Lord, but he at once replied that his followers need have no concern. Men who are guilty of such hypocrisy were evidently not plants of the divine planting and they would surely be rooted up. These boasted teachers were like blind men who were attempting to guide the blind; both they and their followers were certain to come to grief.

Peter turns to ask a fuller explanation of the statement which Jesus had made. The Master at first rebukes him for his lack of spiritual perception, but proceeds to explain most clearly that real uncleanness is not a matter of the body, but of the spirit, or only of the body as directed by the spirit. The only actual defilement is that of the soul. "A man is not made unclean by that which entereth into his mouth but by that which proceeds from his heart!" A man cannot be polluted by eating that which is ceremonially unclean, but only by thinking and doing that which is morally impure. To men of the present age such teaching may seem elementary. There is need, however, for its emphasis and for a new insistence upon reality in religion and upon distinguishing between what is formal and what is essential, between what is external and what is vital. To the Pharisees the teaching was revolutionary. It was a disclosure of their hypocrisy; it was a defiance of their proud claims; it was a defeat of their endeavor to discredit Jesus. It brought the conflict between him and the rulers to a climax. It is not strange that he deemed it necessary to withdraw from Galilee and to enter the Gentile territory near to Tyre and Sidon.

E. FAITH TRIED AND TRIUMPHANT
Ch. 15:21-28

21 And Jesus went out thence, and withdrew into the parts of Tyre and Sidon. 22 And behold, a Canaanitish

*woman came out from those borders, and cried, saying,
Have mercy on me, O Lord, thou son of David; my daughter is grievously vexed with a demon. 23 But he answered
her not a word. And his disciples came and besought him,
saying, Send her away; for she crieth after us. 24 But he
answered and said, I was not sent but unto the lost sheep
of the house of Israel. 25 But she came and worshipped
him, saying, Lord, help me. 26 And he answered and
said, It is not meet to take the children's bread and cast it
to the dogs. 27 But she said, Yea, Lord: for even the dogs
eat of the crumbs which fall from their masters' table. 28
Then Jesus answered and said unto her, O woman, great
is thy faith: be it done unto thee even as thou wilt. And
her daughter was healed from that hour.*

Only once during his earthly ministry did Jesus leave
the land of his birth. It was in those days when he wished
to avoid both the opposition of his enemies and the interruption of the crowds in order that he might find quiet
and retirement in which to teach his disciples the great
truths they were to proclaim after his rejection and death
which he now saw clearly approaching. He withdrew
across the border of Galilee "into the parts of Tyre and
Sidon." There he is met by a woman whose trust in him
is so surprising that she wins from our Lord the word of
unique praise: "O woman, great is thy faith." Jesus
seldom spoke in that way and it is well worth inquiring
what it was in the faith of this woman which he regarded
as so strange. Of course it is notable that she was a
Canaanitish woman; that is, one who in modern speech
would be called a heathen. She may have known little of
the religion of Israel. She had been reared among the
Gentiles. She had never seen our Lord perform a miracle,
yet she addressed Jesus as the true Messiah, and asks him
to heal her daughter who is grievously vexed with a demon. It is remarkable that a stranger and a foreigner
should have made such a difficult request. However, these
are not the circumstances which distinguish her faith. Its

greatness lies in the fact that when it was tested, it stood the test; when it was tried, it was triumphant.

It was tested first by the silence of Jesus, "He answered her not a word." This was surprising. She had heard of the sympathy of Christ, and of his willingness to help and to heal; she comes to him with her broken heart; she pleads for a daughter "grievously vexed with a demon"; but Jesus makes to her petition no reply. It is like the test which comes to the followers of Christ today when, to the earnest cry of their hearts, there seem to be no answer and no response. They are tempted to doubt the efficacy of prayer or the love of the Master.

The silence of Jesus, however, does not still the cry of this eager woman. She follows Jesus so persistently that the disciples, moved by a selfish desire to be freed from the annoyance, request him to give her what she asks and to send her away. Jesus then states a law of his earthly ministry which would render it apparently impossible for him to grant the request of the woman, "I was not sent but unto the lost sheep of the house of Israel." In the few years allotted for his task, it was wise and necessary that Jesus should confine his efforts to a limited area and to the people best prepared for his mission. It was, therefore, aside from his immediate purpose to perform miracles for people of other lands. Such statements concerning the reign of law are used in modern days to discourage those who have faith in Christ, and particularly such as trust in his willingness and power to answer prayer. The woman does not pretend to explain the difficulty involved. She turns to Jesus with undiminished fervor; she falls before him and cries, "Lord, help me." In hours of great need, men who are troubled by the problems of philosophy thus turn to Christ in simple, trustful prayer.

Jesus, however, replies in words which, of all those which ever fell from his lips, seem to be most nearly cruel. The unkindness, however, was not real. His actual love must have been revealed by the accents of his voice, "It is not meet to take the children's bread and cast it to the dogs." This might have seemed a heartless reply to the sorrowing mother, but she saw the tender irony it contained and also the possible promise for her relief. Jesus seemed to be saying that his own people, who had rejected him, regarded the Gentiles as dogs, and that his ministry had been intended for them and not for the Gentiles. He uses, however, the word which implies the "little dogs," which in Eastern lands belong to the household. On this suggestion the woman seizes. It is not exactly right to say that she "entraps the Master in his words"; he rather points out the path which her ready wit and eager faith at once followed, "Yea, Lord: for even the dogs eat of the crumbs which fall from their masters' table." She admits that she is a Gentile and has no claim upon the help of Christ; but she believes that the granting of her request will be no real departure from the law of his earthly ministry. She suggests that even Gentiles may receive something from his overflowing grace. In fact, she makes her humble position the very ground of her plea.

Modern followers of Christ are sometimes tempted to cease from prayer by the consciousness of their own unworthiness. True faith, however, clings to Christ; it places no confidence in itself; it makes personal unworthiness a plea for grace. It is never disappointed. Thus Jesus turns to the woman with his matchless word of praise and love, "O woman, great is thy faith: be it done unto thee even as thou wilt." Her faith had triumphed over all the tests, "and her daughter was healed from that hour." Why, however, did Jesus so test her faith? Not to discover its quality; he knew that in advance, but that it might be developed and that his disciples and the multitude might understand the conditions on which her request was granted. If the faith of a Christian is tested today, it is not that the Lord may learn its temper but that the relationship of the believer to him may be more clearly defined; that the faith itself may be developed, and that others like the disciples may be instructed, and still others, like the multitude, may be shown the willingness of Christ to answer and reward those who put their trust in him.

F. THE MIRACLES IN DECAPOLIS
Ch. 15:29-39

29 And Jesus departed thence, and came nigh unto the sea of Galilee; and he went up into the mountain, and sat there. 30 And there came unto him great multitudes, having with them the lame, blind, dumb, maimed, and many others, and they cast them down at his feet; and he healed them: 31 insomuch that the multitude wondered, when they saw the dumb speaking, the maimed whole, and the lame walking, and the blind seeing: and they glorified the God of Israel.

32 And Jesus called unto him his disciples, and said, I have compassion on the multitude, because they continue with me now three days and have nothing to eat: and I would not send them away fasting, lest haply they faint on the way. 33 And the disciples say unto him, Whence should we have so many loaves in a desert place as to fill so great a multitude? 34 And Jesus saith unto them, How many loaves have ye? And they said, Seven, and a few small fishes. 35 And he commanded the multitude to sit down on the ground; 36 and he took the seven loaves and the fishes; and he gave thanks and brake, and gave to the disciples, and the disciples to the multitudes. 37 And they all ate, and were filled: and they took up that which remained over of the broken pieces, seven baskets full. 38 And they that did eat were four thousand men, besides women and children. 39 And he sent away the multitudes, and entered into the boat, and came into the borders of Magadan.

Even in the regions of Tyre and Sidon, outside the border of his native land, Jesus has been unable to escape from the crowds. He has there been asked to perform a cure for a believing woman and the fame of the miracle has attracted the multitudes so that he now journeys with his disciples farther to the east and the south. He goes to the farther shore of the Sea of Galilee. Yet there again he is soon surrounded by "great multitudes," having with them the "lame, blind, dumb, maimed, and many others." He has not come with the purpose of performing miracles. He is seeking a place of retirement and an opportunity of teaching his disciples, but his compassion never fails. He healed them "insomuch that the multitude wondered, when they saw the dumb speaking, the maimed whole, and the lame walking, and the blind seeing." It was a region, the inhabitants of which were largely Gentiles. It was a fitting sequel to the miracle performed just previously in the region of Tyre and Sidon at the request of a Canaanitish woman. It was an intimation of the wider work which the true King was to perform among all nations. It is significant that as he heals these multitudes "they glorified the God of Israel."

It is this fact of a ministry among Gentiles which forms the distinguishing feature of the great miracle which Jesus now proceeds to perform. As he beholds the multitudes hungering and fainting, he supplies them food by multiplying for their need seven loaves of bread and a few small fishes. There are those who imagine that this is but another account of the feeding of the five thousand. It is true that many of the features are the same. In both cases Jesus reveals his patient compassion. He has been seeking for retirement with his disciples, but when the crowds gather about him he sacrifices his own plan and comfort; he resumes his work of teaching and he ministers to the bodies, as well as the souls, of those who have thronged about him. We should notice also the unbelief of the disciples. When Jesus suggests the need of food they seem to have forgotten utterly the former miracle. Some commentators insist that such doubt is incredible and that this portion of the story, at least, must have been borrowed by the writer from the former narrative. Some of us are too conscious of similar unbelief in ourselves, in spite of repeated miracles of grace, to wonder long at the blindness of the apostles.

In both miracles we note the abundant supply for the hungry multitudes and we remember the message of supreme importance which Jesus attached to the miracle, namely, that he himself is the true Bread for the soul and that they who trust in him shall have eternal life. It is in relation to this symbolic teaching that the two similar miracles contain their slightly differing suggestions. The five thousand who were miraculously fed were probably all Jews; among the four thousand were probably many Gentiles; and this latter miracle may be an intimation that Jesus, although rejected by his own people, is to give his life for the world and is to be the living Bread for all nations.

G. THE LEAVEN OF THE PHARISEES AND OF THE SADDUCEES Ch. 16:1-12

1 And the Pharisees and Sadducees came, and trying him asked him to show them a sign from heaven. 2 But he answered and said unto them, When it is evening, ye say, It will be fair weather: for the heaven is red. 3 And in the morning, It will be foul weather to-day: for the heaven is red and lowering. Ye know how to discern the face of the heaven; but ye cannot discern the signs of the times. 4 An evil and adulterous generation seeketh after a sign; and there shall no sign be given unto it, but the sign of Jonah. And he left them, and departed.

5 And the disciples came to the other side and forgot to take bread. 6 And Jesus said unto them, Take heed and beware of the leaven of the Pharisees and Sadducees. 7 And they reasoned among themselves, saying, We took no bread. 8 And Jesus perceiving it said, O ye of little faith, why reason ye among yourselves, because ye have no bread? 9 Do ye not yet perceive, neither remember the five loaves of the five thousand, and how many baskets ye took up? 10 Neither the seven loaves of the four thou-

sand, and how many baskets ye took up? 11 How is it that ye do not perceive that I spake not to you concerning bread? But beware of the leaven of the Pharisees and Sadducees. 12 Then understood they that he bade them not beware of the leaven of bread, but of the teaching of the Pharisees and Sadducees.

As Jesus returns to the west shore of the lake his enemies again assail him bitterly. It is the very climax and final crisis of his ministry in Galilee. The desperate hostility of the rulers is evidenced by the fact that a coalition has been formed by the Pharisees and Sadducees, two parties usually violently opposed but now drawn together by their common hatred of Jesus. They "asked him to show them a sign from heaven." It was an impertinence and an insult. He had filled the land with wonder at his signs. They had been countless in number and of many kinds. They had been sufficient to prove him to be the Christ, the predicted Messiah. Just what his enemies now wished it is difficult to say; possibly some voice from heaven, evidently some strange portent which would compel them to believe. However, to ask for another sign is a hypocritical way of throwing doubt and discredit upon the miracles which Jesus already has performed, and of suggesting that his enemies are quite ready to accept his claims if only he will present sufficient proof.

Jesus replies that their unbelief is not due to lack of evidence, but to want of spiritual discernment; the difficulty is not with the character of his proofs, but with the state of their hearts. They were wise enough to see indications of good or bad weather in a golden sunset or in a lowering morning, but in all the gracious works of Jesus they were too stupid to see the signs of his royalty and of the nearness of his Kingdom. His miracles were "the signs of the time," the indications that the King had come. His enemies would have understood these signs had it not been that their sight was dimmed by sin, and their hearts were "adulterous" in their disloyalty to God. Jesus again, as on a former occasion, declares that only one distinct and unique sign is yet to be given, "the sign of Jonah"; the resurrection of Jesus, prefigured by the experience of the great prophet, was to be the crowning demonstration of his claims. One who will not believe in Christ in view of his resurrection is self-condemned; his condition is hopeless, his unbelief is fatal.

As Jesus crosses the lake with his disciples, he takes occasion to warn them against the false teaching of the enemies whose demand for a sign had revealed their true character. "Take heed and beware of the leaven of the Pharisees and Sadducees." According to Mark, Jesus added a warning against the "leaven of Herod." As afterward explained, Jesus used "leaven" as a symbol of false doctrine. The Pharisees were the formalists of the day; they reduced religion to a system of ceremonies, and regarded a ritual as more important than moral law. The Sadducees were rationalists and materialists; they did not believe in resurrection, or angel, or spirit. They were like those of the present day, who as far as possible, deny and descredit the supernatural in revelation and in religion. The Herodians may represent the modern secularists; they cared little for religion; they placed their hopes in political readjustment, and lived for the prizes and pleasures of the world.

Men of such beliefs and sympathies can have no place in their hearts for Christ; no wonder that they rejected him, and that he warned his disciples against them. In the present day the church needs to be guarded against the same forms of false teaching. The leaven of formalism and materialism and worldliness is still spreading and against its insidious influences the followers of Christ need to be warned.

The disciples failed at first to understand what Jesus meant. They thought he referred to literal leaven, or to bread, and more naturally, as they had provided no bread for their journey. Jesus reminds them of the two miracles he had wrought in feeding the multitudes, so that if physical food had been needed he could have supplied that; but he was concerned about the more important matter of spiritual food. He was thinking of the false teaching to which his disciples would be exposed. Against this peril he ever wishes his disciples to be warned.

VIII
THE PERSON AND WORK
OF THE KING
Chs. 16:13 to 17:27

A. JESUS APPROVES THE CONFESSION
OF PETER Ch. 16:13-20

13 Now when Jesus came into the parts of Cæsarea Philippi, he asked his disciples, saying, Who do men say that the Son of man is? 14 And they said, Some say John the Baptist; some, Elijah; and others, Jeremiah, or one of the prophets. 15 He saith unto them, But who say ye that I am? 16 And Simon Peter answered and said, Thou art the Christ, the Son of the living God. 17 And Jesus answered and said unto him, Blessed art thou, Simon Bar-Jonah: for flesh and blood hath not revealed it unto thee, but my Father who is in heaven. 18 And I also say unto thee, that thou art Peter, and upon this rock I will build my church; and the gate of Hades shall not prevail against it. 19 I will give unto thee the keys of the kingdom of heaven: and whatsoever thou shall bind on earth shall be bound in heaven; and whatsoever thou shalt loose on earth shall be loosed in heaven. 20 Then charged he the disciples that they should tell no man that he was the Christ.

At Caesarea Philippi, in the secluded regions of northern Galilee, relieved for a time from the attacks of his enemies and the interruptions of the crowds, Jesus at last found an opportunity to be alone with his disciples, and it was then that he reached the climax of his teaching concerning his divine Person. It was then also that he began his teaching concerning his atoning work.

For nearly three years, by parable and miracle, by Scripture reference and by the constant messages of his daily life, Jesus had revealed himself to his disciples as the Messiah, the predicted King, the Son of God. To discover how far they have learned the lesson, or to impress it upon them more deeply, he asks them two questions: first, "Who do men say that the Son of man is?" Their answer is unsatisfactory but kindly. They might have replied that many regarded Jesus as a fanatic, an impostor, even a glutton and a drunkard; they were too considerate for that; they replied that the men of his day regarded him as a great prophet, in fact, a reincarnation of one of the greatest prophets. It is exactly the answer the world is giving today, "Jesus was a man, the best of men, a man who spoke for God, but still a man." Such a reply did not meet the approval of our Lord; it never does; and so he asks his second question, "But who say ye that I am?" Simon Peter answered, and he spoke for his fellow disciples and for believers in all ages, "Thou art the Christ, the Son of the living God." By the "Christ," the "Anointed One," he of course, meant the predicted "Messiah," the Redeemer, the Savior of the world. By "the Son of God" he meant all those words could signify as contrasted with the prophets and saints of all ages; and we are right in taking the phrase upon our lips to denote a Being who, while truly man, is truly God; a unique Being to whom we can pray, in whose unseen presence we can trust, before whom each of us can fall and exclaim, as did Thomas, "My Lord and my God."

Jesus did not rebuke Thomas; and here he pronounces a blessing upon Peter. This blessing transforms "Peter's great confession" into Christ's great claim; he accepted the homage, and declared that only divine illumination could have enabled Peter to utter these words, "Blessed art thou, Simon Bar-Jonah: for flesh and blood hath not revealed it unto thee, but my Father who is in heaven." Thus the deity of Christ is a divinely revealed truth; if one does not see this reality, we are not to despise him and not to argue with him; we can pity, we can pray for him;

and should he, like Peter, continue to listen to the great words and to witness the great works of Christ, and should he follow the Master faithfully, someday he, too, may come to worship him.

This truth is also a fundamental truth, "And I also say unto thee, that thou art Peter, and upon this rock I will build my church," not merely on Peter, but a Peter confessing the deity of Christ; and not confessing it as a conclusion of his own reason, but upon Peter confessing his acceptance of the truth which God has revealed to his soul. Upon such a man, and such men, the church was founded; and of such men the church of all ages has been composed. Such a church, too, is imperishable; "the gates of Hades," i.e., "death," the entrance to the underworld, "shall not prevail against it."

To such as confess this knowledge of Christ he gives the power of opening to others his Kingdom and of revealing to them what is permitted and what is forbidden in that Kingdom. Such possibly is the meaning of the further promise which Christ gives to Peter, before he forbids him to tell others the truth he had just confessed. Why this strange prohibition, "Then charged he the disciples that they should tell no man that he was the Christ"? Because the multitude was not yet ready for that truth, they would have misunderstood his claims; only when his work was complete, only then his disciples, guided by his Spirit, could proclaim the truth concerning his divine Person.

B. JESUS PREDICTS HIS DEATH AND RESURRECTION Ch. 16:21-28

21 From that time began Jesus to show unto his disciples, that he must go unto Jerusalem, and suffer many things of the elders and chief priests and scribes, and be killed, and the third day be raised up. 22 And Peter took him and began to rebuke him, saying, Be it far from thee, Lord: this shall never be unto thee. 23 But he turned, and said unto Peter, Get thee behind me, Satan: thou art a stumblingblock unto me: for thou mindest not the things of God, but the things of men. 24 Then said Jesus unto his disciples, If any man would come after me, let him deny himself, and take up his cross, and follow me. 25 For whosoever would save his life shall lose it: and whosoever shall lose his life for my sake shall find it. 26 For what shall a man be profited, if he shall gain the whole world, and forfeit his life? or what shall a man give in exchange for his life? 27 For the Son of man shall come in the glory of his Father with his angels; and then shall he render unto every man according to his deeds. 28 Verily I say unto you, There are some of them that stand here, who shall in no wise taste of death, till they see the Son of man coming in his kingdom.

The two fundamental and supreme doctrines of Christianity are the truths concerning the divine Person and the atoning work of Jesus Christ. Other truths are vital; others are inseparably related to these; but these doctrines are absolutely essential; without them Christianity would cease to be a distinct religion, if it continued to be a religion at all. When at Caesarea Philippi, Jesus had brought to a climax his teaching concerning the first of these truths, he "began to show unto his disciples, that he must go unto Jerusalem, and suffer many things of the elders and chief priests and scribes, and be killed, and the third day be raised up." This is an actual beginning. Before this Jesus has made veiled allusions to the cross. Now, however, with definiteness and clearness he states the certainty and necessity of his death. It was necessary because of the divine purpose which makes the death of Christ the very essence of his atoning work. He teaches them also of his resurrection, although this they seem utterly unable to believe. To his mind, however, it is the certain, glorious issue of all he is to endure.

"And Peter took him, and began to rebuke him." To the mind of this devoted disciple who had just acknowledged Jesus as the Christ, the prediction of death seems like a confession of defeat, a contradiction of the Messianic claim, an admission unworthy of his Lord.

But Jesus, rebuked by Peter, turns to rebuke Peter. "Get thee behind me, Satan: thou art a stumbling-block unto me: for thou mindest not the things of God, but the things of men." These words are serious, but not quite so severe as they may seem. Jesus does not mean that Peter is really satanic and depraved, but that in urging Christ to shrink from death he is playing the part of the tempter and is siding with men, not with God. The offense of the cross has never ceased. It is still human and natural to insist that the death of Christ was not necessary; but "the preaching of the cross" is the very "wisdom of God" and the "power of God."

Jesus then turns to his disciples and declares the inevitable law of Christian life. The servant is not above his master, and if the King is to be crucified, it is not strange that his follower must also bear the cross. "If any man would come after me, let him deny himself, and take up his cross, and follow me." The death of Christ will avail for none but those who are willing to die to sin and self, and to follow Christ as his servants. To "deny himself" does not mean to deny something to himself, but to renounce self. To "take up his cross" does not mean to endure some little or great irritation, or burden, or distress, but to go to the place of crucifixion, to die. Following Christ involves the denial and the death of self.

The result, however, is a larger, fuller, freer, truer life. This is what Jesus means by the promise which he adds, "For whosoever would save his life shall lose it: and whosoever shall lose his life for my sake shall find it." One who suffers for the sake of Christ will enjoy eternal life in heaven; this is true; but the promise is of a present experience as well. Jesus is not urging sacrifice for its own sake, but, quite definitely, sacrifice for his sake and the gospel's. Such sacrifice results in the enrichment and the enlargement of life, and in the enjoyment of all that is worthy the name of life. To lose this larger, fuller life, for the sake of all the pleasure, or sin, or satisfaction, which the world has to offer, would be folly, "for what shall a man be profited, if he shall gain the whole world, and forfeit his life?" Should he make such a tragic bargain, his choice would be irrevocable; life could never be regained, for "what shall a man give in exchange for his life" if that life is once lost? The gain or the loss is likewise eternal. Following Christ involves a present experience; but the issues are abiding, and the full realization will be had only when Christ returns in glory, "for the Son of man shall come in the glory of his Father with his angels; and then shall he render unto every man according to his deeds." Although he was to be rejected and crucified he was to rise and to ascend, and someday, to reappear. It would be far better for one to endure the shame and scorn of a present evil world than to be excluded from the perfected Kingdom of God which would be manifest at the glorious reappearing of Christ. This coming of Christ is the third great theme on which our Lord instructs the disciples while at Caesarea Philippi. His coming and Kingdom were to be the hope and expectation of his followers, as indeed they have been of the church through all the centuries. Some of his immediate followers were to catch a foregleam of the glory, not many days after, when they saw their Lord, with Moses and Elijah, in heavenly splendor, on the Mount of Transfiguration. As Jesus said to his disciples, "Verily I say unto you, There are some of them that stand here, who shall in no wise taste of death, till they see the Son of man coming in his kingdom."

C. JESUS IS TRANSFIGURED Ch. 17:1-8

1 And after six days Jesus taketh with him Peter, and James, and John his brother, and bringeth them up into a high mountain apart: 2 and he was transfigured before them; and his face did shine as the sun, and his garments became white as the light. 3 And behold, there appeared unto them Moses and Elijah talking with him. 4 And Peter answered, and said unto Jesus, Lord, it is good for us to be here: if thou wilt, I will make here three tabernacles; one for thee, and one for Moses, and one for Elijah. 5 While he was yet speaking, behold, a bright cloud overshadowed them: and behold, a voice out of the cloud, saying, This is my beloved Son, in whom I am well pleased; hear ye him. 6 And when the disciples heard it, they fell on their face, and were sore afraid. 7 And Jesus came and touched them and said, Arise, and be not afraid. 8 And lifting up their eyes, they saw no one, save Jesus only.

The transfiguration of our Lord, while he prays on the slopes of Mt. Hermon, is closely and vitally related to the teaching he has been giving to the disciples near the villages of Caesarea Philippi. He has accepted Peter's great confession as to his divine person, and now, out of the heavenly glory, comes the voice of the Father saying, "This is my beloved Son." He has taught them particularly of his approaching death; and now, upon the mountain, Moses and Elijah appear, talking with him, as Luke affirms, "of his decease which he was about to accomplish at Jerusalem." He has predicted his return in glory, and now, as Peter afterward declared, he gives the disciples a foretaste of what that glory would be.

Just what is meant by the statement, "He was transfigured before them," it is difficult for us to understand. It is surely an experience quite different from that of Moses on the mountain. The face of Moses shone with a reflected light; but, in the case of Jesus, a glory from within bursts forth and irradiates his whole being, until not only his face but his very garments are radiant with a dazzling light. Matthew has been picturing to us the career of the King. It is as if the monarch had been walking in disguise; only occasionally beneath his humble garment has been revealed a glimpse of the purple and the gold. Here, for an hour, the disguise is withdrawn and the King appears in his real majesty and in the regal splendor of his divine glory.

Jesus had been alone, with Peter, James, and John, when the startling change in his appearance occurred; but as the disciples gazed on him in wonder, "behold, there appeared unto them Moses and Elijah talking with him." The two men whose departure from the world had been veiled in mystery were chosen for this mysterious return. Moses is commonly supposed to represent the Law and Elijah the Prophets; both had pointed forward by symbol and prediction to the atoning work of Christ; these men could speak with Jesus intelligently concerning his coming death. Then, too, these men had been prepared peculiarly, by personal experiences, to understand the grace of God, and therefore, they best of all could comprehend the love of God in the gift of his Son.

"And Peter answered," that is, his remark was called forth by the startling experience, "Lord, it is good for us to be here: if thou wilt, I will make here three tabernacles; one for thee, and one for Moses, and one for Elijah." Peter was dazed by the wonder and mystery of the scene. He did not know what to say. His words seem absurd; beings from the unseen world would hardly care for huts on the mountainside; it would not be a kindness long to detain here on earth visitors from heaven. However, his suggestion is far from meaningless; Peter is not to be ridiculed; he realized the blessedness of his experience; however clumsily expressed, his desire was to prolong such an ecstatic vision; in spite of his fear, he wished to continue in such blissful companionship.

Even while Peter was speaking, a bright cloud came and overshadowed them all. The scene was about to end; but first there came out of the cloud the voice of the Father conveying the supreme message of the hour, "This is my beloved Son, in whom I am well pleased." There was no need of detaining Moses and Elijah. He had come, of whom Moses in the Law and the Prophets had testified, even Jesus, the divine Son of God. The time had come when those who wished to know the nature and will and saving grace of God could find them completely and finally revealed in Jesus Christ his Son.

"And when the disciples heard it, they fell on their face, and were sore afraid. And Jesus came and touched them and said, Arise, and be not afraid. And lifting up their eyes, they saw no one, save Jesus only." They needed none other; him they were to hear; yet for a time the heavenly light grew dim; they were to follow him into the dark valley of the shadow of death; but they could never forget the vision of his revealed glory; henceforth he was to them more truly than ever a divine Lord and the coming King.

This unique experience was of deep significance to our Lord himself. It prepared him for the pain and death he so soon was to endure. It assured him again of his divine sonship; it reminded him that if he lost his life he would find it, if he endured the cross he would surely rise from the dead and meet the saints of old in a state of glory, in a position of supreme power.

This event was of still greater significance to the disciples. They, too, needed to be prepared for the experiences which lay before them. Their belief in the divine nature of their Lord was strengthened by this vision of his glory; the mysterious predictions of his death and resurrection were confirmed by what they had seen and heard; the splendor of his final coming was henceforth more real, and in view of its certainty they were more ready than before to take up the cross and come after him.

No less important are the messages for his followers today. They are reminded that by faith in him, as they now behold his glory, they can be "transformed into the same image," "transfigured," not by an outward imitation of Christ but by the operation of an inner power "even as from the Lord the Spirit."

So, too, we see predicted more clearly the circumstances of his future appearing; then some, who like Moses have died, and whose bodies have disappeared in burial, will appear in bodies deathless and immortal; others like Elijah, who never died, will not taste of death, but will be transformed, transfigured, "in a moment, in the twinkling of an eye" and "be caught up . . . to meet the Lord in the air"; but the splendor of the scene will be embodied and centered in the majestic form and radiant face of the returning triumphant King.

D. JOHN THE BAPTIST AND ELIJAH
Ch. 17:9-13

9 And as they were coming down from the mountain, Jesus commanded them, saying, Tell the vision to no man, until the Son of man be risen from the dead. 10 And his disciples asked him, saying, Why then say the scribes that Elijah must first come? 11 And he answered and said, Elijah indeed cometh, and shall restore all things: 12 but I say unto you, that Elijah is come already, and they knew him not, but did unto him whatsoever they would. Even so shall the Son of man also suffer of them. 13 Then understood the disciples that he spake unto them of John the Baptist.

The vision of their transfigured Lord and of the heavenly visitors had strengthened and inspired the three apostles, but it was not intended for the curious, ignorant crowds that awaited the return of Jesus. "As they were coming down from the mountain, Jesus commanded them, saying, Tell the vision to no man, until the Son of man be risen from the dead." This command of secrecy is similar to that given to those whom Jesus had healed during this period of retirement; but to it is added a strange limitation, "until the Son of man be risen from the dead." After his resurrection they were to be witnesses of his divine glory; but for such testimony they were not yet prepared, nor would it have been understood by the multitude. A report of such a heavenly vision might occasion ridicule or result in a fanatical uprising. Only those who believe in Christ are prepared for a full revelation of his divine glory.

As they descended the mountains the minds of Peter and James and John were full of questions as to what had been meant by the experiences which had been theirs, by the vision of their transfigured Lord and of Moses and Elijah. As the transfiguration had been a foregleam of the coming of Christ in glory, it called to their remembrance a prediction concerning the coming of a messenger to prepare the way for the King, "And his disciples asked him, saying, Why then say the scribes that Elijah must first come?" The question was occasioned by the appearance of Elijah on "the holy mountain." There was a popular expectation that this great prophet would prepare the way before the Messiah. It was based upon the closing words of Malachi: "Behold, I will send you Elijah the prophet before the great and terrible day of Jehovah come. And he shall turn the heart of the fathers to the children, and the heart of the children to their fathers; lest I come and smite the earth with a curse." What puzzled the disciples was the fact that Jesus had come and had so far performed his ministry before Elijah had appeared. Jesus explained to them that the prophecy had at least its initial fulfillment in the work of John the Baptist who had come "in the spirit and power of Elijah." He had turned the nation back to God in repentance and had revived the hope of the coming Messiah. However, as Jesus declared, he had not been recognized, but they had done unto him "whatsoever they would." In the treatment of his forerunner, Jesus foresaw what he himself would endure as the predicted King. As Elijah had suffered at the hands of Ahab and Jezebel; as John had been murdered by Herod and Herodias, so Jesus was to be rejected by the Jews and crucified by the order of Pilate. In the death of John, Jesus saw a portent of his own approaching sufferings and thus clearly predicted to his disciples a second time his approaching death, "Even so shall the Son of man also suffer of them." Thus even with the light of the transfiguration still lingering on his countenance did Jesus definitely predict his crucifixion; thus too, in veiled symbol, does he refer to his coming glory, of which he had caught a foregleam in the splendors of "the holy mount."

E. JESUS HEALS THE EPILEPTIC BOY
Ch. 17:14-20

14 And when they were come to the multitude, there came to him a man, kneeling to him, and saying, 15 Lord, have mercy on my son: for he is epileptic, and suffereth grievously; for oft-times he falleth into the fire, and oft-times into the water. 16 And I brought him to thy disciples, and they could not cure him. 17 And Jesus answered and said, O faithless and perverse generation, how long shall I be with you? how long shall I bear with you? bring him hither to me. 18 And Jesus rebuked him; and the demon went out of him: and the boy was cured from that hour.

19 Then came the disciples to Jesus apart, and said, Why could not we cast it out? 20 And he saith unto them, Because of your little faith: for verily I say unto you, If ye have faith as a grain of mustard seed, ye shall say unto this mountain, Remove hence to yonder place; and it shall remove; and nothing shall be impossible unto you.

When the artist Raphael painted the picture of the transfiguration of Jesus, he sketched on the same canvas this scene of the demoniac boy surrounded by the nine disciples at the foot of the mountain. Of course the incidents occurred on different days; but this combination heightens the contrast of the experience of Jesus in the splendors of the mountain summit and his experience amid the shadows of human sorrow and distress which he entered on the plain below. It was not the first time he had exchanged heavenly glory for earthly gloom; and how majestically he bore himself amid the shadows! Surely this is the picture of a King. Matthew has omitted many of the details included in the story by Mark; but the omissions do not diminish, they rather emphasize, the impression of royalty.

There is the distressed father, kneeling as a suppliant before Jesus; there is the poor boy whose disease has been occasioned by an evil spirit or has been the occasion for the mastery of the spirit; there are the disciples, helpless in their imperfect faith; then the word of royal command, the rebuke of the demon, and the cure is complete.

However, there is deep human sympathy in the heart of the King. There is no aloofness in his manner. He is touched by the anguish of the father, and by the suffering of the boy, but most of all he is troubled by the unbelief which has needlessly delayed the cure. Never does Jesus appear more sensitive to the lack of faith by which his ministry has been attended, never does he confess more clearly his willingness to escape from such surroundings. "O faithless and perverse generation," he cries, "how long shall I be with you?" The unbelief is "perverse" because it is due, not to lack of evidence, but because the evidence has been rejected or neglected.

Jesus must have had in mind the multitude, the doubting father, and the hostile Pharisees, as well as the nine disappointed disciples; but the latter did not seem to perceive any rebuke to themselves until they came to Jesus privately and were told definitely that their failure has been due to their "little faith." Yet Jesus adds a word of gracious promise which may hearten modern disciples depressed by conscious failure, "If ye have faith as a grain of mustard seed," that is, real trust, however small, "ye shall say unto this mountain, Remove hence to yonder place; and it shall remove"; that is, any obstacle may be overcome. Jesus is speaking in Oriental imagery, and his words are not to be pressed too literally; nor yet when he adds "and nothing shall be impossible unto you."

There are limitations to the powers granted to the followers of Christ; yet within the sphere of his commands and commission, in accomplishing the task he assigns, in bearing the burdens he imposes, nothing is impossible to those who trust and obey.

The twenty-first verse is omitted by the Revisers; it had been copied from the Gospel of Mark and in this sense forms a real part of the message. "This kind goeth not out save by prayer." Let our faith be expressed in believing petition, and our Master will have no occasion to grieve over the inefficiency of our service.

F. JESUS AGAIN PREDICTS HIS DEATH
Ch. 17:22-23

22 *And while they abode in Galilee, Jesus said unto them, The Son of man shall be delivered up into the hands of men; 23 and they shall kill him, and the third day he shall be raised up. And they were exceeding sorry.*

For the last time Jesus is about to revisit Capernaum. While he lingers in northern Galilee one great theme occupies his thoughts and his teachings. It is his death which he soon is to suffer at Jerusalem. He has spoken of it before, and with increasing definiteness; here, however, he uses a novel phrase, "The Son of man shall be delivered up into the hands of men; and they shall kill him." What is this "delivered up"? It was formerly translated "betrayed," and suggested such treachery as that of Judas; this betrayal Jesus clearly foresaw and it added bitter drops to his cup of coming suffering. More probably the word here refers to the handing over of Jesus to the Roman authorities to be crucified; however, there may be even an intimation of the surrender of the Son by the Father for the redemption of the world. It may be an echo of that sacred message, "God so loved the world, that he gave his only begotten Son." Certain it is that Jesus never regarded his death as a mere incident in his career, or as an experience which other men might share. His death was unique; he declared it to be "a ransom for many," and "for the remission of sins." As before he had expressed the divine necessity by saying that he "must go unto Jerusalem, . . . and be killed," so now he may be intimating the divine purpose as he speaks of being "delivered up into the hands of men."

However, the death of Christ is not set forth as an isolated event; he unites it with another, from which it is inseparable, namely, his resurrection. "And the third day he shall be raised up." His predictions were not the gloomy forebodings of a human martyr, but the clear anticipations of a divine Savior. He sees the necessity for his atoning death, but also the certainty of his resurrection victory. The cross is a fit symbol for much that is essential in our Christian faith, but it never should be allowed to hide the majestic form of the risen, glorified, ascended King.

"They were exceeding sorry." It was the sorrow of sympathy and of devoted love; yet it was partly the sorrow of unbelief. They had begun to understand what he meant by "death," but the meaning of this "rising again" they could not conceive. So, too, our mourning should be radiated by the comfort born of the resurrection of Christ, that we "sorrow not, even as the rest, who have no hope."

G. JESUS PROVIDES THE TEMPLE TAX
Ch. 17:24-27

24 And when they were come to Capernaum, they that received the half-shekel came to Peter, and said, Doth not your teacher pay the half-shekel? 25 He saith, Yea. And when he came into the house, Jesus spake first to him, saying, What thinkest thou, Simon? the kings of the earth, from whom do they receive toll or tribute? from their sons, or from strangers? 26 And when he said, From strangers,

Jesus said unto him, Therefore the sons are free. 27 But, lest we cause them to stumble, go thou to the sea, and cast a hook, and take up the fish that first cometh up; and when thou hast opened his mouth, thou shalt find a shekel: that take, and give unto them for me and thee.

This incident is to be found in no other Gospel. Here it properly belongs. This is the "Gospel of the King" and this striking story is the story of a King. It includes a royal claim, a royal concession, and a royal command.

Jesus had just been teaching his disciples concerning his divine Person and his atoning work. Peter had confessed him to be the Son of God. As they returned to Capernaum, Peter was asked whether his Master would pay "the half-shekel" which was required of every Israelite as an annual tax for the support of the Temple worship. Peter immediately replied, "Yea." Was it, however, so simple a question? Was he, who in the hearing of Peter claimed to be "greater than the temple," to submit to the demands of the Temple? Was he, whom Peter confessed to be "the Son of God," compelled to support the house of God? Was he, who came to give his life "a ransom for many," to pay the "ransom money" which the Jewish ritual required?

Peter evidently began to feel a little uneasy in his own mind; and as soon as he came into the presence of his Lord he sought to vindicate himself; but Jesus anticipated him with a definite rebuke, as he claimed exemption from the tax. It was a royal claim and was embodied in a brief parable: "What thinkest thou, Simon? the kings of the earth, from whom do they receive toll or tribute? from their sons, or from strangers? And when he said, From strangers, Jesus said unto him, Therefore the sons are free." The meaning is perfectly plain: Jesus claimed to be the divine Son of God, and as the Son of God he declared that he need pay no tribute to support the worship of God. What a claim! Was it not blasphemy unless it was true?

Then followed a royal concession, "But, lest we cause
them to stumble, go thou . . . and give unto them for
me and thee." "Lest we cause them to stumble," thus
Jesus was careful to avoid needless offense. The people of
Capernaum did not understand that he was the Son of
God. Had he refused to pay that simple tax he would
have been regarded as irreligious and profane. With a
kingly condescension he waived his royal rights. Yet
those who knew him to be the Son of God needed to know
that he was abating no claim. Peter needed to know on
what ground Jesus would pay the tax; and the followers of
Jesus today need to be reminded, not only of the divine
claims of Christ, but of his example as he warns them not
always to insist upon their rights, but with princely generosity to yield their rights when otherwise they might be
misunderstood and might cause needless offense.

Lastly Jesus gave a royal command, "Go thou to the
sea, and cast a hook, and take up the fish that first cometh
up; and when thou hast opened his mouth, thou shalt
find a shekel: that take, and give unto them for me and
thee." That promised miracle must have made its peculiar appeal to the old fisherman, Simon Peter; but it has
its message for every follower of Christ. Who but he
could have given such a command? Surely this must be
the divine King who has dominion over "whatsoever passeth through the paths of the seas."

Note too that closing touch, "Give unto them for me
and thee," not, "for us." Peter paid the tax on a different
ground; he could not claim to be the Son of God; he
needed a ransom for his soul. Such a ransom we need;
and it has been provided for us graciously by the divine
King.

IX
THE SERVANTS
OF THE KING
Chs. 18 to 20

A. JESUS WARNS AGAINST GIVING OFFENSE
Ch. 18:1-14

1 In that hour came the disciples unto Jesus, saying, Who then is greatest in the kingdom of heaven? 2 And he called to him a little child, and set him in the midst of them, 3 and said, Verily I say unto you, Except ye turn, and become as little children, ye shall in no wise enter into the kingdom of heaven. 4 Whosoever therefore shall humble himself as this little child, the same is the greatest in the kingdom of heaven. 5 And whoso shall receive one such little child in my name receiveth me: 6 but whoso shall cause one of these little ones that believe on me to stumble, it is profitable for him that a great millstone should be hanged about his neck, and that he should be sunk in the depth of the sea.

7 Woe unto the world because of occasions of stumbling! for it must needs be that the occasions come; but woe to that man through whom the occasion cometh! 8 And if thy hand or thy foot causeth thee to stumble, cut it off, and cast it from thee: it is good for thee to enter into life maimed or halt, rather than having two hands or two feet to be cast into the eternal fire. 9 And if thine eye causeth thee to stumble, pluck it out, and cast it from thee: it is good for thee to enter into life with one eye, rather than having two eyes to be cast into the hell of fire. 10 See that ye despise not one of these little ones: for I say unto you, that in heaven their angels do always behold the face of my Father who is in heaven. 12 How think ye? if any man have a hundred sheep, and one of them be gone astray, doth he not leave the ninety and nine, and go unto

*the mountains, and seek that which goeth astray? 13
And if so be that he find it, verily I say unto you, he re-
joiceth over it more than over the ninety and nine which
have not gone astray. 14 Even so it is not the will of your
Father who is in heaven, that one of these little ones should
perish.*

The eighteenth, nineteenth, and twentieth chapters of
this Gospel are mainly concerned with the series of discourses delivered by Christ to his disciples. They are all
designed to instruct the servants of the King. Those of the
eighteenth chapter were delivered at Capernaum during
the last visit of Jesus in that city. Those of the next two
chapters were delivered as Jesus journeyed through Perea
on his way to Jerusalem and the cross.

The occasion of the first discourse was a question which
had arisen among his followers as to which of them should
be greatest in the Kingdom of Heaven. There was something admirable in their discussion, for it revealed the fact
that they believed the promises of Christ and regarded his
Kingdom as something glorious and a high place in this
Kingdom as something supremely desirable to attain. Of
course there was much of pride and of self-confidence in
their debate, and therefore Jesus rebuked them. He called
a little child and set him in the midst of them and said,
"Verily I say unto you, Except ye turn, and become as
little children, ye shall in no wise enter into the kingdom
of heaven." They were faced in the wrong direction.
They needed to turn, if they were to attain positions of
greatness; if indeed they were even to be admitted to the
Kingdom. Jesus had previously told them that the Kingdom belonged to the poor in spirit and now, to rebuke
their pride, he points them to a little child, for he wished
to suggest that what they needed was the trust, and the
conscious dependence and humility, which, if not found in
all children, are associated with childhood and constitute
what is known as a childlike spirit. Jesus assures them
that humility is the path to the highest position in the

Kingdom of Heaven. However, by humility he means not merely a low opinion of self, nor merely diffidence, but a willingness and a desire to render humble service for the sake of the King; for he adds, "Whoso shall receive one such little child in my name receiveth me." To be willing to care even for a little child, to undertake gladly so humble a task is a sign of that spirit which constitutes true greatness in the sight of the King.

Having thus bestowed his praise on those who are childlike, the King proceeded to warn his followers, lest they might cause one of these little ones to stumble. When Jesus spoke of the "little ones," he did not mean merely those who are young in years, but those who, like children, are limited in experience or strength or knowledge or opportunity. It is the willingness to care for such that Jesus declares to be the sign of greatness. On the other hand, to be willing to lead one such little one into sin, to cause one of these helpless and dependent ones to stumble or to fall, is so great a crime that our Lord declares that, it would be better for such a one "that a great millstone should be hanged about his neck, and that he should be sunk in the depth of the sea"; such a fate would be preferable to that which awaits one who has been guilty of offending one of these children of the King.

Jesus declares that the world is full of temptations and "occasions of stumbling"; but he warns his followers lest any one of them should willingly cause others to fall. Even his followers would be capable of such a disgraceful course. Therefore, the sternest self-discipline would be necessary. At a sacrifice, no matter how great, one must secure himself against such a possible crime. If necessary he must be willing to sacrifice what may be as precious as a hand or a foot. Even the most bitter loss, even the yielding of what was most precious to the heart, would be far better than to be cast into the eternal fire.

Having pointed out the peril of causing to stumble one of these little ones who trust in him, Jesus further warns his disciples against despising these trustful and dependent followers of his. He does so on the ground that they are so precious to his Father who is in heaven. He declares that the angels who serve, or protect or represent them, are nearest to the throne of God, and therefore his followers cannot think lightly of those who are so dear to God. He further uses a familiar and beautiful illustration. He suggests how deeply a shepherd is concerned over a sheep which has gone astray and how he rejoices when it is found. Even so he declares, "It is not the will of your Father who is in heaven, that one of these little ones should perish." Thus if the Father so loves them, we must love them too and avoid aught that might offend them or cause them to fall. If, like the disciples of old, we are at all conscious of superior powers and opportunities, let us not feel that these entitle us to the chief places in the Kingdom unless they are gladly and constantly used in helping, guiding, and comforting the weaker and more obscure servants of the King.

B. JESUS TEACHES HOW OFFENDERS ARE TO BE TREATED Ch. 18:15-35

15 And if thy brother sin against thee, go, show him his fault between thee and him alone: if he hear thee, thou hast gained thy brother. 16 But if he hear thee not, take with thee one or two more, that at the mouth of two witnesses or three every word may be established. 17 And if he refuse to hear them, tell it unto the church: and if he refuse to hear the church also, let him be unto thee as the Gentile and the publican. 18 Verily I say unto you, What things soever ye shall bind on earth shall be bound in heaven; and what things soever ye shall loose on earth shall be loosed in heaven. 19 Again I say unto you, that if two of you shall agree on earth as touching anything that they shall ask, it shall be done for them of my Father who is in heaven. 20 For where two or three are gathered together in my name, there am I in the midst of them.

21 Then came Peter, and said to him, Lord, how oft shall my brother sin against me, and I forgive him? until seven times? 22 Jesus saith unto him, I say not unto thee, Until seven times; but, Until seventy times seven. 23 Therefore is the kingdom of heaven likened unto a certain king, who would make a reckoning with his servants. 24 And when he had begun to reckon, one was brought unto him, that owed him ten thousand talents. 25 But forasmuch as he had not wherewith to pay, his lord commanded him to be sold, and his wife, and children, and all that he had, and payment to be made. 26 The servant therefore fell down and worshipped him, saying, Lord, have patience with me, and I will pay thee all. 27 And the lord of that servant, being moved with compassion, released him, and forgave him the debt. 28 But that servant went out, and found one of his fellow-servants, who owed him a hundred shillings: and he laid hold on him, and took him by the throat, saying, Pay what thou owest. 29 So his fellow-servant fell down and besought him, saying, Have patience with me, and I will pay thee. 30 And he would not: but went and cast him into prison, till he should pay that which was due. 31 So when his fellow-servants saw what was done, they were exceeding sorry, and came and told unto their lord all that was done. 32 Then his lord called him unto him, and saith to him, Thou wicked servant, I forgave thee all that debt, because thou besoughtest me: 33 shouldest not thou also have had mercy on thy fellow-servant, even as I had mercy on thee? 34 And his lord was wroth, and delivered him to the tormentors, till he should pay all that was due. 35 So shall also my heavenly Father do unto you, if ye forgive not every one his brother from your hearts.

In warning his followers against giving offense, Jesus clearly tells them that, in this present world, offenses are sure to come, and he now proceeds to show how the disciples are to treat those who are guilty of sinning against their fellow Christians. His directions are calculated to guide each individual believer, but they are also designed for the instruction of the united body of believers which constitutes his church. If then an offense has been committed, one is first of all to go to the offender alone and to seek for a reconciliation. It is possible that the offender may repent and that friendship may be restored. If, however, the offender is unwilling to confess his fault, then the one against whom the sin has been committed is to take with him one or two fellow Christians that in their presence the charge may be made and the appeal for penitence and reparation. However, in case these private efforts fail, then the matter is to be referred to the authority of the church, and if the offender is still unmoved, he is to be excluded from the communion and companionship of the Christian body. He is to be regarded "as the Gentile and the publican." When discipline is thus carefully and sympathetically administered, the decisions of the Christian brotherhood will receive the sanction of God, they will be "bound in heaven." However, the church must seek guidance in prayer. The Master promises his presence and assures them of definite replies. The promise first of all concerns these immediate cases of discipline, but its implications are much larger and its encouragement to united petition is inspiring. "If two of you shall agree on earth as touching anything that they shall ask, it shall be done for them of my Father who is in heaven."

In all this teaching as to the treatment of offenders, Jesus had been implying that pardon should always be granted to the penitent. It is not strange then that his disciples questioned whether there were not limits to this generous forgiveness of offenders. "Then came Peter, and said to him, Lord, how oft shall my brother sin against me, and I forgive him? until seven times? Jesus saith unto him, I say not unto thee, Until seven times; but, Until seventy times seven." Of course our Lord was not speaking literally, but he did mean to teach that for a Christian there can be no limit set upon his willingness to forgive. To pardon the penitent reveals the princely spirit of a true follower of the King. It shows also a grateful appreciation of the pardon which Christ has secured for each one who has enlisted in his service. It was to illustrate this further truth that Jesus related the parable of the unmerciful servant. It is recorded by no other writer; and it is in exact harmony with this Gospel of the King, for the story relates to "a certain king" to whom one debtor owed ten thousand talents. It was an almost impossible sum for anyone to pay in a lifetime. Its present equivalent would be more than twelve millions of dollars. When the creditor had nothing to pay, and cried out for mercy, the king "being moved with compassion, released him, and forgave him the debt." This is evidently a picture of our relation to God and of his pardoning grace. Surely we have nothing to pay. Day by day our debt has been increasing; it is beyond all measure and we have no hope of payment. Though one should live a perfect life in the future he would have nothing to offer for his failure in the past to render the obedience and service which have been daily owed to the heavenly King. Yet he has freely forgiven us all our debt; he has canceled every obligation for the sake of his own dear Son, "in whom we have our redemption through his blood, the forgiveness of our trespasses, according to the riches of his grace."

By way of striking contrast Jesus described another servant of the same king who owed the forgiven debtor a trifling sum of one hundred shillings, probably less than fifteen dollars; yet when he begged for mercy he was cast into prison "till he should pay that which was due." Is it not a searching picture of the ingratitude which we show when we feel unkindly and are unforgiving toward our fellow Christian whose offense against us has been so little in comparison with the debt which God has forgiven us? It is not strange that Jesus concluded his parable by telling us of the rebuke the king administered to the heartless debtor he had forgiven; and how "He was wroth, and delivered him to the tormentors, till he should pay all that was due." Then he added impressively, "So shall also my heavenly Father do unto you, if ye forgive not every one his brother from your hearts." Surely the forgiveness of God cannot be claimed or enjoyed by those who are unwilling to forgive their fellow men; but in view of the grace of God revealed to us in our Savior, we should remember the words of the apostle, "Be ye kind one to another, tenderhearted, forgiving each other, even as God also in Christ forgave you."

C. JESUS TEACHES CONCERNING MARRIAGE
Ch. 19:1-12

1 And it came to pass when Jesus had finished these words, he departed from Galilee, and came into the borders of Judæa beyond the Jordan; 2 and great multitudes followed him, and he healed them there.

3 And there came unto him Pharisees, trying him, and saying, Is it lawful for a man to put away his wife for every cause? 4 And he answered and said, Have ye not read, that he who made them from the beginning made them male and female, 5 and said, For this cause shall a man leave his father and mother, and shall cleave to his wife; and the two shall become one flesh? 6 So that they are no more two, but one flesh. What therefore God hath joined together, let not man put asunder. 7 They say unto him, Why then did Moses command to give a bill of divorcement, and to put her away? 8 He saith unto them, Moses for your hardness of heart suffered you to put away your wives: but from the beginning it hath not been so. 9 And I say unto you, Whosoever shall put away his wife, except for fornication, and shall marry another, committeth adultery: and he that marrieth her when she is put away committeth adultery. 10 The disciples say unto him, If the case of the man is so with his wife, it is not expedient to marry. 11 But he said unto them, Not all men can receive this saying, but they to whom it is given. 12 For there are eunuchs, that were so born from their mother's womb: and there are eunuchs, that were made eunuchs by men: and there are eunuchs, that made themselves eunuchs for

*the kingdom of heaven's sake. He that is able to receive
it, let him receive it.*

Jesus has left Galilee for the last time. He is journeying
southward through Perea. This country is not named in
the New Testament, but the strip of territory which is so
called and which lay east of the Jordan was largely in-
habited by Jews and through it lay the favorite route of
travel for those who were going from Galilee to Judea.
Jesus is no longer seeking retirement. He is surrounded
by great multitudes, many of whom he heals. However,
he is still teaching his disciples, both by his works of divine
power and by his discourses which he delivers as occasions
suggest. The first three themes concern the social life
of the followers of Christ. They relate to marriage, to
childhood, and to wealth.

The first of these subjects is suggested by an attack
made upon Jesus by his enemies. The Pharisees are determined upon his destruction. They come to him with a
question designed to entangle and embarrass him and if
possible to discredit him with the crowds and to furnish
a possible occasion for his arrest. The question proposed
relates to divorce. Rabbis of the day were divided in their
views as to the teaching of the law; some held that divorce
was lawful only on the ground of infidelity; others held
that it was allowable for any one of a large variety of
causes, even for personal dislike. Jesus avoids their snare
and lays down a principle fundamental to the stability of
human society. Not only does he agree with those who
held the stricter view of marriage, he insists that the bond
was designed to be indissoluble. He refers to the law of
marriage as divinely established at creation. "Have ye
not read, that he who made them from the beginning
made them male and female?" Jesus quotes the words of
Adam as embodying the will of God, "For this cause shall
a man leave his father and mother, and shall cleave to his
wife; and the two shall become one flesh." Jesus suggests

that the union is physical as well as spiritual. The marriage tie cannot be broken save by unfaithfulness to the marriage vow. A divorce, which is merely an act of human legislation, cannot set aside a union which is divinely constituted. "What therefore God hath joined together, let not man put asunder." How much the world today is in need of the same solemn teachings of the Lord. Marriage is not to be entered into lightly or inadvisedly, nor can the bond be loosed on grounds of incompatibility of temper, disagreeable habits, or loss of love. The tie is one which only death or sin can break.

While the enemies of Jesus are not wholly surprised at his strict view of the marriage tie, they are elated to find, as they suppose, that his teaching contradicts the Law of Moses, "They say unto him, Why then did Moses command to give a bill of divorcement, and to put her away?" Jesus at once replies, "Moses for your hardness of heart suffered you to put away your wives: but from the beginning it hath not been so." Moses did not encourage divorce, he limited it and regulated it. He recognized the hardness of heart of the very people of God. Divorce was not ideal. It would be unnecessary were hearts pure and sinless. As marriage was first established it was a union which could not be broken.

Among the Jews the granting of a divorce carried with it the right of remarriage. It is well for us in the present day to distinguish between these two ideas. There seems to be a common belief that even the guilty party in a suit of divorce has a right to remarry. This case Jesus does not discuss. It may indeed be advisable for parties who are guilty of immorality to secure legal separations which bear the name of divorce. It is surely allowable for a divorce to be granted in case the marriage tie has actually been broken by unfaithfulness; but it is quite another matter to teach that one who has been at fault is justified, when a divorce has been granted, in marrying when and whom he will. There is something peculiarly searching in the words of the Lord, "Whosoever shall put away his wife, except for fornication, and shall marry another, committeth adultery: and he that marrieth her when she is put away committeth adultery."

This strict interpretation of the law startles the disciples of our Lord. If one cannot possibly escape even from an undesirable and an unfortunate marriage, they conclude that "it is not expedient to marry." Jesus replies that for some it may not be expedient, and that, while marriage should be the rule for all, there are some who may be excepted. Some, as Jesus declares, are so constituted by nature and disposition that they should not marry; others are in conditions and circumstances which make marriage inadvisable, and there are some who voluntarily refrain from marriage because of special service which, as celibates, they can best render to Christ. Thus while Jesus intimates that celibacy is allowable he does not urge it upon his followers, and he considers it expedient, only in unusual cases.

D. JESUS RECEIVES LITTLE CHILDREN
Ch. 19:13-15

13 Then were there brought unto him little children, that he should lay his hands on them, and pray: and the disciples rebuked them. 14 But Jesus said, Suffer the little children, and forbid them not, to come unto me: for to such belongeth the kingdom of heaven. 15 And he laid his hands on them, and departed thence.

Something is added to the significance of this beautiful scene by the setting in which it is placed. Jesus has been speaking of the sanctity of the marriage tie by which the safety of the home is secured; he now teaches the sacredness of childhood which brings to the home its completeness, its glory, and its ennobling care. "Then were brought unto him little children that he should lay his hands on them, and pray." These children were probably carried in the arms of their parents. What was desired for them was that blessing by the Master which may well symbolize the personal relation and spiritual contact with Christ which all parents with equal eagerness should seek for their children.

"And the disciples rebuked them"; they seemed to feel that the children were too insignificant to be allowed to interfere with the work or to demand the care of Christ. Many things today tend to keep parents from bringing their children to the Master: custom and carelessness and indifference and fear and diffidence, even friends, seem to play the part of those "disciples" and to conspire to prevent and to rebuke those who really desire to see their children brought to Christ.

The reply of Jesus has cast an unfading halo about the face of every helpless child, "Suffer the little children, and forbid them not, to come unto me." Their innocent helplessness appealed to the King. Should it not affect us, and should we not feel that no work is more Christlike, none more blessed than the care of children? We are true servants of the King only as we feel the appeal of childhood, and only as we seek to supply to children their physical and mental and spiritual needs.

"For to such belongeth the kingdom of heaven." It is theirs by right; not those particular children, not all children in general; but all of whatever age who are childlike in their trust and dependence and purity, all those who cast themselves upon the King and upon his sustaining grace will enter his glorious Kingdom.

"And he laid his hands on them, and departed thence." But his blessing has brought its benediction wherever his name has been heard. Christianity is peculiarly the religion which has regarded the rights of children. Where Christ is known and trusted and followed, there infancy is sacred and childhood is secure.

E. JESUS TEACHES CONCERNING SACRIFICE AND REWARDS Chs. 19:16 to 20:16

1. THE RICH YOUNG MAN Ch. 19:16-22

16 And behold, one came to him and said, Teacher, what good thing shall I do, that I may have eternal life? 17 And he said unto him, Why askest thou me concerning that which is good? One there is who is good: but if thou wouldest enter into life, keep the commandments. 18 He saith unto him, Which? And Jesus said, Thou shalt not kill, Thou shalt not commit adultery, Thou shalt not steal, Thou shalt not bear false witness, 19 Honor thy father and thy mother; and, Thou shalt love thy neighbor as thyself. 20 The young man saith unto him, All these things have I observed: what lack I yet? 21 Jesus said unto him, If thou wouldest be perfect, go, sell that which thou hast, and give to the poor, and thou shalt have treasure in heaven: and come, follow me. 22 But when the young man heard the saying, he went away sorrowful; for he was one that had great possessions.

Here is the striking story of one who, in spite of riches, youth, position, and power, is not satisfied. He comes to Jesus and says, "Teacher, what good thing shall I do, that I may have eternal life?" Jesus at once rebukes him: "Why askest thou me concerning that which is good? One there is who is good." It is a mistake to suppose that Jesus here denies his own sinlessness, or disclaims divinity. As to the latter, many assert that Jesus is suggesting that he is "either not good, or is God." This is true enough but it is not the point. Jesus wishes to convict the young man of his moral need. He intimates that the thoughtless use of the word "good," in addressing one whom he regards as a human teacher, is an index to his superficial view of goodness. In the sight of a holy God, and judged by a divine standard of righteousness, can the young inquirer claim to be good? Can any man call himself righteous, in the light of divine holiness?

Jesus now proposes the test of the revealed will of God; he mentions the commandments, at least such as concern man's relation to man. The self-righteous inquirer at once replies that he has kept these from his youth. Jesus looks with love upon the young man whose moral purpose has been so high, but he now applies the deep probe which shows that the man has never observed the spirit of the commandments even though he believes he has kept the letter. Jesus sees the real selfishness of the heart. He proposes the supreme test, "Go, sell that which thou hast, and give to the poor, and thou shalt have treasure in heaven: and come, follow me." In this sentence Jesus convicts the man of having broken the second table of the Law which requires one to love his neighbor as himself; he promises an eternal recompense for sacrifice, and he offers, by his personal companionship, the power and influence which will make the keeping of the Law more possible and complete. No one can claim to be righteous when judged by the Commandments as interpreted by Christ; our only hope is to come to him for guidance and help. He will lay bare the secret selfishness of our hearts and he will develop the spirit of self-renunciation and love which forms the essence of eternal life; and in his Kingdom we ultimately shall be recompensed for every loss.

Our Lord does not demand that all his followers shall sacrifice their worldly possessions. He is dealing with a specific case. He does demand that each one shall give up anything which keeps one from open, honest fellowship with him. In the case of this inquirer, Jesus makes plain to him that his goodness is superficial and inadequate. Love of money is the canker which is hidden in his soul; Jesus further shows him that he must choose between his wealth and the eternal life which Jesus alone can give. No wonder the young man "went away sorrowful." He had made a fatal choice. His was "the great refusal." His riches had never satisfied him before, still less will they satisfy him now. He realized his weakness and his need;

but he kept his wealth and he rejected his Savior. He desired the highest good; he yearned for eternal life; but he was not willing to pay the price.

2. THE QUESTION OF PETER Ch. 19:23-30

23 And Jesus said unto his disciples, Verily I say unto you, It is hard for a rich man to enter into the kingdom of heaven. 24 And again I say unto you, It is easier for a camel to go through a needle's eye, than for a rich man to enter into the kingdom of God. 25 And when the disciples heard it, they were astonished exceedingly, saying, Who then can be saved? 26 And Jesus looking upon them said to them, With men this is impossible; but with God all things are possible. 27 Then answered Peter and said unto him, Lo, we have left all, and followed thee; what then shall we have? 28 And Jesus said unto them, Verily I say unto you, that ye who have followed me, in the regeneration when the Son of man shall sit on the throne of his glory, ye also shall sit upon twelve thrones, judging the twelve tribes of Israel. 29 And every one that hath left houses, or brethren, or sisters, or father, or mother, or children, or lands, for my name's sake, shall receive a hundredfold, and shall inherit eternal life. 30 But many shall be last that are first; and first that are last.

The disciples had witnessed a tragic incident. They had seen a young man who had been offered eternal life but who had been ready to barter his soul for gold. Jesus now startles them by the statement of a truth which is illustrated by the scene they had witnessed, "Verily I say unto you, It is hard for a rich man to enter into the kingdom of heaven." This was particularly surprising to Jews. They imagined that wealth was a positive proof of the favor of God. What, then, could Jesus mean? He did not intend to teach that the possession of riches is sinful, nor that poverty is necessarily virtuous, nor that private property is a social wrong. He meant to indicate that riches may possibly keep their possessor from Christian discipleship and that one who seeks to satisfy himself with wealth, one "who trusts in riches" cannot enter the Kingdom of God. Jesus even adds a pardonable hyperbole, "It is easier for a camel to go through a needle's eye, than for a rich man to enter into the kingdom of God." One who would enter that Kingdom must be as a little child; he must abandon all trust in self, in self-attainment, in self-righteousness. He must be willing to sacrifice anything which stands between himself and Jesus Christ. When the disciples hear it they are astonished, saying, "Who then can be saved?" Our Lord replies, "With men this is impossible; but with God all things are possible." It does require resolution and decision and sacrifice, but God is ready to supply all needed grace; his Spirit can give strength to those who turn to him in trust.

As the rich man sweeps away sorrowfully in his costly robes, Peter looks upon him with apparent scorn, and turns to Jesus with self-complacency to say, "Lo, we have left all, and followed thee; what then shall we have?" It was not a noble question. It expressed a commercial, worldly spirit; but Jesus refrains from uttering a rebuke; a moment later he will correct Peter by telling him the story of the laborers in the vineyard; but first of all he gives to Peter a promise, and some of the followers of Christ today need to be assured by that promise. Sometimes a whisper steals into their hearts and they feel like asking what recompense they are to receive for their sacrifices made for the sake of Christ. Jesus replies with a kingly promise. He declares that "in the regeneration," in the age to come, when Jesus has returned and has made all things new, then those who have followed him through the scenes of present trial and sacrifice will share with him the glory of his throne. Nor was the promise for his immediate followers alone. It is for everyone who has sacrificed for his sake; all such will "receive a hundredfold" and will "inherit eternal life." Jesus adds, however, a word of warning; Peter must beware of self-confident pride. "Many shall be last that are first; and first that are last." That is to say, many, like Peter, who have had the opportunity of being nearest to Christ in this present life may not receive the greatest reward. Men will be judged according to faithfulness. Still more solemn is the warning to such as the rich man, who cling to their wealth and refuse the service of the King. Their power and riches put them now in the first place of opportunity. They may be the last to accept Christ and the eternal life which he offers.

3. THE PARABLE OF THE LABORERS IN THE VINEYARD   Ch. 20:1-16

1 For the kingdom of heaven is like unto a man that was a householder, who went out early in the morning to hire laborers into his vineyard. 2 And when he had agreed with the laborers for a shilling a day, he sent them into his vineyard. 3 And he went out about the third hour, and saw others standing in the marketplace idle; 4 and to them he said, Go ye also into the vineyard, and whatsoever is right I will give you. And they went their way. 5 Again he went out about the sixth and the ninth hour, and did likewise. 6 And about the eleventh hour he went out, and found others standing; and he saith unto them, Why stand ye here all the day idle? 7 They say unto him, Because no man hath hired us. He saith unto them, Go ye also into the vineyard. 8 And when even was come, the lord of the vineyard saith unto his steward, Call the laborers, and pay them their hire, beginning from the last unto the first. 9 And when they came that were hired about the eleventh hour, they received every man a shilling. 10 And when the first came, they supposed that they would receive more; and they likewise received every man a shilling. 11 And when they received it, they murmured against the householder, 12 saying, These last have spent but one hour, and thou hast made them equal unto us, who have borne the burden of the day and the scorching heat. 13 But he answered and said to one of them, Friend, I do thee no wrong: didst not thou agree with me for a shilling?   14 Take up that which is thine, and go thy way; it is my will to give unto this last, even as unto thee.   15 Is it not lawful for me to do what I will with mine own? or is thine eye evil, because I am good?   16 So the last shall be first, and the first last.

The interpretation of this parable has been found difficult simply because it has been separated from the story of the rich young man and from the question of Peter to which it really belongs.   It was really designed to indicate the peril of refusing to enter the service of Christ and the danger of a commercial spirit in seeking for rewards in such service.   The story illustrates the great principle stated in the verse which precedes and in the verse with which it closes, "Many shall be last that are first; and first that are last."   Peter seemed to imagine that, because he had sacrificed for Christ, the Master was bound to give him a great reward.   Jesus did promise the reward, but he wished to rebuke the spirit which prompted one to serve, not in love and gratitude, but for the sake of the recompense which may be given.   He tells the story of the laborers who early in the morning made a hard and fast bargain for "a shilling a day," and of others who were engaged at the third and sixth and ninth and even at the eleventh hour, who made no agreement with the householder, but who trusted in his honesty and generosity, and who when the evening was come received as much as those who had been hired in the early morning.   The latter complained, not because they failed to receive the wage for which they had bargained, but because others who had rendered a less service had received an equal reward.   Thus Jesus would correct the commercial spirit which sometimes animates his followers.   He shows that everyone will receive all that he deserves, all, indeed, for which he may bargain, but there will be surprises; not that anyone receives so little, but that some will receive so much.

He is absolutely sovereign in bestowing his eternal rewards. He recognizes that some have less opportunity for the service; their ability and the time of their service is limited; but if they trust in him and depend upon his grace, they will be surprised at the liberality of the King. Rewards are certain, but they are not the true motive of service. We should follow the King and seek to please him because this is in itself the highest and truest life, but chiefly because he has done so much for us. Gratitude will make sacrifice easy. His love can be trusted for a surprising and unmerited reward.

F. JESUS TEACHES TRUE GREATNESS
Ch. 20:17-28

17 And as Jesus was going up to Jerusalem, he took the twelve disciples apart, and on the way he said unto them, 18 Behold, we go up to Jerusalem; and the Son of man shall be delivered unto the chief priests and scribes; and they shall condemn him to death, 19 and shall deliver him unto the Gentiles to mock, and to scourge, and to crucify: and the third day he shall be raised up.

20 Then came to him the mother of the sons of Zebedee with her sons, worshipping him, *and asking a certain thing of him. 21 And he said unto her, What wouldest thou? She saith unto him, Command that these my two sons may sit, one on thy right hand, and one on thy left hand, in thy kingdom. 22 But Jesus answered and said, Ye know not what ye ask. Are ye able to drink the cup that I am about to drink? They say unto him, We are able. 23 He saith unto them, My cup indeed ye shall drink: but to sit on my right hand, and on* my *left hand, is not mine to give; but* it *is for them for whom it hath been prepared of my Father. 24 And when the ten heard it, they were moved with indignation concerning the two brethren. 25 But Jesus called them unto him, and said, Ye know that the rulers of the Gentiles lord it over them, and their great ones exercise authority over them. 26 Not so shall it be among you: but whosoever would become great among you shall*

be your minister;   27 and whosoever would be first among
you shall be your servant: 28 even as the Son of man
came not to be ministered unto, but to minister, and to give
his life a ransom for many.

The request of Salome that her two sons might occupy
the chief places in the coming Kingdom of Christ was
made at the very time that Jesus had again predicted his
suffering and death. This often has been called the third
prediction, but more accurately it is the fourth recorded by
Matthew, and is evidently an example of the repeated references made by Christ since he gave the first great disclosure at Caesarea Philippi. Here details of cruelty are
added. Not only is he to die, but he is to be mocked and
scourged and crucified. That Jesus saw so minutely all
the agonies awaiting him, enhances the picture of his
matchless heroism as he moves forward with such majestic
tread to accomplish his redeeming work.

That this request was made for James and John at such
a time marks the contrast between the self-sacrifice of the
King and the self-seeking of his followers, and it adds
meaning to the message which he now delivers relative to
the nature of true greatness.

There are aspects of beauty in the request made by
Salome. It discloses a mother's fondness which assumes
that nothing could be too good for her sons. It also reveals a mother's faith. In that prophet of Nazareth, whom
the rulers hated and despised, Salome saw one who was yet
to be King of kings and Lord of lords. She wished her
sons to have the highest places in that Kingdom, and this
is a desire which all parents may properly share. However, it did betray on the part of James and John, for
whom this mother was speaking, much of pride and jealousy and misunderstanding, and these Jesus lovingly rebukes. He addresses to them the question, "Are ye able
to drink the cup that I am about to drink?" They assure
him that they are able to share that cup of suffering. He

then explains to them that while indeed that cup is for
them to drink, the honor which they claim is not to be
given in mere caprice, nor to be arbitrarily assigned; it
must be earned. The high places in his Kingdom are not
matters of appointment but of achievement; they are not
secured by influence but by merit. "To sit on my right
hand, and on my left hand, is not mine to give; but it is
for them for whom it hath been prepared of my Father."
The rewards indeed may be given at last by Christ, but
they will not be given independently of real desert; for
time and eternity, the highest places in his Kingdom are
prepared for those by whom they are deserved.

This request of James and John fills their fellow disciples with indignation; but we are not to conclude that this
was "righteous indignation"; they are not merely troubled
because James and John are lacking in discernment, because their request is unjust, because their attitude is selfish. It seems that "the ten" are equally mistaken, equally
at fault; they are jealous; they covet and claim for themselves exactly the thing James and John have requested.
We are commonly tempted to be most indignant at those
faults in others of which we ourselves are guilty.

Jesus does not rebuke his disciples, but he takes the
occasion to declare the law of true greatness. This he
contrasts with the standards of the world, by which his
followers are ever in danger of being affected. Among
the Gentiles, among the nations, those are accounted as
the leaders, those are called great, who rule over others
and who are served by many; but among the followers of
Christ different ideals must prevail; those are the greatest
who are of the most service to others. In contrast with
heathen standards Jesus sets forth a principle, which may
be translated, "Whosoever would become great among you
shall be your servant: and whosoever would be first among
you shall be your slave." Service is the law of greatness
in the Kingdom of Christ; and from this law the King was
not exempt. Rather, he is himself the great Exemplar,

"Even as the Son of man came not to be ministered unto, but to minister, and to give his life a ransom for many." This willing sacrifice, this death in the place of many, this redeeming love, recognized and accepted by his followers, is the motive for service, and it is likewise the measure of true greatness. We are not Christians because we serve others; we serve others because we are Christians. Self-sacrifice and helpfulness are not substitutes for faith in Christ; they are the natural expressions of our faith and love. The more humble and patient and faithful our service, the nearer we ever shall be to him whose greatness is supreme, who loved us, and gave himself up for us.

G. JESUS GIVES SIGHT TO THE BLIND
Ch. 20:29-34

29 And as they went out from Jericho, a great multitude followed him. 30 And behold, two blind men sitting by the way side, when they heard that Jesus was passing by, cried out, saying, Lord, have mercy on us, thou son of David. 31 And the multitude rebuked them, that they should hold their peace: but they cried out the more, saying, Lord, have mercy on us, thou son of David. 32 And Jesus stood still, and called them, and said, What will ye that I should do unto you? 33 They say unto him, Lord, that our eyes may be opened. 34 And Jesus, being moved with compassion, touched their eyes; and straightway they received their sight, and followed him.

The journey through Perea has ended; Jesus is nearing Jerusalem; the last great city has been passed, but as he departs from Jericho he performs a cure which illustrates his kingly power and reveals his tender sympathy. Two blind men cry out to him for mercy. One of these elsewhere is called Bartimaeus. The spiritual sight of these men seems to be clearer than that of the nation which is about to reject its King, for they recognize him as the true Messiah; they salute him as the "son of David," they trust in his divine power, and they receive his gracious help and are instantly delivered from their distress.

This miracle is also a parable of the saving work of Christ. He opens the "eyes of the understanding" and gives spiritual sight to those who need to see life clearly with its duties, its demands, and its problems in relation to man and to God. There is, first of all, the picture of pitiful need; poor and helpless because blind, with none to sympathize and none to aid, these men form a striking picture of those today who are lacking spiritual sight. Nearby, in striking contrast, stands the majestic form of the King; he is passing for the last time; he is able to heal if only he can be reached.

Then there is the picture of the obstacles to be overcome, of the doubts and difficulties that lie in the way of those who need the healing touch of Christ. "The multitude rebuked them, that they should hold their peace." Often do those who yearn for light and healing hear words to discourage and suggestions which lead to hopelessness and despair.

Then there is the picture of eager determination, "They cried out the more, saying, Lord, have mercy on us, thou son of David."

Lastly is the picture of complete relief. "Jesus, being moved with compassion, touched their eyes; and straightway they received their sight, and followed him." How many likewise have found the Master able and willing to give them spiritual vision; their eyes have been opened to see things unseen and eternal, to follow the Master with joyful footsteps as they journey toward the celestial city where they will see the King in his beauty and will be like him when they see him as he is.

X
THE REJECTION
OF THE KING

Chs. 21 to 23

A. THREE ACTED PARABLES OF WARNING
Ch. 21:1-22

1. THE ROYAL ENTRY   Ch. 21:1-11

1 And when they drew nigh unto Jerusalem, and came unto Bethphage, unto the mount of Olives, then Jesus sent two disciples, 2 saying unto them, Go into the village that is over against you, and straightway ye shall find an ass tied, and a colt with her: loose them, *and bring* them *unto me. 3 And if any one say aught unto you, ye shall say, The Lord hath need of them; and straightway he will send them. 4 Now this is come to pass, that it might be fulfilled which was spoken through the prophet, saying,*
5. Tell ye the daughter of Zion,
*   Behold, thy King cometh unto thee,*
*   Meek, and riding upon an ass,*
*   And upon a colt the foal of an ass.*
6 And the disciples went, and did even as Jesus appointed them, 7 and brought the ass, and the colt, and put on them their garments; and he sat thereon. 8 And the most part of the multitude spread their garments in the way; and others cut branches from the trees, and spread them in the way. 9 And the multitudes that went before him, and that followed, cried, saying, Hosanna to the son of David: Blessed is he that cometh in the name of the Lord; Hosanna in the highest. 10 And when he was come into Jerusalem, all the city was stirred, saying, Who is this? 11 And the multitudes said, This is the prophet, Jesus, from Nazareth of Galilee.

No incident in the life of our Lord is more in harmony with the purpose of Matthew than the royal entry into Jerusalem. Of course it forms an essential part of the story of all the Gospels, but in none does it constitute a more definite climax or conform to a more evident design.

Matthew is the Gospel of the King, and here Jesus issues a royal command; he makes a royal progress; he receives a royal acclaim. To his command it is assumed that no refusal is possible; he enters the city mounted and attended as an Oriental monarch; he is hailed by the multitude as the Son of David, the King, and as worthy of supreme homage and praise.

Matthew is the Gospel of Fulfillment, and this incident is shown to correspond in minutest detail to a prophecy which is here quoted. However, Matthew is also the Gospel which emphasizes the rejection of Jesus; and here after the deadly hatred of his enemies has been revealed; after the predictions of his death have been so solemnly repeated; even while the multitudes shout with passing emotion, the silence of the rulers is ominous of tragedy. Jesus evidently is offering himself to the nation, but it is about to refuse him and to allow him to be destroyed. By this temporary outburst of popular enthusiasm no reader is for a moment deceived. Upon the bright picture there rests the shadow of the cross.

This royal entry was an acted parable. No one supposes that Jesus meant the borrowed colt, or the caparisons of rustic garments, or the peasants who attended him, were to be parts of the furnishings of an Oriental court. They were the symbols of royalty by which he definitely presented himself to his people as the promised Messiah; he was making an appeal for the trust and obedience and homage of human hearts; but he was warning the rulers that in rejecting him they would be rejecting their King; they would be defeating their highest hopes. Someday, however, he is to appear in glory; that humble pageant which moves through the streets of Old Jerusalem is but the faint symbol of the true coming of the King. Those who now accept him and offer him the willing homage of their hearts will then rejoice and will enter with gladness into the blessedness of his perfected Kingdom.

2. CLEANSING THE TEMPLE   Ch. 21:12-17

12 And Jesus entered into the temple of God, and cast out all them that sold and bought in the temple, and over-threw the tables of the money-changers, and the seats of them that sold the doves; 13 and he saith unto them, It is written, My house shall be called a house of prayer: but ye make it a den of robbers. 14 And the blind and the lame came to him in the temple; and he healed them. 15 But when the chief priests and the scribes saw the wonder-ful things that he did, and the children that were crying in the temple and saying, Hosanna to the son of David; they were moved with indignation, 16 and said unto him, Hearest thou what these are saying? And Jesus saith unto them, Yea: did ye never read, Out of the mouth of babes and sucklings thou hast perfected praise? 17 And he left them, and went forth out of the city to Bethany, and lodged there.

The abuse, which Jesus here rebukes, had arisen from what was at first a public convenience, namely, the sale to pilgrims in the neighborhood of the Temple, of sacri-fices which they could not bring from their distant homes. Gradually the traffic had pressed nearer until the mer-chants had entered the Temple area and were desecrating the sacred courts by their distracting noises, their greed, their extortions, and their fraud.

The act of our Lord in expelling these intruders from the sacred courts was not merely an example of power which one man, conscious of the right and justice of his cause, may exercise over those whom guilt of conscience makes weak and timid; nor yet was this merely the work of a reformer who was correcting an evil custom. It was on the part of our Lord an acted parable. It was a rebuke of the nation, the spiritual state of which was indicated by their apparent disregard of the sacredness of the house of God. It was a symbol, warning of the judgment which was to be visited upon them because of their apostasy and unbelief.

Furthermore, this was a claim on the part of Jesus to be the real Lord of the Temple. He identifies himself with God whom he declares to be his own Father and he supports this claim by proceeding to perform miracles of healing within the Temple courts. He is thus making a public claim, as on the day before, to be the promised Messiah, and he emphasizes this claim by his reply to the rulers when they rebuke him for allowing the children to hail him with their "Hosannas." He declares that they are justified in welcoming him as "the son of David"; and he further quotes, as applying to himself, a psalm which speaks of the universal sovereignty predicted as belonging to man, a psalm, however, which was to be fulfilled by the Messiah, and which pictured the unlimited rule which he would exercise as the appointed King. Jesus declares that such praises have the divine warrant and sanction and are appropriately bestowed upon himself. Such claims were so obvious, the meaning of his symbolic actions were becoming so clear, that the rulers were filled with even more deadly hate. It was, therefore, not merely for the sake of rest but to avoid a more open conflict that Jesus withdrew for the night to lodge with his friends in Bethany.

3. THE BARREN FIG TREE   Ch. 21:18-22

18 Now in the morning as he returned to the city, he hungered. 19 And seeing a fig tree by the way side, he came to it, and found nothing thereon, but leaves only; and he saith unto it, Let there be no fruit from thee henceforward for ever. And immediately the fig tree withered away. 20 And when the disciples saw it, they marvelled, saying, How did the fig tree immediately wither away? 21 And Jesus answered and said unto them, Verily I say unto you, If ye have faith, and doubt not, ye shall not only do what is done to the fig tree, but even if ye shall say unto

this mountain, Be thou taken up and cast into the sea, it
shall be done. 22 And all things, whatsoever ye shall ask
in prayer, believing, ye shall receive.

The withering of the fruitless fig tree was not only a
miracle wrought by the power of Christ, it was a parable
of the punishment which was to be visited upon Israel for
its sin and unbelief. On a fig tree the green fruit is first
formed and then the foliage is produced, so that fruit
might be expected on a tree in full leaf; but on this tree
Jesus found none. This fruitless tree with its show of
leaves was, however, a symbol of Israel; the nation had
made a profession of holiness; it had maintained its pretentious ritual; it had preserved a form of godliness, but
when the King had come, he had found none of the real
fruits of righteousness; and now his rejection was to be followed by the national disaster of which the withering of
the tree was a parable and a warning.

The story may contain a note of admonition for all who
now bear the name of Christ; their lives must correspond
with their profession, their deeds with their claims. However, for his immediate followers the King found in the
miracle a message of inspiration and cheer. As his disciples marveled at his power he declared that similar
power was at their command; it was the power of believing
prayer, it could remove mountains; not that a literal attempt was to be made, but that it could do things otherwise impossible. Of course there are other familiar
conditions, but our temptation is to limit too far the implications of the promise, "All things, whatsoever ye shall
ask in prayer, believing, ye shall receive."

B. THE CLAIMS OF DIVINE AUTHORITY
Ch. 21:23-27

23 And when he was come into the temple, the chief
priests and the elders of the people came unto him as he
was teaching, and said, By what authority doest thou these

> things? and who gave thee this authority? 24 And Jesus
> answered and said unto them, I also will ask you one ques-
> tion, which if ye tell me, I likewise will tell you by what
> authority I do these things. 25 The baptism of John,
> whence was it? from heaven or from men? And they rea-
> soned with themselves, saying, If we shall say, From
> heaven; he will say unto us, Why then did ye not believe
> him? 26 But if we shall say, From men; we fear the multi-
> tude; for all hold John as a prophet. 27 And they an-
> swered Jesus, and said, We know not. He also said unto
> them, Neither tell I you by what authority I do these things.

As Jesus reaches the city he is at once attacked by all
the Jewish rulers and leaders. They challenge him to state
by what authority he is acting in receiving honors as the
Messiah or in driving the traders from the Temple as on
the day past. Their question is framed with subtle skill,
"By what authority doest thou these things? and who gave
thee this authority?" They place Jesus in a dilemma; if
he claims that authority had been delegated to him, then
he may be accused of disloyalty and of schism in supplant-
ing the recognized "authorities" of the Jewish state; if he
claims inherent divine authority, as one with God, he may
be condemned for blasphemy.

Jesus silences his enemies with a question which involves them in a counterdilemma, "The baptism of John,
whence was it? from heaven or from men?" They cannot
say "from heaven," for they had rejected John; they do not
dare to say "from men," for they fear the people by whom
John was regarded as a prophet. They try to escape by
the cowardly reply, "We know not." Agnosticism is usually cowardly and deserving of little respect.

Jesus does more than silence them; he answers them.
His question is no irrelevant riddle by which he meets a
difficulty and delays the necessity of a reply. He definitely
implies that the authority of John was divine, and that his
own authority is the same; but as they were afraid to deny
the divine authority of John they are powerless to deny

that of Jesus; and further he implies that if they had accepted the message of John, they would be prepared to accept Jesus. It is true that if we are afraid to accept the logical conclusions of our doubts and denials, we never can hope to discover truth.

Jesus further rebukes and exposes his enemies. When they say, "We know not," Jesus knows, and they know, and the crowd knows, that they are not honest; the Lord has laid bare their hypocrisy; he has made it perfectly evident that the real question at issue is not authority but obedience. The enemies of Jesus pretend that they want to know more of his credentials; they really want to discredit and to entrap him. The modern enemies of our Lord declare that they want more proofs, more evidence; what they really lack is love for him and submission to his will. Those who do not repent when John preaches, will not believe when Jesus offers to save. The world needs today, not more proof of divine authority, but more obedience to the divine will.

Jesus absolutely discredited his enemies in the sight of the people. They were the constituted authorities in all matters civil and religious, and yet they were made to confess publicly that they were not competent to judge a clear, familiar, important case relating to religious authority. They really abdicated their position. They, therefore, were disqualified to pass an opinion on the exactly parallel case of the authority of Jesus. Jesus had defeated them with their own weapon. No wonder that subsequently, when on trial before such judges, he refused to answer them a word. He had shown their incompetence, their insincerity, their unbelief. Honest doubters are deserving of sympathy; but professed seekers after truth, who are unwilling to accept the consequences of belief, should expect to receive no further light. An increasing knowledge of divine truth is conditioned upon humble submission of the heart and the will to what already has been revealed.

C. THREE PARABLES OF JUDGMENT
Chs. 21:28 to 22:14

1. THE TWO SONS Ch. 21:28-32

28 But what think ye? A man had two sons; and he came to the first, and said, Son, go work to-day in the vineyard. 29 And he answered and said, I will not: but afterward he repented himself, and went. 30 And he came to the second, and said likewise. And he answered and said, I go, sir: and went not. 31 Which of the two did the will of his father? They say, The first. Jesus saith unto them, Verily I say unto you, that the publicans and the harlots go into the kingdom of God before you. 32 For John came unto you in the way of righteousness, and ye believed him not; but the publicans and the harlots believed him: and ye, when ye saw it, did not even repent yourselves afterward, that ye might believe him.

In replying to the hostile rulers, Jesus has made a claim of divine authority; he now adds three parables which condemn his enemies and pronounce judgment upon them and the nation. The first is very brief, but pointed. Two sons are described: one, who refused to obey his father, repented and served him; the other promised to serve but continued to disobey; to the one Jesus compared those of the publicans and harlots who, after lives of notorious sin, had repented at the preaching of John; to the other Jesus compared the rulers, who with all their profession of righteousness and with all their boasted ceremonies, continued to live in real rebellion against God. He thus rebuked the rulers for their pretense that they were willing to accept Jesus if only sure that his authority was divine; he declares that their real difficulty is unwillingness to obey the divine will. He affirms that they, and all who like them are impenitent and insincere, can never enter the Kingdom of God; he promises that even the worst sinners may repent and be saved.

2. THE WICKED HUSBANDMEN   Ch. 21:33-46

33 Hear another parable: There was a man that was a householder, who planted a vineyard, and set a hedge about it, and digged a winepress in it, and built a tower, and let it out to husbandmen, and went into another country. 34 And when the season of the fruits drew near, he sent his servants to the husbandmen, to receive his fruits. 35 And the husbandmen took his servants, and beat one, and killed another, and stoned another. 36 Again, he sent other servants more than the first: and they did unto them in like manner. 37 But afterward he sent unto them his son, saying, They will reverence my son. 38 But the husbandmen, when they saw the son, said among themselves, This is the heir; come, let us kill him, and take his inheritance. 39 And they took him, and cast him forth out of the vineyard, and killed him. 40 When therefore the lord of the vineyard shall come, what will he do unto those husbandmen? 41 They say unto him, He will miserably destroy those miserable men, and will let out the vineyard unto other husbandmen, who shall render him the fruits in their seasons. 42 Jesus saith unto them, Did ye never read in the scriptures,

The stone which the builders rejected,
The same was made the head of the corner;
This was from the Lord,
And it is marvellous in our eyes?

43 Therefore say I unto you, The kingdom of God shall be taken away from you, and shall be given to a nation bringing forth the fruits thereof. 44 And he that falleth on this stone shall be broken to pieces: but on whomsoever it shall fall, it will scatter him as dust. 45 And when the chief priests and the Pharisees heard his parables, they perceived that he spake of them. 46 And when they sought to lay hold on him, they feared the multitudes, because they took him for a prophet.

To the malicious challenge of his enemies, Jesus has already replied, claiming for himself divine authority and condemning them for their guilty unbelief. He now adds a second parable more clearly stating his claims and more solemnly rebuking these hostile rulers and pronouncing judgment upon the nation they represent. He tells the story of a householder who establishes and equips a vineyard and lets it to tenants. He lives at a distance and expects as rent a certain portion of the vintage. However, when he sends for the fruit, his messengers are abused and killed; at last his own son is slain. He determines to come and to exact justice and to deliver his vineyard to tenants who are more worthy.

The parable was so plain that even the enemies of Jesus understood its meaning. The householder is Jehovah; the vineyard is Israel; the husbandmen are the rulers to whom the nation had been intrusted; the servants are the prophets sent to summon the people to repent and to render to God the fruits of righteousness; the son is Jesus himself, who thus claimed a unique relation to God, distinct from the prophets and all human messengers, and who definitely foresees his own rejection and death; the return of the householder is the coming visitation of divine judgment and the rejection of Israel, and the call of the Gentiles. It is aside from the present purpose of Jesus to refer to the individual Jews who will accept him and to the future conversion of the nation of which Paul writes. He wishes now to emphasize his own rejection, and the guilt and punishment of the nation. He declares, however, that his death will issue in his exaltation and triumph; he is "the stone which the builders rejected, the same was made the head of the corner." He also warns his enemies that all who in unbelief stumble on that stone, all who reject him, will be "broken to pieces," and all who attempt to drag down that stone will be ground and scattered as dust.

3. The Marriage Feast Ch. 22:1-14

1 And Jesus answered and spake again in parables unto them, saying, 2 The kingdom of heaven is likened unto a

*certain king, who made a marriage feast for his son,   3 and
sent forth his servants to call them that were bidden to the
marriage feast: and they would not come.   4 Again he sent
forth other servants, saying, Tell them that are bidden, Behold, I have made ready my dinner; my oxen and my
fatlings are killed, and all things are ready: come to the
marriage feast.   5 But they made light of it, and went their
ways, one to his own farm, another to his merchandise;
6 and the rest laid hold on his servants, and treated them
shamefully, and killed them.   7 But the king was wroth;
and he sent his armies, and destroyed those murderers, and
burned their city.   8 Then saith he to his servants, The
wedding is ready, but they that were bidden were not
worthy.   9 Go ye therefore unto the partings of the highways, and as many as ye shall find, bid to the marriage
feast.   10 And those servants went out into the highways,
and gathered together all as many as they found, both bad
and good: and the wedding was filled with guests.   11 But
when the king came in to behold the guests, he saw there
a man who had not on a wedding-garment: 12 and he
saith unto him, Friend, how camest thou in hither not having a wedding-garment? And he was speechless.   13 Then
the king said to the servants, Bind him hand and foot, and
cast him out into the outer darkness; there shall be the
weeping and the gnashing of teeth.   14 For many are
called, but few chosen.*

The picture of the Kingdom of the Messiah as a banquet at which Israel would be seated and from which Gentiles would be excluded, was familiar enough to the Jews;
but Jesus reverses the figure with details reported only by
Matthew, and with the main purpose of pronouncing
judgment upon the nation which is rejecting him.

Matthew is the Gospel of the King and it is interesting to
note that the parable which Jesus now gives presents to us
a feast prepared by a King, it is indeed "a marriage feast
for his son"; while the companion picture in Luke describes merely a great supper given by "a certain man."
So the treatment of the invitation, according to the story

of Matthew, is a much more serious matter. It is despised and neglected while those who bear it are abused and killed. The consequent punishment of the offenders is more severe; they are destroyed and their city is burned. The whole incident is here narrated with marks of royalty which are in perfect harmony with the character of this Gospel.

The purpose of our Lord, as in the similar parable in Luke, is to show by the picture the guilt of the nation which is rejecting the invitation to enter the Kingdom of Heaven. He plainly indicates the consequent rejection of Israel, the suffering of the nation, and the destruction of Jerusalem. Quite as plainly it shows that from among the Gentiles many both good and bad will be gathered into the Christian church. There is, however, to be a final separation before the blessings of the Kingdom will be enjoyed. This is pictured by the fate of the man who was found among the guests but "who had not on a wedding-garment." He is cast "into the outer darkness." Those who are to enjoy the glory of the Kingdom must be arrayed in the robe of righteousness which the King requires and which he is ready to provide for all who accept of Christ. "For many are called, but few chosen." Eternal life is represented as a free choice on the part of man, and as a divine election on the part of God. As among the Jews "the many" rejected their Messiah, so among professed Christians there will be those who will lack the garment of righteous life and character and so will lose, at last, the approval of the King and the joys of his palace. Thus in this parable of the marriage feast Jesus predicts the judgment of Israel, the call of the Gentiles, and the demand for righteousness in those who are at last to share the glories of his Kingdom.

D. THREE ENSNARING QUESTIONS
Ch. 22:15-40

1. TRIBUTE TO CAESAR? Ch. 22:15-22

15 Then went the Pharisees, and took counsel how they might ensnare him in his talk. 16 And they send to him their disciples, with the Herodians, saying, Teacher, we know that thou art true, and teachest the way of God in truth, and carest not for any one: for thou regardest not the person of men. 17 Tell us therefore, What thinkest thou? Is it lawful to give tribute unto Cæsar, or not? 18 But Jesus perceived their wickedness, and said, Why make ye trial of me, ye hypocrites? 19 Show me the tribute money. And they brought unto him a denarius. 20 And he saith unto them, Whose is this image and superscription? 21 They say unto him, Cæsar's. Then saith he unto them, Render therefore unto Cæsar the things that are Cæsar's; and unto God the things that are God's. 22 And when they heard it, they marvelled, and left him, and went away.

Early in this memorable day of public teaching, Jesus has been attacked by the elders and chief priests and scribes; but he has defeated them, exposed them to ridicule, and indicted them as apostates and murderers. In their furious hate they would have him killed at once; but they fear the multitudes with whom Jesus is so popular. To compass his death, therefore, they must first discredit him with the people; they must entangle him in his teaching. Thus to entrap him, they now return with a series of three crafty questions; but Jesus evades each snare, he answers each question fairly and completely, and then asks a question by which his enemies are finally silenced.

The first question relates to the payment of tribute to the Roman Government. The more conservative Jews held that God was the ruler of Israel and that it was possibly wrong to pay taxes to support a heathen state. The more liberal party sided with the Herods, who owed their power to Rome. Therefore the enemies of Jesus send to him representatives of both parties, Pharisees and Herodians, so that if he avoids offending one party he will displease the other. They approach Jesus with the flattering assurance that he is so truthful and courageous that he will not hesitate to express his true convictions; and then they propose their artful question, "Is it lawful to give tribute unto Cæsar, or not?" Shall Jesus say, "Yes"? Then he will cease to be a popular idol, for the people loathe the hateful oppression of Rome. Shall Jesus say, "No"? Then his enemies will hurry him away to the Roman governor and the cross, as a traitor and a rebel. The dilemma seems complete; yet Jesus not only escapes the snare, but, in his reply, he enunciates a law for all time, "Render therefore unto Cæsar the things that are Caesar's; and unto God the things that are God's."

To make plain his meaning, Jesus first calls for a Roman coin, and asks whose image and superscription it bears. They, of course, reply, "Cæsar's." Jesus therefore insists that if they accept the coins of Caesar, they must pay taxes to Caesar. That is, if one accepts the protection of a government, and the privileges provided by a government, then one is under obligation to support that government. Christianity never should be identified with any political party or social theory, but Christians ever should take their stand for loyalty, for order, and for law.

It is not the whole of life, however, to "render . . . unto Cæsar the things that are Cæsar's"; one must also "render unto God the things that are God's." The latter higher allegiance includes the former. The enemies of Jesus suggested a conflict of duties; he showed that there was perfect harmony. He intimated, however, that there was danger of forgetting God, and our obligations to him of trust, service, worship, love. The true basis for citizenship is devotion to God, and no political theory or party allegiance can be taken as a substitute for loyalty to him. The enemies of Jesus were answered and rebuked, and his followers were given guidance for all the coming years.

2. Is There a Resurrection?   Ch. 22:23-33

23 On that day there came to him Sadducees, they that say that there is no resurrection: and they asked him, 24 saying, Teacher, Moses said, If a man die, having no children, his brother shall marry his wife, and raise up seed unto his brother. 25 Now there were with us seven brethren: and the first married and deceased, and having no seed left his wife unto his brother; 26 in like manner the second also, and the third, unto the seventh. 27 And after them all, the woman died. 28 In the resurrection therefore whose wife shall she be of the seven? for they all had her. 29 But Jesus answered and said unto them, Ye do err, not knowing the scriptures, nor the power of God. 30 For in the resurrection they neither marry, nor are given in marriage, but are as angels in heaven. 31 But as touching the resurrection of the dead, have ye not read that which was spoken unto you by God, saying, 32 I am the God of Abraham, and the God of Isaac, and the God of Jacob? God is not the God of the dead, but of the living. 33 And when the multitudes heard it, they were astonished at his teaching.

Jesus defeated the Pharisees and the Herodians. He is now attacked by the Sadducees, who were the priestly, and most powerful, party among the Jews. They questioned the immortality of the soul, and believed neither in angels nor in spirits; they represented the modern materialists. It is to be noted, however, that the question with which they approached Jesus is not in reference to immortality but to the resurrection of the body. They propose the case of a woman, married successively to seven brothers from each of whom she was separated by death; and they ask, "In the resurrection therefore whose wife shall she be of the seven?" They hope that Jesus will either deny the orthodox belief as to the resurrection or make some statement which will contradict the law of Moses which made the successive marriages lawful. The reply of Jesus is one which is applicable to many modern skeptics, "Ye do err, not knowing the scriptures, nor the power of God." This twofold ignorance caused them to imagine a contradiction which really did not exist. First, as to "the power of God": he is able to provide a life in which there is no death, or birth, or marriage, but where the relations are even higher than the most blessed relationship of earth. Such an existence, with its higher laws, is consistent with the facts and laws of our present life. Second, as to "the scriptures": what do they declare that God has promised to do? Jesus answers this question by quoting from the very system of law to which the Sadducees have referred, "I am the God of Abraham, and the God of Isaac, and the God of Jacob," and then he adds, "God is not the God of the dead." He means to establish the fact of the continued existence of the dead; yet not merely this, but to prove the resurrection of the dead. The latter is the question at issue. Life, as used by our Lord, indicated normal life, not that of a disembodied soul, but of an immortal soul clothed with a deathless body. "The living" are therefore the risen. The confident expectation of such a future state is based on our relation to God. If he is truly our God, and we are his people, the triumph of death is not real and permanent, but will be ended by the glory of a resurrection from the dead. Many beliefs which men scout because they seem to contradict known laws of science will some day be explained by the discovery of higher laws. It is for us to ask what has been written, and then to believe in the power of God to perform.

3. WHICH IS THE GREAT COMMANDMENT?
Ch. 22:34-40

34 But the Pharisees, when they heard that he had put the Sadducees to silence, gathered themselves together. 35 And one of them, a lawyer, asked him a question, trying him: 36 Teacher, which is the great commandment in the law? 37 And he said unto him, Thou shalt love the Lord thy God with all thy heart, and with all thy soul, and with all thy mind. 38 This is the great and first commandment.

39 And a second like unto it is this, Thou shalt love thy neighbor as thyself. 40 On these two commandments the whole law hangeth, and the prophets.

The third question addressed to our Lord embodies a familiar problem which the scribes liked to discuss, namely, as to which among the commandments is the most important. Their code of morality was most complex, and consisted in an infinite number of minute requirements and regulations. The reply of Jesus is startling in its insight and its simplicity; he declares that the whole duty of man, the full sum of moral obligations, the essence of all divine law, is embodied and expressed in one word, "love." This love must be exercised in two directions, first toward God, and second toward men. All the Ten Commandments and all other divine requirements are but expressions of this one supreme principle. "The first commandment" therefore is love to God: this is the fulfillment of the "first table of the law"; but "the second" is inseparable from it; it comprehends the rest of the commandments, as it requires love for men. What must have startled the hearers was the fact that both "these two commandments" are quoted from the Old Testament, and the first was so familiar that it was repeated twice daily by all Jews. So simple and so unquestioned is the principle of love, by which all moral problems can be solved, by which all moral obligations can be fulfilled.

E. THE QUESTION OF JESUS   Ch. 22:41-46

41 Now while the Pharisees were gathered together, Jesus asked them a question, 42 saying, What think ye of the Christ? whose son is he? They say unto him, The son of David. 43 He saith unto them, How then doth David in the Spirit call him Lord, saying,
44 The Lord said unto my Lord,
   Sit thou on my right hand,
   Till I put thine enemies underneath thy feet?

45 If David then calleth him Lord, how is he his son? 46 And no one was able to answer him a word, neither durst any man from that day forth ask him any more questions.

Three questions have been asked to entangle Jesus and to discredit him with the people; his answers not only foil his enemies but declare universal principles for the guidance of his followers. The first relates to political and civic duties, the second concerns natural and physical laws, the third is in the realm of morals and ethics. Now Jesus proposes a counterquestion; it embodies the supreme problem in the sphere of philosophy and religion. The question concerns the person of Christ: Is he to be regarded as man or God, or as at once God and man? Where is Christ to be placed in the scale of being? Or, as Jesus voiced the problem, how could David speak of the coming Messiah as both his Son and his Lord? There was but one answer; there can be but one: Christ is both human and divine, he is the Son of David and also the Son of God. The incarnation is the only solution of our most serious difficulties in the sphere of religious belief. Jesus has absolutely defeated and silenced his enemies; and he concludes the long controversy by this expression of his supreme claim to be the Christ of whom David has prophesied, the Messiah, the King.

F. THE WARNING AGAINST THE PHARISEES
Ch. 23:1-12

1 Then spake Jesus to the multitudes and to his disciples, 2 saying, The scribes and the Pharisees sit on Moses' seat: 3 all things therefore whatsoever they bid you, these do and observe: but do not ye after their works; for they say, and do not. 4 Yea, they bind heavy burdens and grievous to be borne, and lay them on men's shoulders; but they themselves will not move them with their finger. 5 But all their works they do to be seen of men: for they make broad their phylacteries, and enlarge the borders of their gar-

ments, *6 and love the chief place at feasts, and the chief seats in the synagogues, 7 and the salutations in the marketplaces, and to be called of men, Rabbi. 8 But be not ye called Rabbi: for one is your teacher, and all ye are brethren. 9 And call no man your father on the earth: for one is your Father, even he who is in heaven. 10 Neither be ye called masters: for one is your master, even the Christ. 11 But he that is greatest among you shall be your servant. 12 And whosoever shall exalt himself shall be humbled; and whosoever shall humble himself shall be exalted.*

In no other Gospel is the guilt of rejecting Jesus made more prominent; in none is the cruel opposition of his enemies more emphasized; and correspondingly, no other writer records more severe condemnation uttered by Jesus against the hostile rulers. These rebukes reach their climax in this chapter. Jesus has vanquished his opponents in argument; he now publicly warns his followers against them and then pronounces upon them a series of seven solemn "woes." The essence of his rebuke is embodied in the repeated term of bitter reproach "hypocrites."

It is the hypocrisy of the Pharisees which Jesus so severely condemns. It has always been remarked that the most bitter denunciations of our Lord are addressed to the men whose outward lives were respectable and whose religious professions were the loudest. We are to be on our guard, however, against concluding that open vice and flagrant sin are better than even selfish and proud morality. We are to be warned, however, that religious privileges and exalted position involve large responsibility, and that immorality and sin are especially repulsive when they accompany proud claims of spiritual leadership and ostentatious performances of religious rites.

The hypocrisy of the Pharisees is stated in the first words of warning which Jesus spoke to his followers. He is careful, however, to distinguish between the office of those false religious teachers and their actual practice. He recognizes that they are worthy of being heard, so far as they upheld the Mosaic law. They were said to "sit on Moses' seat"; that is, to be acting in his place and to proclaim his laws as teachers of the revealed will of God. Insofar as they were true to such a sacred office they were to be obeyed. It was their practices, however, which were to be avoided, especially their failure to follow their own precepts. While guilty of moral faults, they also were to be condemned for adding to the requirements of the law minute and countless rules, most of which they had received by tradition, which together formed a wearisome and confusing round of ritual observances and bound the conduct of men every hour of the day and in every act of life, so that they constituted a burden which was intolerable and which the Pharisees made no effort to relieve. Such teachers, lacking in sincerity and in sympathy, were to be neither trusted nor followed, least of all to be imitated.

Jesus further warns against their ostentation, "All their works they do to be seen of men." Jesus gives two examples of this pretentious ceremonialism. One is that "They make broad their phylacteries"; by which he referred to the cases of leather which the Jews bound upon their arms and upon their foreheads, and in which were written certain extracts from the law. They also "enlarge the borders of their garments," making a display of their careful observance of the minutest requirements of the ceremonial law. Jesus also warns against their pride and love of praise, as they desire the chief places at feasts and in synagogues and delight in public notice and in being recognized as religious leaders.

In warning his followers against these Pharisees, our Lord specially emphasizes the last point. His warning is applicable in the present day. When he insists, however, that no man is to be called "Rabbi" or "Father" or "Master," the terms are not to be interpreted too literally. These very words might be used as titles of respect or to indicate definite duties and positions of responsibility and trust; but the warning is needed today which is implied in the prohibition which our Lord here gives. There has always been danger in the church arising from love of place and from a desire for special recognition and the longing to be regarded as superior to other followers of Christ. Our Lord does remind us of our equality as believers and that in the truest sense, he alone is the Teacher; he alone is to be regarded with reverence: he alone is Master and Lord. In contrast with the spirit of the Pharisee the follower of Christ is to be humble, the greatest among them is to take the part of a servant, lowliness is the true path to exaltation.

G. THE WOES UPON THE PHARISEES
Ch. 23:13-39

13 But woe unto you, scribes and Pharisees, hypocrites! because ye shut the kingdom of heaven against men: for ye enter not in yourselves, neither suffer ye them that are entering in to enter.

15 Woe unto you, scribes and Pharisees, hypocrites! for ye compass sea and land to make one proselyte; and when he is become so, ye make him twofold more a son of hell than yourselves.

16 Woe unto you, ye blind guides, that say, Whosoever shall swear by the temple, it is nothing; but whosoever shall swear by the gold of the temple, he is a debtor. 17 Ye fools and blind: for which is greater, the gold, or the temple that hath sanctified the gold? 18 And, Whosoever shall swear by the altar, it is nothing; but whosoever shall swear by the gift that is upon it, he is a debtor. 19 Ye blind: for which is greater, the gift, or the altar that sanctifieth the gift? 20 He therefore that sweareth by the altar, sweareth by it, and by all things thereon. 21 And he that sweareth by the temple, sweareth by it, and by him that dwelleth therein. 22 And he that sweareth by the heaven, sweareth by the throne of God, and by him that sitteth thereon.

23 Woe unto you, scribes and Pharisees, hypocrites! for

ye tithe mint and anise and cummin, and have left undone
the weightier matters of the law, justice, and mercy, and
faith: but these ye ought to have done, and not to have left
the other undone.   24 Ye blind guides, that strain out the
gnat, and swallow the camel!

25 Woe unto you, scribes and Pharisees, hypocrites! for
ye cleanse the outside of the cup and of the platter, but
within they are full from extortion and excess.   26 Thou
blind Pharisee, cleanse first the inside of the cup and of
the platter, that the outside thereof may become clean also.

27 Woe unto you, scribes and Pharisees, hypocrites! for
ye are like unto whited sepulchres, which outwardly appear
beautiful, but inwardly are full of dead men's bones, and of
all uncleanness.   28 Even so ye also outwardly appear
righteous unto men, but inwardly ye are full of hypocrisy
and iniquity.

29 Woe unto you, scribes and Pharisees, hypocrites! for
ye build the sepulchres of the prophets, and garnish the
tombs of the righteous, 30 and say, If we had been in the
days of our fathers, we should not have been partakers with
them in the blood of the prophets.   31 Wherefore ye witness to yourselves, that ye are sons of them that slew the
prophets.   32 Fill ye up then the measure of your fathers.
33 Ye serpents, ye offspring of vipers, how shall ye escape
the judgment of hell?   34 Therefore, behold, I send unto
you prophets, and wise men, and scribes: some of them
shall ye kill and crucify; and some of them shall ye scourge
in your synagogues, and persecute from city to city: 35
that upon you may come all the righteous blood shed on
the earth, from the blood of Abel the righteous unto the
blood of Zachariah son of Barachiah, whom ye slew between the sanctuary and the altar.   36 Verily I say unto
you, All these things shall come upon this generation.

37 O Jerusalem, Jerusalem, that killeth the prophets, and
stoneth them that are sent unto her! how often would I
have gathered thy children together, even as a hen gathereth her chickens under her wings, and ye would not!
38 Behold, your house is left unto you desolate.   39 For I
say unto you, Ye shall not see me henceforth, till ye shall
say, Blessed is he that cometh in the name of the Lord.

No more terrible denunciations ever fell from the lips of Jesus than those which are recorded in this chapter. It may be imagined how his enemies must have quailed before these burning words of righteous indignation. There is, however, no trace of malice, no suggested loss of self-control. The scene forms a necessary complement to the more familiar picture of the meekness and gentleness of Jesus. He is not to be suspected of showing any weak tolerance of sin. He was great enough to be angry with evil. He was brave enough to denounce duplicity and corruption in high places and among the rulers of the people. There is such a thing as "the wrath of the Lamb." Even in these stern judgments, however, there is some suggestion of pity and of sorrow, and the "woe" which Jesus pronounces possibly may be interpreted as meaning "Alas for you."

Yet these solemn sentences are of interest not merely for the light they throw upon the character of Christ, nor because they form the last words of the public ministry which began with Beatitudes and now ends with rebuke; but because they furnish for all coming ages a necessary warning against pretense and unreality in religion, against all ecclesiastical tyranny and proud proselyting bigotry, against all insincerity and shams.

1. The first of these "woes" is against religious leaders who actually make men irreligious. The picture is that of a great company moving toward the open gates of the Kingdom and led by the scribes and Pharisees, but the latter refuse to enter and obstruct the way and endeavor to close the gates. The enemies of Christ are really thus treating their followers by refusing to receive John the Baptist and by rejecting Jesus, both of whom came preaching repentance that men might be ready to enter the Kingdom. There are those today who profess the name of Christ, who even preach his Gospel, who, however, live so inconsistently, who are so uncharitable in their judgments, so narrow in their prejudices, so bitter in their enmities as to turn others away from Christ and his church.

2. The second of these "woes" rebukes the fanatical party spirit which masquerades as zeal for religion. The Pharisees spared no effort to win proselytes not to Judaism merely, but to their own sect, and they showed such bitterness and selfishness that those whom they won became more truly deserving of condemnation than they were before. So many today who press some peculiar religious propaganda and win adherence to their own narrow party imagine that they are serving God, whereas in reality their bigotry and spiritual pride infect and corrupt and debase those whose support they secure.

3. The third "woe" accuses the Pharisees of spiritual blindness, of pitiful, moral stupidity. It exhibits the absurdity of the casuistry which distinguishes between oaths which are binding and those which need not be regarded because differing slightly in form; as though one could break a promise to which he had sworn by one oath but was bound to perform the same promise if he swore by another even less solemn. The fault includes the perversion of conscience which is too prevalent at the present day, according to which it is felt that actual wrong can be affected by circumstances, that things absolutely sinful are justified under certain conditions, and that the laws of God are altered by accidents and details of time and place.

4. The first three "woes" deal with false teaching, the last three concern wrong actions; the fourth rebukes a fault both in precept and in practice. It warns against the loss of moral perspective. The Pharisees were in some particulars even more scrupulous than the law required; tithes were exacted from all who reaped the harvests of corn and of fruit, but the Pharisees extended their tithing to small garden herbs like mint and cummin. Jesus does not rebuke them for their excessive zeal. To be most scrupulous is not wrong in itself, but when it is combined with indifference to the broad principles of morality, then it is monstrous and forms the truest badge and proof of insincerity and hypocrisy.

5. The fifth "woe" is a warning against mere external

purity. It is folly to cleanse the outside of the cup and platter, thus to insist that they shall be ceremonially clean, when the contents of these vessels have been defiled by dishonesty, cruelty, and wrong. It is surely wise to maintain a proper demeanor and to preserve a fair reputation among men, but what is far more necessary is the maintenance of a clean heart and of purity in thought and motive and desire.

6. The sixth "woe" was a severe rebuke to all those who maintained merely an outward show of morality, while their inner lives were impure and full of uncleanness. It was the special fault of the Pharisees, who outwardly appeared righteous to men, but who were like the sepulchers which were painted white that they might be clearly seen so that men might avoid the pollution which contact with these sepulchers might cause. Jesus somewhat alters the figures and intimates the peril which the Pharisees caused to all who approached them, who, instead of being warned against their impurity, were only deceived, and therefore the more endangered by the outward show of holiness and ceremonial purity.

7. The last "woe" rebukes those who are self-deceived, or who falsely profess to surpass their forefathers in righteousness. They build the tombs of the prophets who are dead, even at the time they are plotting to kill a prophet who is living in their midst. While professing themselves to be so superior to the ancient murderers, they show that they are of the same moral character even as they are children by physical descent. It is always easy to feel we are superior to others simply because our faults are of a different kind and our sins are committed under different conditions.

8. Our Lord follows these seven "woes" by a stern word of judgment. He insists that the crimes of the fathers have been shared by their sons, and that God will visit upon them the punishment due to their sins. The rulers whom Jesus is denouncing will be responsible for the faults

of the people whom they guide and represent.   They cannot escape the sentence of condemnation which rests upon them.   Jesus sums up the guilt of the past generations as it is recorded from the first to the last book of their Scriptures, that is, from the murder of Abel recorded in Genesis, to the murder of Zacharias recorded in Chronicles; and he declares that the judgment was hastening, it was about to come on that very generation.

9. It is with this doom in view that Jesus pronounces his matchless lament over the city which he loved.   His heart seems to be breaking as he remembers how long God has sought in vain to secure the repentance of his people and how he himself has pleaded with them to receive him and his salvation.   It is the pathetic cry of rejected love.   It is the prediction of approaching penalty and destruction for the sacred city.   Yet the last word contains a note of hope: Jesus is finishing his public ministry, he clearly foresees his own rejection and the consequent desolation of Jerusalem; but he looks forward to a time when he would return in glory, when his people would look in penitence "on him whom they pierced," whom they would cry, "Blessed is he that cometh in the name of the Lord." The hope of Israel and of the world centers in the coming of the King.

XI
THE PROPHECIES
OF THE KING'S RETURN
Chs. 24; 25

A. THE PRESENT AGE Ch. 24:1-14

1 And Jesus went out from the temple, and was going on his way; and his disciples came to him to show him the buildings of the temple. 2 But he answered and said unto them, See ye not all these things? verily I say unto you, There shall not be left here one stone upon another, that shall not be thrown down.

3 And as he sat on the mount of Olives, the disciples came unto him privately, saying, Tell us, when shall these things be? and what shall be the sign of thy coming, and of the end of the world? 4 And Jesus answered and said unto them, Take heed that no man lead you astray. 5 For many shall come in my name, saying, I am the Christ; and shall lead many astray. 6 And ye shall hear of wars and rumors of wars; see that ye be not troubled: for these things must needs come to pass; but the end is not yet. 7 For nation shall rise against nation, and kingdom against kingdom; and there shall be famines and earthquakes in divers places. 8 But all these things are the beginning of travail. 9 Then shall they deliver you up unto tribulation, and shall kill you: and ye shall be hated of all the nations for my name's sake. 10 And then shall many stumble, and shall deliver up one another, and shall hate one another. 11 And many false prophets shall arise, and shall lead many astray. 12 And because iniquity shall be multiplied, the love of the many shall wax cold. 13 But he that endureth to the end, the same shall be saved. 14 And this gospel of the kingdom shall be preached in the whole world for a testimony unto all the nations; and then shall the end come.

Jesus clearly saw and predicted his death and resurrection, but he just as definitely foretold his return in glory at the end of the present age. In describing this return he used a term which is truly royal; the word translated "coming," which was often employed of the visit of an emperor. It became among Christians the accepted term to describe the coming of the King. This coming in one sense was to be a return, a reappearing; from another point of view, it was to be the real coming of Christ; as the Messiah in full reality he was thus to appear for the first time. This personal, visible, glorious return of Christ has been through all the ages the inspiring hope of his followers. It will introduce the glories of his perfected Kingdom upon earth.

As to the details and attendant events of this return, there have been widely divergent beliefs among Christians. These differences are not surprising. First of all, it must be remembered that we have here only a partial report of the discourse of Jesus. It is necessary to compare the records of Mark and of Luke, and even then to consider that we probably have been given but a fraction of the entire prophecy.

Then again, it must be noted that Jesus employs Oriental imagery and uses at times figures of speech which need to be interpreted with caution and reserve.

In the third place, it is evident that our Lord is describing not one event, but two; he is prophesying the literal overthrow of the holy city by the armies of Rome, but he is using the colors of this tragic scene to paint the picture of his own coming in glory. So interwoven are these two series of predictions that it is extremely difficult at times to be certain whether the reference is to the nearer or to the more remote of these great events. It is, therefore, evident that in the study of these chapters there is no place for dogmatism or uncharitable self-confidence. One needs to be guarded against bigotry and fanaticism as well as against indifference and unbelief.

The discourse was occasioned by questions of the disciples addressed to Jesus as to the time of the two events of which he had before spoken. On this day as he withdraws for the last time from the Temple and from the holy city, the disciples call his attention to the splendor of the Temple structures. Conscious of his rejection and of the impending doom of the city, Jesus sadly replies, "There shall not be left here one stone upon another, that shall not be thrown down." Subsequently, as Jesus pauses to rest on the western slope of the Mount of Olives, the disciples approach him with the questions as to when this prediction was to be fulfilled, and further as to the signs which might precede his coming and the end of the age when his coming was to occur. Jesus assures them, first of all, that these events are not to be in the immediate future. While the disciples must be watchful and expectant, much time is to elapse before these great events may occur. This was true in reference to the destruction of Jerusalem, much more was it true of the coming of the King. Therefore, Jesus sketches for his disciples the character of the present age down to its very end, and describes the experiences of his followers and defines their supreme and continuing task. According to his description, the present age is to be characterized by the appearance of many deceivers who will claim allegiance and assume to take the place of Christ, the true Savior and King. There are also to be wars and rumors of wars, and in addition to these political agitations, there are to be famines and earthquakes. Yet these disturbances are to be regarded as characteristics of the present age and not as signs of its approaching end. The followers of Christ are to be hated and persecuted among all nations for his sake; many of them will prove false and treacherous and will hate their fellow Christians; many will lose their love for Christ; but those who continue faithful are certain of ultimate deliverance. In spite of all these difficulties and disturbances the work of his followers is to be pressed. Their task is clear. Until it has been completed, the King will not return. "This gospel of the kingdom shall be preached in the whole world for a testimony unto all the nations; and then shall the end come." Whatever differences of opinion may exist among the servants of the King relative to the details of his return, all shall be united in the accomplishment of their common task and inspired by the same blessed hope.

B. THE GREAT TRIBULATION
Ch. 24:15-28

15 When therefore ye see the abomination of desolation, which was spoken of through Daniel the prophet, standing in the holy place (let him that readeth understand), 16 then let them that are in Judæa flee unto the mountains: 17 let him that is on the housetop not go down to take out the things that are in his house: 18 and let him that is in the field not return back to take his cloak. 19 But woe unto them that are with child and to them that give suck in those days! 20 And pray ye that your flight be not in the winter, neither on a sabbath: 21 for then shall be great tribulation, such as hath not been from the beginning of the world until now, no, nor ever shall be. 22 And except those days had been shortened, no flesh would have been saved: but for the elect's sake those days shall be shortened. 23 Then if any man shall say unto you, Lo, here is the Christ, or, Here; believe it not. 24 For there shall arise false Christs, and false prophets, and shall show great signs and wonders; so as to lead astray, if possible, even the elect. 25 Behold, I have told you beforehand. 26 If therefore they shall say unto you, Behold, he is in the wilderness; go not forth: Behold, he is in the inner chambers; believe it not. 27 For as the lightning cometh forth from the east, and is seen even unto the west; so shall be the coming of the Son of man. 28 Wheresoever the carcass is, there will the eagles be gathered together.

Before the reappearing of Christ, the opposition to his followers, their sufferings and distresses will reach their climax in a "great tribulation" which immediately precedes the appearing of the King. This event is painted so vividly in colors borrowed from the destruction of Jerusalem by the Romans, that it is difficult to distinguish between the references to the two events. The sign which immediately precedes the beginning of the great tribulation is described as "the abomination of desolation." In the case of the destruction of Jerusalem, this is supposed by many to have been the royal standards, or the Roman armies; but in the case of the tribulation at the end of the age, it is understood to refer to the appearance of the "antichrist," the "man of sin," to whom the other New Testament writers refer. It is under his rule and tyranny that there will be "great tribulation, such as hath not been from the beginning of the world until now, no, nor ever shall be." Were it not for the divine intervention that has been determined, it would appear that none would survive this reign of savagery and horror. As men yearn for escape and deliverance they will be misled easily by the many false Christs and false prophets who will manifest such signs and wonders as to lead astray the very followers of Christ. The servants of the King, however, should not be misled. They are not to look for a human deliverer who is to be found in the wilderness nor in any secret place of the city. Their Deliverer is to appear from heaven; his coming is to be "as the lightning cometh forth from the east, and is seen even unto the west." It will bring with it judgment upon his enemies and destruction to all who are morally corrupt and the servants of evil, for "Wheresoever the carcase is, there will the eagles be gathered together."

C. THE COMING OF CHRIST Ch. 24:29-31

29 But immediately after the tribulation of those days the sun shall be darkened, and the moon shall not give her light, and the stars shall fall from heaven, and the powers

of the heavens shall be shaken: 30 and then shall appear
the sign of the Son of man in heaven: and then shall all the
tribes of the earth mourn, and they shall see the Son of
man coming on the clouds of heaven with power and great
glory. 31 And he shall send forth his angels with a great
sound of a trumpet, and they shall gather together his elect
from the four winds, from one end of heaven to the other.

The great tribulation at the end of the age is to be ended
by the glorious appearing of the King. His return, however, will be immediately preceded by certain definite
signs, so startling and so terrifying that they can leave no
doubt as to the certainty of the event which is to follow.
They are described, however, in figures which are as mysterious as they are impressive, "The sun shall be darkened, and the moon shall not give her light, and the stars
shall fall from heaven, and the powers of the heavens
shall be shaken." Then occurs the event toward which
all the ages are moving, for which the weary world has
waited, by which the work of the church will be crowned
and her hopes fulfilled, namely, the personal, glorious appearing of the crucified, risen, ascended Lord, "Then shall
appear the sign of the Son of man in heaven." Whether
this "sign" is to be distinguished from the event itself, and
if so, what its nature may be, it is useless to conjecture.
The event is gloriously stated: it is to be an appearing of
the Son of Man "coming on the clouds of heaven with
power and great glory." For his enemies it is a time of
dread and of terror: "All the tribes of the earth mourn";
for his followers it is to be a time of deliverance and of
triumph: "He shall send forth his angels with a great
sound of a trumpet, and they shall gather together his
elect from the four winds, from one end of heaven to the
other." This is the time when his persecuted, suffering,
and faithful servants will rejoice in the visible presence of
their Lord, in the triumph and in the reign of the King.

D. THE EXHORTATION TO WATCHFULNESS
Ch. 24:32-51

32 Now from the fig tree learn her parable: when her branch is now become tender, and putteth forth its leaves, ye know that the summer is nigh; 33 even so ye also, when ye see all these things, know ye that he is nigh, even at the doors. 34 Verily I say unto you, This generation shall not pass away, till all these things be accomplished. 35 Heaven and earth shall pass away, but my words shall not pass away. 36 But of that day and hour knoweth no one, not even the angels of heaven, neither the Son, but the Father only. 37 And as were *the days of Noah, so shall be the coming of the Son of man. 38 For as in those days which were before the flood they were eating and drinking, marrying and giving in marriage, until the day that Noah entered into the ark, 39 and they knew not until the flood came, and took them all away; so shall be the coming of the Son of man. 40 Then shall two men be in the field; one is taken, and one is left: 41 two women* shall be *grinding at the mill; one is taken, and one is left. 42 Watch therefore: for ye know not on what day your Lord cometh. 43 But know this, that if the master of the house had known in what watch the thief was coming, he would have watched, and would not have suffered his house to be broken through. 44 Therefore be ye also ready; for in an hour that ye think not the Son of man cometh.*

45 Who then is the faithful and wise servant, whom his lord hath set over his household, to give them their food in due season? 46 Blessed is that servant, whom his lord when he cometh shall find so doing. 47 Verily I say unto you, that he will set him over all that he hath. 48 But if that evil servant shall say in his heart, My lord tarrieth; 49 and shall begin to beat his fellow-servants, and shall eat and drink with the drunken; 50 the lord of the servant shall come in a day when he expecteth not, and in an hour when he knoweth not, 51 and shall cut him asunder, and appoint his portion with the hypocrites: there shall be the weeping and the gnashing of teeth.

With this great event in view Jesus urges upon his followers a spirit of watchfulness. For them, his coming is not to be unexpected; the signs to which he has just referred will as clearly warn them of his approach as the budding of the trees in the springtime suggest the approach of spring. Even the generation then living was to witness the destruction of Jerusalem which was in itself to be a type and a sign of the greater event which lay in the more distant future. However long the delay might be, the predictions were certain to be fulfilled; Jesus declared that his words "shall not pass away." The exact time of his return, however, was known to no one; of it he, who became man and humbled himself, was voluntarily ignorant; it was known only to the Father. It was, however, to be at a time when the great world would be indifferent and careless. As in the days of Noah men were absorbed in their usual worldly occupations until the very time of the Flood; so at the very close of the present age, men will be indifferent and careless as to the return of the King. The event will at last come with startling suddenness, fellow workers will be separated in the field and in the home; one will be taken to meet the King; another left to the impending doom. In view of such an event our Lord urges watchfulness, such as should be shown by one who is on his guard against the approach of a thief; and still more, as one who is a servant and desires to be found faithfully employed at his task when his master returns. So Jesus urges upon his followers such conduct as becomes those who are waiting for the return of their Lord. This parable of the unfaithful servants seems to refer particularly to those of his followers who are appointed to positions of peculiar trust and power. It is one of three parables connected with the prophecy of the coming of the King. It was probably spoken with immediate reference to his disciples. They were to be guarded against carelessness, indifference, self-indulgence, and self-confidence. They were not to abuse their power or their privileges.

Unfaithfulness would be met by severe penalties, but the faithful and wise servants would be rewarded when their Lord returned. His coming was to be the motive of fidelity and loyal service.

E. THE PARABLE OF THE TEN VIRGINS
Ch. 25:1-13

1 Then shall the kingdom of heaven be likened unto ten virgins, who took their lamps, and went forth to meet the bridegroom. 2 And five of them were foolish, and five were wise. 3 For the foolish, when they took their lamps, took no oil with them: 4 but the wise took oil in their vessels with their lamps. 5 Now while the bridegroom tarried, they all slumbered and slept. 6 But at midnight there is a cry, Behold, the bridegroom! Come ye forth to meet him. 7 Then all those virgins arose, and trimmed their lamps. 8 And the foolish said unto the wise, Give us of your oil; for our lamps are going out. 9 But the wise answered, saying, Peradventure there will not be enough for us and you: go ye rather to them that sell, and buy for yourselves. 10 And while they went away to buy, the bridegroom came; and they that were ready went in with him to the marriage feast: and the door was shut. 11 Afterward came also the other virgins, saying, Lord, Lord, open to us. 12 But he answered and said, Verily I say unto you, I know you not. 13 Watch therefore, for ye know not the day nor the hour.

The meaning of this beautiful and pathetic parable is not difficult to discover. Jesus is teaching his followers to be ready for his return. His coming should be for them a time of supreme joy. He therefore compares it here with the time of a marriage feast. For some, however, it will be an hour of disillusion, of judgment, and of despair.

Jesus describes himself as the heavenly Bridegroom. His followers are represented by ten virgins, some of whom are foolish and some are wise. No mention is made here of the bride, for one purpose of the parable is to show that the professing church may be divided into two classes. There are the true and the false followers of the King. Both the foolish and the wise virgins regarded themselves as friends of the bridegroom, but only the wise were ready to enter with him into the marriage feast, for according to the Oriental imagery only those who carried lights and formed a part of the marriage procession were admitted to the wedding festival. Both the foolish and the wise virgins carried lamps, but only the wise "took oil in their vessels with their lamps." Among the followers of Christ mere outward profession is not enough. Preparation for the coming of Christ demands inward grace, and such an influence of the Holy Spirit as will be manifested in a life which will be a light shining in a dark world.

"While the bridegroom tarried" they all slumbered and slept. This tarrying of the bridegroom accords with the continual teaching of Jesus relative to his return. His coming was not to be immediate; long years first were to pass. It was, however, to be sudden. When at last the time arrived it would be unexpected. The fact that the virgins "slept" indicates no special fault. It is, rather, stated in order to emphasize the suddenness of the return of Christ. Both the wise and the foolish were asleep, but suddenly "at midnight there is a cry, Behold, the bridegroom! Come ye forth to meet him." It is then that the real difference appears between the foolish and the wise; the former have no oil for their lamps. They are not ready to take their places in the joyful procession and to enter with the bridegroom into the feast. The refusal of the wise to share their oil with the foolish is not a suggestion of selfishness, but a statement of the serious truth that moral life and spiritual graces cannot be divided and shared in a time of testing or of need. When the Bridegroom is about to appear, it will then be too late to prepare for his coming and it will be futile to turn to friends and associates for help. Such too is the solemn teaching of the exclusion of the foolish virgins from the marriage supper. When the door has been shut and when they are crying, "Lord, Lord, open to us," it is of course a picture which does not belong to the present. Jesus is now willing to receive all who come to him; but in the hour of his return when he has admitted to his Kingdom those who have been true to him and were ready for his coming, it will be too late for those who were so foolish as to waste the time of grace, so reckless as to make no provision for their spiritual life, to then cry out for mercy and to ask for entrance into the Kingdom of Heaven. It is here that the deep pathos of the scene appears. The tragic words are those which are spoken by the Bridegroom, "Verily I say unto you, I know you not." When Jesus has come in his glory, it will then be too late to begin a new life, to develop spiritual graces, and to show our friendship for him. Such necessary preparation for his return belongs to the present time. We must be ready for his return. This is the meaning of his closing warning, "Watch therefore, for ye know not the day nor the hour."

F. THE PARABLE OF THE TALENTS
Ch. 25:14-30

14 For it is *as* when *a man, going into another country, called his own servants, and delivered unto them his goods. 15 And unto one he gave five talents, to another two, to another one; to each according to his several ability; and he went on his journey. 16 Straightway he that received the five talents went and traded with them, and made other five talents. 17 In like manner he also that* received *the two gained other two. 18 But he that received the one went away and digged in the earth, and hid his lord's money. 19 Now after a long time the lord of those servants cometh, and maketh a reckoning with them. 20 And he that received the five talents came and brought other five talents, saying, Lord, thou deliveredst unto me five talents: lo, I have gained other five talents. 21 His lord said unto him, Well done, good and faithful servant:*

thou hast been faithful over a few things, I will set thee over many things; enter thou into the joy of thy lord. 22 And he also that received the two talents came and said, Lord, thou deliveredst unto me two talents: lo, I have gained other two talents. 23 His lord said unto him, Well done, good and faithful servant: thou hast been faithful over a few things, I will set thee over many things; enter thou into the joy of thy lord. 24 And he also that had received the one talent came and said, Lord, I knew thee that thou art a hard man, reaping where thou didst not sow, and gathering where thou didst not scatter; 25 and I was afraid, and went away and hid thy talent in the earth: lo, thou hast thine own. 26 But his lord answered and said unto him, Thou wicked and slothful servant, thou knewest that I reap where I sowed not, and gather where I did not scatter; 27 thou oughtest therefore to have put my money to the bankers, and at my coming I should have received back mine own with interest. 28 Take ye away therefore the talent from him, and give it unto him that hath the ten talents. 29 For unto every one that hath shall be given, and he shall have abundance: but from him that hath not, even that which he hath shall be taken away. 30 And cast ye out the unprofitable servant into the outer darkness: there shall be the weeping and the gnashing of teeth.

Jesus is still teaching his followers to be prepared for his coming. He is impressing upon them the need of watchfulness. Watching, however, does not imply idleness. It suggests such glad anticipation as was symbolized by the faithful and wise servant who was looking for his lord's return, and by such spiritual preparation as was pictured by the wise virgins whose lamps were trimmed and burning; but it further includes such faithful service as is pictured in this parable of the talents. Those who are faithful in their work are in a true sense watching for the coming of the King.

In this parable again, Jesus plainly teaches that there will be a long delay before he returns. He pictures himself as a man who goes on a long journey "into another country" and who returns "after a long time." In his absence, however, he entrusts his goods to his servants; to one he gives five talents, to another two, to another one; "to each according to his several ability." This last phrase does not mean to limit the teaching of the parable to the opportunities which Jesus gives to his servants as distinguished from the abilities of these servants. The phrase is merely a necessary part of the drapery of the picture; the familiar teaching is that different followers of Christ are given both varying capacities and opportunities for serving him; some with small capacity have large opportunity, and some with large abilities have limited opportunities; in some cases both are great, in others both are small. The real message of the parable is the need of faithfulness and the certainty of reward, however great or small the abilities or opportunities may be. It is just here that the difference must be noted between the somewhat similar parable of the pounds recorded by Luke. The latter parable shows that the greater the faithfulness, the greater will be the reward. This parable of the talents indicates that equal faithfulness, however limited the opportunities, merits an equal reward. On his return, in making his reckoning, the master addresses the same words to the servant whose five talents "gained other five," and to the servant whose two talents "gained other two": "Well done, good and faithful servant: thou has been faithful over a few things, I will set thee over many things; enter thou into the joy of thy lord."

There is, however, another and a darker side to the picture. It is possible for one to neglect his gift, to refuse to develop his ability, and to waste his opportunity for service. This is the special temptation of those who feel that their place in life is obscure and that the possibilities for serving the Lord are small and insignificant. It was the servant who received only one talent who went away and hid his talent in the earth. The excuse which he

offered to the master on his return was foolish and condemned himself. He declared that he feared the severity
of the master. He showed that he had no conception of
the true character of his lord. It is sometimes true that
those who have small ability neglect their opportunities for
service, because they do not realize the grace and kindness
of the Lord who gives, with every talent, grace for its
proper use and never allows any real effort for him truly to
fail. All he expects is that one shall do his best. For those
who are timid and distrustful, or merely idle and indifferent, the picture in this parable is full of solemn warning.
The talent is taken away and the servant is cast "into
the outer darkness." It is a familiar truth that the neglect
of a talent always results in its loss; while the wise use
of gifts and abilities and opportunities always results in
their enlargement. There is a subtle touch here in the
statement that the talent which is taken from "the wicked
and slothful servant" is given to him who had the ten
talents. It is true that equal faithfulness receives an equal
reward, but it requires more fidelity rightly to employ five
talents than two. Greater responsibility accompanys
greater opportunity. It may be possible, however, for all
the servants of the King to be so faithful to him in the
accomplishment of daily tasks, in the use of the simplest
occasions for service, in accomplishing the special work
which he may assign, that when he appears they may meet
him without fear and may receive his word of blessed
assurance, "Well done, good and faithful servant."

G. THE JUDGMENT Ch. 25:31-46

*31 But when the Son of man shall come in his glory, and
all the angels with him, then shall he sit on the throne of
his glory: 32 and before him shall be gathered all the nations: and he shall separate them one from another, as the
shepherd separateth the sheep from the goats; 33 and he
shall set the sheep on his right hand, but the goats on the*

left. 34 Then shall the King say unto them on his right hand, Come, ye blessed of my Father, inherit the kingdom prepared for you from the foundation of the world: 35 for I was hungry, and ye gave me to eat; I was thirsty, and ye gave me drink; I was a stranger, and ye took me in; 36 naked, and ye clothed me; I was sick, and ye visited me; I was in prison, and ye came unto me. 37 Then shall the righteous answer him, saying, Lord, when saw we thee hungry, and fed thee? or athirst, and gave thee drink? 38 And when saw we thee a stranger, and took thee in? or naked, and clothed thee? 39 And when saw we thee sick, or in prison, and came unto thee? 40 And the King shall answer and say unto them, Verily I say unto you, Inasmuch as ye did it unto one of these my brethren, even these least, ye did it unto me. 41 Then shall he say also unto them on the left hand, Depart from me, ye cursed, into the eternal fire which is prepared for the devil and his angels: 42 for I was hungry, and ye did not give me to eat; I was thirsty, and ye gave me no drink; 43 I was a stranger, and ye took me not in; naked, and ye clothed me not; sick, and in prison, and ye visited me not. 44 Then shall they also answer, saying, Lord, when saw we thee hungry, or athirst, or a stranger, or naked, or sick, or in prison, and did not minister unto thee? 45 Then shall he answer them, saying, Verily I say unto you, Inasmuch as ye did it not unto one of these least, ye did it not unto me. 46 And these shall go away into eternal punishment: but the righteous into eternal life.

The New Testament contains no scene of more impressive majesty than this which is sketched by the pen of Matthew alone. It is peculiarly in harmony with the purpose of his Gospel. He is writing the story of the King, and here alone is the picture of the Son of Man seated on the throne of his glory and determining who among all the nations of the world can enter and who is to be excluded from his heavenly Kingdom. It is undoubtedly a difficult scene to interpret. If one attempts to press too far the possible suggestions of each minor detail, if one forgets that there are other passages of Scripture with which any seeming teaching must be compared, and further, if one neglects to notice that Jesus is still dealing in parables and imagery rich with Oriental color, he will undoubtedly find himself confronted by problems difficult to solve and will reach conclusions contrary to the plainest teachings of the Bible. Thus it is absurd to conclude that our Savior here teaches that eternal life can be secured by being kind to the poor regardless of any relationship to him, and in spite of lack of moral character or faith. On the other hand, it is unwise to reason as though this were the only passage which deals with the matter of coming judgment or which throws light upon the events which belong to the end of the present age. What we do have here are great elemental realities sketched for us with surpassing impressiveness and grandeur. For example, here is the picture in which Jesus declares for the only time in the Gospel that he is himself "the King"; elsewhere it is implied; here it is plainly stated. He claims that he is the royal Judge, who, some day, will say to the righteous, "Come, ye blessed of my Father, inherit the kingdom prepared for you from the foundation of the world." It is thus first of all a picture which sketches for us the kingly dignity of our Lord.

Just as obviously it suggests that the time is coming when there will be a separation among men. Judgment is a reality. In the parables which immediately precede we are reminded not only that the followers of Christ must be watching for his return but that the time of his coming will be a time of separation, and of division. Here that latter teaching is emphasized as possibly in no other portion of the Gospels. It declares that there is such a thing as a final division. There is reality in "eternal punishment" and in "eternal life."

The third great truth is just as obvious. Jesus surely intends to teach that the judgment of men will be determined by their moral character and that this character is indicated by their deeds. Charity to the poor and neglected is but one example of the many forms in which men may reveal their actual attitude toward that which is right, and the real state of mind toward the King and toward his brethren by whom alone he is represented in this present age. The real attitude of the heart and mind toward Christ, expressed in outward act, is the test by which life is to be judged. Those who are ready for the coming of the King must possess the spiritual grace suggested in the parable of the virgins; they must wisely use their opportunities, as set forth in the parable of the talents, and they must possess the character depicted by the righteous in this august scene of judgment, if at last they are to share a place in the glorious Kingdom of our Lord.

XII
THE TRIAL, DEATH,
AND RESURRECTION
OF THE KING

Chs. 26 to 28

A. THE DEVOTION OF MARY AND THE TREACHERY OF JUDAS Ch. 26:1-16

1 And it came to pass, when Jesus had finished all these words, he said unto his disciples, 2 Ye know that after two days the passover cometh, and the Son of man is delivered up to be crucified. 3 Then were gathered together the chief priests, and the elders of the people, unto the court of the high priest, who was called Caiaphas; 4 and they took counsel together that they might take Jesus by subtlety, and kill him. 5 But they said, Not during the feast, lest a tumult arise among the people.

6 Now when Jesus was in Bethany, in the house of Simon the leper, 7 there came unto him a woman having an alabaster cruse of exceeding precious ointment, and she poured it upon his head, as he sat at meat. 8 But when the disciples saw it, they had indignation, saying, To what purpose is this waste? 9 For this ointment *might have been sold for much, and given to the poor. 10 But Jesus perceiving it said unto them, Why trouble ye the woman? for she hath wrought a good work upon me. 11 For ye have the poor always with you; but me ye have not always. 12 For in that she poured this ointment upon my body, she did it to prepare me for burial. 13 Verily I say unto you, Wheresoever this gospel shall be preached in the whole world, that also which this woman hath done shall be spoken of for a memorial of her.*

14 Then one of the twelve, who was called Judas Iscariot, went unto the chief priests, 15 and said, What

are ye willing to give me, and I will deliver him unto you?
And they weighed unto him thirty pieces of silver. 16
And from that time he sought opportunity to deliver him
unto them.

The form of Jesus never appears more majestic than
when he moves through the closing scenes of this Gospel
story and stands under the shadow of the cross. In dark
contrast are his cowardly foes, foully plotting to kill him
but, in fear of the people, planning to delay the murder
until after the passover feast. Jesus with divine prevision
sees that this feast is precisely the time when the passover
lamb must be slain. He predicts that within two days he
will be crucified. All the Old Testament types and predictions are being fulfilled voluntarily by the King.

In even deeper contrast appear the deeds of Mary and
of Judas, as one anoints Jesus with precious perfume, and
the other betrays him for the price of a slave. This Mary
of Bethany is not to be confused with Mary of Magdala,
nor is either to be mistaken for the penitent woman who
bathed the feet of Jesus with her tears. At the home of
Mary and Martha and Lazarus, in Bethany, Jesus has been
spending each night of the last memorable week. When
in his honor a feast is being given by Simon, whom Jesus
seems to have cured of leprosy, Mary enters and pours
upon the head of Jesus a flask of costly ointment. Some
of the disciples are indignant at what they regard as a
purposeless waste, and intimate that the perfume might
better have been sold for the relief of the poor. As Jesus
defends and praises the deed of devotion, he teaches:
(1) No gift to him can be too great if made in grateful
love, "She hath wrought a good work upon me"; an act
may be morally beautiful even though not pratically useful. (2) Care for the poor and other duties which are of
perpetual obligation may give way before an opportunity
for service which cannot recur; sometimes even charity is
not the highest expression of Christian devotion, "Ye have

the poor always with you; but me ye have not always."
(3) Jesus appreciates the meaning and motive of our
service; he estimates them at their highest possible value
and interprets them in the light of his own love and knowledge. He declares that the anointing is a preparation of
his body for burial; it surely expresses a sympathy which
is a balm to his lonely bleeding soul. (4) The influence
of an act of Christian sacrifice will never cease. The example of Mary is still filling the earth with the fragrance
of loving service. This Jesus predicted in his words of
unique praise, "Wheresoever this gospel shall be preached
in the whole world, that also which this woman hath done
shall be spoken of for a memorial of her."

Against the background of this charming scene is drawn
the dark form of Judas as he goes to the chief priests, un-
solicited and without excuse, and offers, for thirty pieces
of silver, to deliver his Lord into their hands at a time
and place when the multitudes will not be present. There
is no possibility of making light of this crime, nor is there
any question that the base motive was avarice, as Matthew
here declares. However, the sad truth is that Judas was
no inhuman monster; he is but a warning example of
what finally a man may do, who, while in daily fellowship
with Jesus does not renounce or master his besetting sin.
He was not the last professing Christian guilty of treason
against the King.

B. THE LAST SUPPER Ch. 26:17-35

*17 Now on the first day of unleavened bread the dis-
ciples came to Jesus, saying, Where wilt thou that we make
ready for thee to eat the passover? 18 And he said, Go
into the city to such a man, and say unto him, The Teacher
saith, My time is at hand; I keep the passover at thy house
with my disciples. 19 And the disciples did as Jesus appointed them; and they made ready the passover.*

*20 Now when even was come, he was sitting at meat
with the twelve disciples; 21 and as they were eating, he*

said, Verily I say unto you, that one of you shall betray me. 22 And they were exceeding sorrowful, and began to say unto him every one, Is it I, Lord? 23 And he answered and said, He that dipped his hand with me in the dish, the same shall betray me. 24 The Son of man goeth, even as it is written of him: but woe unto that man through whom the Son of man is betrayed! good were it for that man if he had not been born. 25 And Judas, who betrayed him, answered and said, Is it I, Rabbi? He saith unto him, Thou hast said.

26 And as they were eating, Jesus took bread, and blessed, and brake it; and he gave to the disciples, and said, Take, eat; this is my body. 27 And he took a cup, and gave thanks, and gave to them, saying, Drink ye all of it; 28 for this is my blood of the covenant, which is poured out for many unto remission of sins. 29 But I say unto you, I shall not drink henceforth of this fruit of the vine, until that day when I drink it new with you in my Father's kingdom.

30 And when they had sung a hymn, they went out unto the mount of Olives.

31 Then saith Jesus unto them, All ye shall be offended in me this night: for it is written, I will smite the shepherd, and the sheep of the flock shall be scattered abroad. 32 But after I am raised up, I will go before you into Galilee. 33 But Peter answered and said unto him, If all shall be offended in thee, I will never be offended. 34 Jesus said unto him, Verily I say unto thee, that this night, before the cock crow, thou shalt deny me thrice. 35 Peter saith unto him, Even if I must die with thee, yet will I not deny thee. Likewise also said all the disciples.

The Last Supper of which Jesus partook with his disciples was a passover feast and in a real sense it was the last Passover; for the redemption which the Jewish festival foreshadowed was accomplished on the following day by the death of Christ and henceforth the place of the Passover was taken by the Christian Sacrament which is known as the Supper of our Lord. It may be helpful to review the scene in the upper room at Jerusalem by asking what guidance it may give in observing the Sacrament which Jesus established as a memorial of his death.

1. A place was prepared in which Jesus might meet his followers with no interruption, where he might commune with them alone and give to them the messages which would prepare them for their future service. As he offered to come for this purpose to the home of his friend in the holy city, so Jesus promises to enter every heart which is prepared to commune with him. This preparation may be made by prayer, or by meditation, or by reading some portion of the sacred story, but by some method of our own choosing the heart must be made ready for his messages of grace and love.

2. As the story is sketched, the supreme figure is that of Christ. No artist would dream of painting the picture without placing our Lord in the center of the scene. So those who would truly partake of the Sacrament must center their thoughts upon the Master and must believe that his is a real presence, symbolized indeed by bread and wine, but actual as an unseen, divine Spirit.

3. All disloyal thoughts must be excluded from the mind. During the passover meal and before Jesus instituted his supper he disclosed to Judas the fact that his treachery had been discovered; and there can be little doubt, as the other Evangelists intimate, that the traitor left the room and was not present when the Supper was instituted. It is certain that actual communion with Christ is utterly impossible if sin is cherished and purposes contrary to the will of the Master are retained. The words addressed to Judas were most solemn. They may warn us of the peril of disloyalty which besets the followers of Christ even as they gather about the table of our Lord.

4. Jesus explained to his disciples the meaning of the sacrament that he was establishing. He took bread and broke it, declaring that it was a symbol of his body which was to be broken for them. He declared that the wine was a picture of his blood "poured out for many." And it

is obvious that those who partake of these symbols must fix their thoughts upon the redemption wrought out by Christ for those who put their trust in him. They must believe that he suffered and died that they might be forgiven and might enjoy a larger and fuller life.

5. It was at this time too that Jesus promised to his followers a share in the blessedness of his Kingdom. He was, indeed, to die, but he was to rise from the dead and some day he was to return in power. He now wishes his followers to keep the feast, cheered by the vision of his return. The sacred Supper should point forward our thoughts to a reunion with loved ones, to opening skies, to an age of universal peace, to a reigning King, "For as often as ye eat this bread, and drink the cup, ye proclaim the Lord's death till he come."

6. They sang a hymn and "went out unto the mount of Olives." It was to be a place of trial and of agony, but they went forth with a song of triumph on their lips; and as we turn from the Supper of our Lord it should always be with a new consciousness of strength and of hope and of certain victory as we put our trust in him.

7. We should turn from the Sacrament with new confidence, but it must not be a reliance upon self. It is a time to pledge a new allegiance to the Lord, but it must not be made in pride or in boastfulness. As Jesus is passing from the upper room to the dark scene of trial, the disciples, led by Peter, profess their loyalty to Jesus; they declare absolute willingness to die with him, but in a short time Peter denies him and they all forsake him. There was nothing wrong in their declaration of love; the fault lay in their unwillingness to be warned of their weakness and in their failure to obey the command of their Lord when he bade them to "watch and pray." The Lord's Supper should be a time of deepening devotion. It should be a place for the expression of real affection; but it is there we should cast ourselves anew upon his promised grace by which alone we can pass in triumph

through the trials and the gloom of the lonely night, expecting on some brighter morning the reunion which is promised us in the palace of the King.

C. JESUS IN GETHSEMANE   Ch. 26:36-56

36 Then cometh Jesus with them unto a place called Gethsemane, and saith unto his disciples, Sit ye here, while I go yonder and pray. 37 And he took with him Peter and the two sons of Zebedee, and began to be sorrowful and sore troubled. 38 Then saith he unto them, My soul is exceeding sorrowful, even unto death: abide ye here, and watch with me. 39 And he went forward a little, and fell on his face, and prayed, saying, My Father, if it be possible, let this cup pass away from me: nevertheless, not as I will, but as thou wilt. 40 And he cometh unto the disciples, and findeth them sleeping, and saith unto Peter, What, could ye not watch with me one hour? 41 Watch and pray, that ye enter not into temptation: the spirit indeed is willing, but the flesh is weak. 42 Again a second time he went away, and prayed, saying, My Father, if this cannot pass away, except I drink it, thy will be done. 43 And he came again and found them sleeping, for their eyes were heavy. 44 And he left them again, and went away, and prayed a third time, saying again the same words. 45 Then cometh he to the disciples, and saith unto them, Sleep on now, and take your rest: behold, the hour is at hand, and the Son of man is betrayed into the hands of sinners. 46 Arise, let us be going: behold, he is at hand that betrayeth me.

47 And while he yet spake, lo, Judas, one of the twelve, came, and with him a great multitude with swords and staves, from the chief priests and elders of the people. 48 Now he that betrayed him gave them a sign, saying, Whomsoever I shall kiss, that is he: take him. 49 And straightway he came to Jesus, and said, Hail, Rabbi; and kissed him. 50 And Jesus said unto him, Friend, do that for which thou art come. Then they came and laid hands on Jesus, and took him. 51 And behold, one of them that were with Jesus stretched out his hand, and drew his sword,

*and smote the servant of the high priest, and struck off his
ear.   52 Then saith Jesus unto him, Put up again thy
sword into its place: for all they that take the sword shall
perish with the sword.   53 Or thinkest thou that I cannot
beseech my Father, and he shall even now send me more
than twelve legions of angels?   54 How then should the
scriptures be fulfilled, that thus it must be?   55 In that
hour said Jesus to the multitudes, Are ye come out as
against a robber with swords and staves to seize me?   I
sat daily in the temple teaching, and ye took me not.   56
But all this is come to pass, that the scriptures of the prophets might be fulfilled.   Then all the disciples left him, and
fled.*

The agony of Jesus in the Garden of Gethsemane would
be difficult to explain, one might say that it would be
difficult to excuse, if Jesus were but a man, there quailing
in dread of physical death. He thus would have appeared
less heroic than many of his followers have been. He,
however, was about to die as a divine Sacrifice for sin.
The cup he was to drink contained a bitterness which no
man had ever tasted. That scene in the Garden can be
interpreted only by the words spoken in the upper room,
"This is my blood of the covenant, which is poured out
for many unto remission of sins." It is this agony which
adds to the mystery and the meaning of the cross.

Yet Jesus, too, was a man, and it was but natural to
shrink from torture and from death. His sufferings enable
him to sympathize with a long train of martyrs who follow
in his steps and who taste in part the cup of his anguish.
He himself longed for sympathy. It was for this reason
that he took with him his closest comrades as he entered
the shadows of the garden, but in weariness or in carelessness they fell asleep; and the Master presents a picture of
the loneliness and desolation which is inseparable from all
sorrow and trial.

The supreme recourse of Jesus is found in prayer.
When the agony grips his soul most fiercely, he still prays;

and he is answered; not that the cup is removed, but grace is given to drain its very dregs, death loses its sting, the grave is deprived of victory, and Jesus becomes "unto all them that obey him the author of eternal salvation." The spirit in which Jesus prays is that of willing obedience to his Father. His matchless words are these, "Nevertheless, not as I will, but as thou wilt." He wins his victory by submission to the will of his Father. When the traitor approaches, Jesus is ready; the agony and the storm are past; Jesus steps forth to meet his enemies and his cross with kingly calm.

In contrast with the princely form of Jesus is the contemptible figure of Judas. The manner in which he concludes his foul crime is in perfect keeping with its essential baseness. Into the Garden where he knew Jesus was accustomed to retire for prayer, he leads a great crowd armed with swords and clubs, and there he betrays his Lord with a kiss, a sign agreed upon, that one of the disciples might not be mistaken for the Master. Thus acts of disloyalty to Christ often seem the more repulsive because of the scenes in which they are committed and of the protestations of love by which they are accompanied.

The fearless composure of Jesus is further contrasted with the conduct of his disciples. One of them, with the impulse of mere physical courage, draws his sword and impetuously attacks a servant of the high priest; but Jesus rebukes him, assuring him that the cause of his Master is not to be advanced by physical violence, and then adding a kingly claim appropriately recorded by Matthew alone, "Thinkest thou that I cannot beseech my Father, and he shall even now send me more than twelve legions of angels?" He is conscious of his power, but equally convinced of a divine purpose. He declares that in his arrest and crucifixion the predictions of redemption are being fulfilled. Willingly he offers himself as the Sacrifice. However, he rebukes the guilty agents of his death. He turns to Judas and his accomplices, resenting the im-

plication of their coming to take him by force. He further
protests against the secrecy with which they are making
his arrest; he had never been guilty of violence; his teachings had all been in public. He declares, however, that
even their sinful conduct had been foretold by the prophets. He submits to their insulting and humiliating seizure;
and his heart is saddened as he sees all his disciples forsake him and flee. Only an hour before they had boasted
their loyalty. Thus ignorant are we of our own moral
cowardice; thus does our courage fail in our hour of trial.

D. JESUS BEFORE CAIAPHAS   Ch. 26:57-75

*57 And they that had taken Jesus led him away to the
house of Caiaphas the high priest, where the scribes and the
elders were gathered together. 58 But Peter followed him
afar off, unto the court of the high priest, and entered in,
and sat with the officers, to see the end. 59 Now the chief
priests and the whole council sought false witness against
Jesus, that they might put him to death; 60 and they
found it not, though many false witnesses came. But afterward came two, 61 and said, This man said, I am able to
destroy the temple of God, and to build it in three days.
62 And the high priest stood up, and said unto him, An-
swerest thou nothing? what is it which these witness against
thee? 63 But Jesus held his peace. And the high priest
said unto him, I adjure thee by the living God, that thou
tell us whether thou art the Christ, the Son of God. 64
Jesus saith unto him, Thou hast said: nevertheless I say
unto you, Henceforth ye shall see the Son of man sitting
at the right hand of Power, and coming on the clouds of
heaven. 65 Then the high priest rent his garments, saying,
He hath spoken blasphemy: what further need have we of
witnesses? behold, now ye have heard the blasphemy: 66
what think ye? They answered and said, He is worthy of
death. 67 Then did they spit in his face and buffet him:
and some smote him with the palms of their hands, 68
saying, Prophesy unto us, thou Christ: who is he that struck
thee?*

69 Now Peter was sitting without in the court: and a maid came unto him, saying, Thou also wast with Jesus the Galilæan. 70 But he denied before them all, saying, I know not what thou sayest. 71 And when he was gone out into the porch, another maid saw him, and saith unto them that were there, This man also was with Jesus of Nazareth. 72 And again he denied with an oath, I know not the man. 73 And after a little while they that stood by came and said to Peter, Of a truth thou also art one of them; for thy speech maketh thee known. 74 Then began he to curse and to swear, I know not the man. And straightway the cock crew. 75 And Peter remembered the word which Jesus had said, Before the cock crow, thou shalt deny me thrice. And he went out, and wept bitterly.

When Jesus was arraigned before the high priest Caiaphas and the chief court of the nation, it was supposed that he was on trial for his life; in reality it was the rulers who were being tried and condemned; the fate of the nation was being determined; here was to take place the public rejection of the King.

The judges convict themselves of prejudice, dishonesty, and malice. They do not seek to ascertain the truth that justice may be done, they desire to secure some pretext which may excuse the murder upon which they are bent. They summon witnesses to establish a verdict they already have reached; but these witnesses fail to agree, until two are found who affirm that Jesus had boasted his ability to destroy the Temple and to rebuild it in three days. It was a distorted form of his prediction that when the temple of "his body" had been destroyed, he would rise on the third day. Such public testimony to such a claim should be remembered in connection with the miracle of the resurrection. However, even this testimony as presented is shown to be worthless, and its weakness is emphasized by the continued silence of Jesus which drives the high priest to desperation, as it clearly declares that no evidence worthy of an answer has been produced.

Then Caiaphas solemnly adjures Jesus to answer plainly whether or not he is "the Christ, the Son of God." With absolute distinctness Jesus replies, "I am"; but he proceeds to explain that, while present appearances may contradict his claim, a time will come when they will see him as Daniel predicted the Messiah would be manifested, "sitting at the right hand of Power, and coming on the clouds of heaven."

No wonder Caiaphas rends his garments to express his horror. The action is in a degree theatrical; but it is designed to emphasize the charge of blasphemy which he at once makes against Jesus. As he appeals to the council they pronounce him "worthy of death." They were right; he did deserve to die, unless he was the Messiah, the divine Son of God. There is no middle ground. Where shall we take our stand, with Caiaphas or with Christ?

"Then did they spit in his face . . . and smote him with the palms of their hands." The brutality seems incredible. These men claimed to be the special representatives of God; but the beast in man is nearer the surface than some suppose, and these rulers in their thirst for blood have been made more fierce by the disclosure of their own perfidy and shame.

Meanwhile another pitiful scene is being enacted in the open courtyard of the palace. It is not a revelation of malice but of cowardice. Peter is ashamed to confess that he is a follower of Jesus. He is denying that he knows him. His courage has failed, not his faith. Something should be said in his defense; some allowance made for his weariness, due to the long night of strain and sorrow, to the cold and loneliness, to the bewilderment of the hour and the suddenness of the attack. However, his fall has been shameful and his disgrace distressing. The denial has been repeated three times: at first it has been colored by deceit, then it has been confirmed with an oath, and finally accompanied with anger. It is easy to point the finger of scorn at the great apostle; but there are few of the followers of

Christ who in times of less severe testing have not as truly denied their Lord by word and deed, with cowardice, and deceit and passion.

Then Peter heard the cock crow; and he remembered the word of Jesus, and "he went out, and wept bitterly." Those were tears and cries of repentance, and they prepared the way of pardon and peace. To many a fallen follower of the King there has come some such minute providence which has recalled vows of devotion and tender words of warning and fellowship with a loving Master. The memory has brought bitter tears of penitence, but afterward there has come a bright morning, a meeting with the risen Christ, a new confession of love, and a deeper devotion to his cause.

E. JESUS BEFORE PILATE. Ch. 27:1-26

1 Now when morning was come, all the chief priests and the elders of the people took counsel against Jesus to put him to death: 2 and they bound him, and led him away, and delivered him up to Pilate the governor.

3 Then Judas, who betrayed him, when he saw that he was condemned, repented himself, and brought back the thirty pieces of silver to the chief priests and elders, 4 saying, I have sinned in that I betrayed innocent blood. But they said, What is that to us? see thou to it. 5 And he cast down the pieces of silver into the sanctuary, and departed; and he went away and hanged himself. 6 And the chief priests took the pieces of silver, and said, It is not lawful to put them into the treasury, since it is the price of blood. 7 And they took counsel, and bought with them the potter's field, to bury strangers in. 8 Wherefore that field was called, The field of blood, unto this day. 9 Then was fulfilled that which was spoken through Jeremiah the prophet, saying, And they took the thirty pieces of silver, the price of him that was priced, whom certain of the children of Israel did price; 10 and they gave them for the potter's field, as the Lord appointed me.

11 Now Jesus stood before the governor: and the gov-

ernor asked him, saying, Art thou the King of the Jews? And Jesus said unto him, Thou sayest. 12 And when he was accused by the chief priests and elders, he answered nothing. 13 Then saith Pilate unto him, Hearest thou not how many things they witness against thee? 14 And he gave him no answer, not even to one word: insomuch that the governor marvelled greatly. 15 Now at the feast the governor was wont to release unto the multitude one prisoner, whom they would. 16 And they had then a notable prisoner, called Barabbas. 17 When therefore they were gathered together, Pilate said unto them, Whom will ye that I release unto you? Barabbas, or Jesus who is called Christ? 18 For he knew that for envy they had delivered him up. 19 And while he was sitting on the judgment-seat, his wife sent unto him, saying, Have thou nothing to do with that righteous man; for I have suffered many things this day in a dream because of him. 20 Now the chief priests and the elders persuaded the multitudes that they should ask for Barabbas, and destroy Jesus. 21 But the governor answered and said unto them, Which of the two will ye that I release unto you? And they said, Barabbas. 22 Pilate saith unto them, What then shall I do unto Jesus who is called Christ? They all say, Let him be crucified. 23 And he said, Why, what evil hath he done? But they cried out exceedingly, saying, Let him be crucified. 24 So when Pilate saw that he prevailed nothing, but rather that a tumult was arising, he took water, and washed his hands before the multitude, saying, I am innocent of the blood of this righteous man; see ye to it. 25 And all the people answered and said, His blood be on us, and on our children. 26 Then released he unto them Barabbas; but Jesus he scourged and delivered to be crucified.

The Jews had been deprived by their Roman conquerors of the right to inflict capital punishment. When, therefore, their chief council had decided that Jesus was worthy of death, the rulers brought him to Pilate, the Roman governor, that he might pronounce and execute the cruel sentence. As Jesus stood before Caiaphas, there was sketched by Matthew a pathetic companion-picture of Peter denying his Lord; as Jesus stands before Pilate, Matthew paints the tragic scene of Judas hastening to his dreadful doom. The sin of Peter was not like that of Judas, nor was his subsequent sorrow. The fall of Peter was an act of cowardice in a career which became of great service to Christ and his church. The treachery of Judas was the final step in a downward course. Peter repented; but Judas felt only the pangs of hopeless remorse. That led him to disclose his crime, to hate the pitiful price of his treason, and to end his life in suicide. How pitiless were the rulers who used him as their tool; how scrupulous were these murderers as to the proper use of blood-stained silver; and how unconsciously were they fulfilling the words of ancient prophecy! The guilt of these rulers is more fully revealed as they appear before Pilate to accuse Jesus and to secure his death. They distort the charge upon which their council condemned Jesus into one of treason against the Roman emperor. Their base insincerity is so obvious as to be evident to Pilate who perceives that their motive is envy. They are crafty and skillful enough to turn the multitudes against Jesus, who had been their popular idol, and to persuade them to ask for the release of Barabbas, a robber and murderer, in place of Jesus, whom they asked Pilate to crucify. It was thus due to the influence of the rulers that the people finally called down upon the nation the curse by their cry, "His blood be on us, and on our children"; and there the guilt for the death of Jesus has rested. In the destruction of Jerusalem, and through all the weary centuries, the Jews have suffered the agonies and anguish which can be traced to obeying their false leaders and to rejecting their rightful King.

The center of the scene is occupied, however, not by the Jewish rulers but by the Roman governor. Pilate presents the contemptible picture of a man who lacks the courage of his own convictions, and who is afraid to do right in the present, because of faults committed in the past. From the first he is convinced that Jesus is innocent, but he fears

lest the Jews may find some occasion for reporting to Rome
his previous crimes. He is compelled to disregard his conscience and to obey the subject Jews whom he despises.
Like all men who trifle with conscience he first attempts a
compromise. He offers to release Jesus in place of Barabbas. This will delight the rulers, for it will discredit Jesus
and brand him as a released criminal; it will please the people who have called Jesus their King. So Pilate plans; but
while he waits for the reply of the multitudes he receives an
ominous message from his wife, asserting the innocence of
Jesus, and warning Pilate against offering to him any in-
jury; and then, to his disgust or dismay, comes the report
that he has been outwitted by the rulers; they have persuaded the people to request Barabbas and the crucifixion
of Jesus. He hesitates, and then before the rising storm of
opposition he yields. He washes his hands as a sign that
he is innocent of the blood of Jesus; but guilt is not so
easily shifted. That blood is staining his own hands. The
Roman governor is one with the Jewish rulers and with the
people in crime, in guilt, and in infamy. Before them
stands the divine King. It is never easy to be loyal to him.
Yet it is impossible to be neutral in his presence. This
Pilate attempted; but all who lack the courage of their convictions and who are afraid to take a stand on the side of
Christ are ultimately found in the company of Pilate, who
released Barabbas, "but Jesus he scourged and delivered
to be crucified."

F. THE CRUCIFIXION AND BURIAL Ch. 27:27-66

27 Then the soldiers of the governor took Jesus into the
Prætorium, and gathered unto him the whole band. 28
And they stripped him, and put on him a scarlet robe. 29
And they platted a crown of thorns and put it upon his
head, and a reed in his right hand; and they kneeled down
before him, and mocked him, saying, Hail, King of the
Jews! 30 And they spat upon him, and took the reed and

smote him on the head. *31 And when they had mocked him, they took off from him the robe, and put on him his garments, and led him away to crucify him.*

32 And as they came out, they found a man of Cyrene, Simon by name: him they compelled to go with them, that he might bear his cross.

33 And when they were come unto a place called Golgotha, that is to say, The place of a skull, 34 they gave him wine to drink mingled with gall: and when he had tasted it, he would not drink. 35 And when they had crucified him, they parted his garments among them, casting lots; 36 and they sat and watched him there. 37 And they set up over his head his accusation written, THIS IS JESUS THE KING OF THE JEWS. 38 Then are there crucified with him two robbers, one on the right hand and one on the left. 39 And they that passed by railed on him, wagging their heads, 40 and saying, Thou that destroyest the temple, and buildest it in three days, save thyself: if thou art the Son of God, come down from the cross. 41 In like manner also the chief priests mocking him, with the scribes and elders, said, 42 He saved others; himself he cannot save. He is the King of Israel; let him now come down from the cross, and we will believe on him. 43 He trusteth on God; let him deliver him now, if he desireth him: for he said, I am the Son of God. 44 And the robbers also that were crucified with him cast upon him the same reproach.

45 Now from the sixth hour there was darkness over all the land until the ninth hour. 46 And about the ninth hour Jesus cried with a loud voice, saying, Eli, Eli, lama sabachthani? that is, My God, my God, why hast thou forsaken me? 47 And some of them that stood there, when they heard it, said, This man calleth Elijah. 48 And straightway one of them ran, and took a sponge, and filled it with vinegar, and put it on a reed, and gave him to drink. 49 And the rest said, Let be; let us see whether Elijah cometh to save him. 50 And Jesus cried again with a loud voice, and yielded up his spirit. 51 And behold, the veil of the temple was rent in two from the top to the bottom; and the earth did quake; and the rocks were rent; 52 and the tombs were opened; and many bodies of the saints that had fallen asleep were raised; 53 and coming forth out of the tombs after his resurrection they entered into the holy city and appeared unto many. 54 Now the centurion, and they that were with him watching Jesus, when they saw the earthquake, and the things that were done, feared exceedingly, saying, Truly this was the Son of God. 55 And many women were there beholding from afar, who had followed Jesus from Galilee, ministering unto him: 56 among whom was Mary Magdalene, and Mary the mother of James and Joses, and the mother of the sons of Zebedee.

57 And when even was come, there came a rich man from Arimathæa, named Joseph, who also himself was Jesus' disciple: 58 this man went to Pilate, and asked for the body of Jesus. Then Pilate commanded it to be given up. 59 And Joseph took the body, and wrapped it in a clean linen cloth, 60 and laid it in his own new tomb, which he had hewn out in the rock: and he rolled a great stone to the door of the tomb, and departed. 61 And Mary Magdalene was there, and the other Mary, sitting over against the sepulchre.

62 Now on the morrow, which is the day after the Preparation, the chief priests and the Pharisees were gathered together unto Pilate, 63 saying, Sir, we remember that that deceiver said while he was yet alive, After three days I rise again. 64 Command therefore that the sepulchre be made sure until the third day, lest haply his disciples come and steal him away, and say unto the people, He is risen from the dead: and the last error will be worse than the first. 65 Pilate said unto them, Ye have a guard: go, make it as sure as ye can. 66 So they went, and made the sepulchre sure, sealing the stone, the guard being with them.

The title placed by Pilate above the cross forms a fitting superscription for the Gospel of Matthew, "This is Jesus the King of the Jews." To demonstrate this fact is the unfailing purpose of the author, and on no other page is it more evident than when he sketches the agonizing story of the crucifixion. The title was prepared in derision, but it recalls a claim, it embodies a reality, it suggests a proph-

ecy. For making that claim Jesus was condemned; yet he
is in reality the King of the Jews, and that nation will attain
its predicted glory when in penitence "they shall look on
him whom they pierced," and when they shall welcome
him with the cry, "Blessed is he that cometh in the name
of the Lord."

This title upon the cross was but one of the forms of
derision heaped upon the innocent Sufferer, and all the
others echoed the same claim of kingship and were unin-
tentional testimonials to the same truth. The brutal soldiers hailed him "King of the Jews," they robed him in
scarlet and crowned him with thorns, and gave him a reed
as a scepter and bowed before him in derisive mockery.
The people taunted him with his claim to be the Son of
God. The chief priests and elders cried out in scorn, "He
is the King of Israel." Even the robbers that were crucified with him united in taunting him with his kingly claims.
The reality and truthfulness of the claims were soon attested by the attendant events. Surely Jesus died as a
King; the sun was hidden and "there was darkness over
all the land"; the earth was shaken; "rocks were rent; and
the tombs were opened." Meanwhile the princely Sufferer
utters no word of complaint, only a cry of anguish as he
feels that he is forsaken by his Father; only a cry of victory
and then he "yielded up his spirit." No wonder that the
centurion who was watching Jesus "feared exceedingly,
saying, Truly this was the Son of God." No wonder that
the women who were there "beholding from afar" looked
with breaking hearts upon the scene of terror. They knew
him and loved him and beneath the disguise of his humilia-
tion they had beheld the majesty of a King.

"And behold, the veil of the temple was rent in two from
the top to the bottom." This is the key to the mystery.
Why did he die? Why did the sinless One thus suffer?
Why was the Son of God asked to endure this shame and
agony and death? It was that he might bring us to the
Father; that he might open for us a new and living way
into the divine presence; it was that we might be justified

by faith, that we might have peace with God and might rejoice in the hope of his eternal glory.

Even the burial of Jesus has its touches of royalty. His lifeless body was secured by a rich ruler named Joseph; it was wrapped in costly linen and placed in a new tomb, which had been hewn out of the rock, and which was sealed with a great stone. There Matthew pictures the faithful women seated near by and guarding the sepulcher as the dark day draws to its close. There were other guards, however, appointed to watch the tomb. The chief priests and scribes appealed to Pilate, telling him of a promise which Jesus had made to rise from the dead. They stated their fear lest his disciples should steal his body and the belief in his resurrection should be established and should prove more dangerous than the current belief that he was a King. With the consent of Pilate they sealed the stone which closed the sepulcher and appointed a guard of soldiers. It established the fact that if the tomb was really found empty on the third day, Jesus must have risen from the dead.

G. THE RESURRECTION Ch. 28

1 Now late on the sabbath day, as it began to dawn toward the first day of the week, came Mary Magdalene and the other Mary to see the sepulchre. 2 And behold, there was a great earthquake; for an angel of the Lord descended from heaven, and came and rolled away the stone, and sat upon it. 3 His appearance was as lightning, and his raiment white as snow: 4 and for fear of him the watchers did quake, and became as dead men. 5 And the angel answered and said unto the women, Fear not ye; for I know that ye seek Jesus, who hath been crucified. 6 He is not here; for he is risen, even as he said. Come, see the place where the Lord lay. 7 And go quickly, and tell his disciples, He is risen from the dead; and lo, he goeth before you into Galilee; there shall ye see him: lo, I have told you. 8 And they departed quickly from the tomb with fear and great joy, and ran to bring his disciples word. 9 And behold, Jesus met them, saying, All hail. And they came and took hold of his feet, and worshipped him. 10 Then saith Jesus unto them, Fear not: go tell my brethren that they depart into Galilee, and there shall they see me.

11 Now while they were going, behold, some of the guard came into the city, and told unto the chief priests all the things that were come to pass. 12 And when they were assembled with the elders, and had taken counsel, they gave much money unto the soldiers, 13 saying, Say ye, His disciples came by night, and stole him away while we slept. 14 And if this come to the governor's ears, we will persuade him, and rid you of care. 15 So they took the money, and did as they were taught: and this saying was spread abroad among the Jews, and continueth *until this day.*

16 But the eleven disciples went into Galilee, unto the mountain where Jesus had appointed them. 17 And when they saw him, they worshipped him; *but some doubted. 18 And Jesus came to them and spake unto them, saying, All authority hath been given unto me in heaven and on earth. 19 Go ye therefore, and make disciples of all the nations, baptizing them into the name of the Father and of the Son and of the Holy Spirit: 20 teaching them to observe all things whatsoever I commanded you: and lo, I am with you always, even unto the end of the world.*

No record of the resurrection is more majestic than this of Matthew. Other Gospels add features of value but none contains more evident marks of royalty. This is the story of a King. Strictly speaking, no writer attempts to describe the event, but all unite in giving unanswerable testimony to the fact of the resurrection of Christ. Matthew records the witness of an angel, of two women, of the guards, and of the eleven disciples. Upon such testimony as this is based our belief in the triumph of the King over death and the grave, and our related hope of "the resurrection of the body and the life everlasting."

The appearance of the angel is described in phrases peculiar to Matthew: "There was a great earthquake; for an angel of the Lord descended from heaven, and came and rolled away the stone, and sat upon it. His appearance was as lightning, and his raiment white as snow." The stone was not rolled away to allow Jesus to escape, but to show that the tomb was already empty; the King had departed; his messenger had come to bear his command to his followers. The guards are stupefied with fear, but the startled women are comforted by the assurance that their Lord has actually risen from the dead, and they are bidden by the angel to go into Galilee where they will meet him.

The appearance to the women is described in phrases of equal majesty. Jesus meets them with the kingly salutation, "All hail." They fall before him and worship him. He bids them not to fear, and repeats his command which the angel has spoken, and tells them to bid his disciples to depart into Galilee where they would see him. He calls his disciples his "brethren." He never had used this phrase before. It is the risen Lord who can thus speak of his followers, for as the "firstborn from the dead," he intimates that he is one with those who by faith share with him in a risen and glorified life. It is for this reason that he is declared to be "the firstborn among many brethren."

The guards who hastened in terror from the empty tomb are the next witnesses of the resurrection described by Matthew. They relate the fact to the chief priests and elders and are bribed by them to report that the disciples of Jesus came by night and stole his body while they themselves slept. There is an element of absurdity in this explanation. If the soldiers were asleep, how do they know who came or what was done in the night? Yet is this statement more ridiculous than any modern explanation of the empty tomb which denies the resurrection of Christ? The statement was not even original on the part of the soldiers. The most familiar, modern denials of the resurrection are borrowed from dead skeptics. Is it probable that the body of Jesus was stolen and that he never arose from the dead? Then his disciples were impostors; his own claims were false; and his church has been built upon a falsehood. There is no reason for denying the fact which is the foundation of our Christian faith. There is no other reasonable explanation of the empty tomb.

The words of the angel and the subsequent message of Jesus appointed a meeting for the disciples in Galilee. It is with this scene that Matthew brings his Gospel to its majestic close; there, as Jesus stands on a mountainside surrounded by his worshiping followers, he gives them his Great Commission. These surely are the words of a King. They contain a royal claim, command, and promise. In the first, Jesus declares that all authority has been given him in heaven and on earth. He is not merely King of the Jews, but King of kings and Lord of lords. In view of this fact he commands his messengers to "make disciples of all the nations." Their mission is not merely to the Jews; no longer is their work to be limited to "the house of Israel," but men of all nations are to be called to be followers of Christ, and are to be urged to acknowledge him as King. Those who accept him are to be baptized in the name of the Father and of the Son and of the Holy Spirit. They are to openly acknowledge their allegiance to him as to a divine Lord. Further, they are to be instructed to keep all the commands of the King and to obey his divine orders.

To encourage his disciples in undertaking their difficult task and in carrying out this bold program, there is given the assuring promise of the unfailing presence of the King, "Lo, I am with you always, even unto the end of the world." This does not refer to the end of the physical earth, but to the completion of this present age and the establishment of the Kingdom of glory. It was with confidence in this unseen Presence and in hope of this coming glory that his disciples went forth obeying the command, trusting in the promise, working, and watching for the appearing of the King.